THE
Baseball Research
JOURNAL

Volume 44
Fall 2015
Number 2

Published by
the Society for American Baseball Research

THE BASEBALL RESEARCH JOURNAL, Volume 44, Number 2

Editor: Cecilia M. Tan
Design and Production: Lisa Hochstein
Cover Design: Lisa Hochstein
Fact Checker: Clifford Blau

Front cover photos: National Baseball Hall of Fame and Library, Cooperstown, NY
Published by:
Society for American Baseball Research, Inc.
Cronkite School at ASU
555 N. Central Ave. #416
Phoenix, AZ 85004

Phone: (602) 496-1460
Web: www.sabr.org
Twitter: @sabr
Facebook: Society for American Baseball Research

Copyright © 2015 by The Society for American Baseball Research, Inc.
Printed in the United States of America
Distributed by the University of Nebraska Press

978-1-933599-85-4 (paper)
978-1-933599-84-7 (ebook)

Contents

Letter from the Editor

It's hard to believe that with this issue I begin my fifth year as SABR's publications director, capping off the most productive four years in the publication department's history. The surge in productivity is not my doing, really. I'm like a US President who gets credit for prosperity while in office. SABR's publications output is the convergence of many factors including a stable front office, an engaged publication-happy board, modern book-making technology, and most importantly, the enthusiastic research output of hundreds and hundreds of members. We are currently publishing about one book per month plus three journals per year (two *BRJ*s and one *National Pastime*). My estimate on how many total words we've published in the past year comes close to two million.

And that doesn't count the words on the SABR website. It doesn't count the words written and published by SABR members in other venues and in books for many other publishers. Nowadays I could read nothing but research by SABR members and still not get to it all. It's glorious. I enjoy living in an age when the dissemination of research is easier than ever, and being part of an organization that foments so much knowledge being gleaned, gained, and shared.

This issue of the *BRJ* has our usual mix of history and statistics, including a group of several that are that SABR staple: articles which combine both. Whether analyzing unlikely pitching gems (J.G. Preston), trends in play like stolen bases (John McMurray), switch-hit homers (Cort Vitty), and postseason success (Stuart Shapiro), or records well known and obscure (Douglas Jordan), these authors are in relentless pursuit of understanding what has happened on the field.

The second group of articles all deal with baseball and its effects off the field. Baseball as a cultural force has been part of the history of television (Robert D. Warrington), popular culture (TV, movies, and music *à la* David Krell), and courtroom law (William Lamb). The author team of Warneke, Ogden, and Shorey return to the pages of the *BRJ* with a social psychology study about youth ballplayers and their choice of heroes among big league players. And Matthew Clifford tracks down a case of mistaken identity that persists in the baseball memorabilia biz.

Lastly we have some good old-fashioned history, telling the stories of memorable fans (Hilda Chester by Rob Edelman), performances (Brian Marshall), personalities (Colonel Ruppert and Miller Huggins by Lyle Spatz and Steve Steinberg), icons (Babe Ruth from two angles, by John McMurray and Michael Haupert, Connie Mack by Norman Macht), and seasons (1951 Hazard, Kentucky, by Sam Zygner). We in SABR have a reputation for myth-busting rather than myth-making; that makes these stories no less compelling. In fact, it makes them more so. Baseball is the original "reality TV" and it never "gets old."

Cecilia Tan
November 2015

4

How Did That Guy Do *That*?

The Unlikeliest Pitching Performances in Major League History

J.G. Preston

Don Fisher was working for the electric company and pitching sandlot baseball in Cleveland when he signed with the New York Giants in August 1945. He pitched only two games for the Giants, was sent to the minors in 1946, and won just three games there before his brief professional career came to an end.

But in one of his two major league games he pitched a shutout against the Boston Braves. A *13-inning* shutout.

As unlikely as it seems that someone could pitch a 13-inning shutout in his second and last major league game, less than two months after pitching on the sandlots, it turns out Fisher has some interesting competition for the unlikeliest pitching performance ever in the major leagues.

Here's an imprecise definition of an "unlikely" performance: it's the kind of game that makes you say, "How did that guy do that?" First, it should be a notably good performance, one in which the pitcher worked at least nine innings and allowed no more than one run. (That narrows it down to less than 10 percent of the starting pitcher performances in the post-1914 database in Baseball-Reference.com's Play Index.) I also think the unlikeliest performances are one-of-a-kind, in that the pitcher never had another game remotely as good. As a result, several of the unlikeliest performances I will identify are the only major league game that pitcher won.

A case can be made that the unlikeliest performances are the longest games pitched in major league history, by Joe Oeschger, Leon Cadore, Jack Coombs, and Joe Harris. Oeschger and Cadore each allowed just one run in 26 innings when they faced each other on May 1, 1920. Coombs allowed just one run and struck out 18 in 24 innings on September 1, 1906; his mound opponent Harris allowed just one run in the first 23 innings before giving up three in the 24th.[1]

Those games are not so much a case of "how did that guy do that?" as they are "how did anybody do that?" While it's true that none of these pitchers had another game quite like it (nor has anyone else), they had other unusual performances. Oeschger pitched 20 innings in a game in 1919 and threw a 14-inning

shutout in 1917; Cadore pitched more than 14 innings in a game in 1921; Coombs pitched 16 scoreless innings in a game in which he struck out 18 in 1910.[2]

Harris does merit consideration for the list of unlikeliest performances. He still holds the American League record, one that may never be broken, for most consecutive scoreless innings in a game; in that 1906 game the A's didn't score from the fourth inning through the 23rd, a span of 20 innings.[3] Harris had entered that game with a 2–17 season record; he never won a major league game after that, and he finished his career with a record of 3–30, the most losses ever for a pitcher who won no more than three games. What keeps him, just barely, off my list of unlikeliest pitching performances is his three wins included a shutout and a three-hitter in which he allowed only one run.[4]

How about Philip Humber, who pitched a *perfect game* for the White Sox against Seattle in 2012? That was his only major league complete game, and he has the fewest career wins (16) and by far the highest career ERA (5.31) of anyone who has pitched a perfect game. (Those numbers could change, as Humber could conceivably return to the major leagues. When this was written in 2015, he was 32 years old and pitching in Korea.) But Humber did have three games in which he pitched seven shutout innings and two other games in which he pitched into the eighth and allowed just one run. That's a lot better than some of his competitors for unlikeliest performance can say.

The unlikeliest no-hitter in the twentieth century was pitched by Bobo Holloman, a 30-year-old rookie who held the Athletics hitless in his first major league start on May 6, 1953. Holloman entered the game with an 8.44 major league ERA and won only two games in the majors after that; he was sent to the minors two months after his no-hitter, never to return. All that keeps Holloman off my list of unlikeliest performances is that, in one of his other wins, he pitched eight shutout innings and allowed just two hits.

Billy Rohr was one strike away from a no-hitter in his major league debut on April 14, 1967, finishing with a one-hit shutout of the Yankees. Rohr won just two more games in the major leagues and finished his brief career with a 5.64 ERA. But in his second major league appearance, also against the Yankees, he pitched a complete game and allowed just one run, making his debut seem not quite so unlikely. (Rohr's ERA in his games after his first two starts was 7.80.)

Jack Nabors started 37 games for the Philadelphia A's in 1915–16 and won only one of them, finishing his career with a 1–25 record. That one win would thus seem to be awfully unlikely. Of course, it was unlikely that anybody would win a game for those teams, as the A's had a combined record of 79–226 in those seasons. Nabors' one win was a complete game in which he allowed two runs, both unearned, but he had an identical stat line in one of his losses, plus two other losses in which he pitched eight innings and allowed two runs. It wasn't his performance in his victory that was unlikely, just the outcome.

I looked for pitchers who had a game with an unusually high (for them) "game score," a concept Bill James introduced in his *1988 Baseball Abstract* to roughly rate a starting pitcher's performance.[5] Baseball-Reference.com shows the game score for every start in its database going back (at this writing) to 1914. Sean Forman, the founder of the website, was kind enough to generate for me a list of the pitchers with the biggest difference between their best game score and their second-best game score.[6] Leon Cadore ranks second on this list and Joe Oeschger fourth, as the game score formula is generous to pitchers who pile up a high number of innings, but I still decided to leave them off my list of unlikeliest performances.

So who's on my list? I was going to do a traditional Top Ten, but I couldn't ignore Number 11. Here's the countdown:

11. BOB LACEY, OAKLAND A'S, OCTOBER 4, 1980

Lacey pitched 282 games in relief from 1977–84 and had several good seasons. In his first major league start, on the next-to-last day of the 1980 season, he shut out the Brewers. (It was the last of 94 complete games manager Billy Martin's A's pitched that season, no team has had more since the 1941 White Sox.) In Lacey's only other start, in 1984, he gave up five runs and was knocked out in the third inning. The difference between his game scores is the fifth-highest between any pitcher's two best. Lacey's longest appearance in his career aside from his shutout was 5.2 innings.

10. TROY HERRIAGE, KANSAS CITY A'S, MAY 22, 1956

After winning 15 games in the Class A South Atlantic League in 1955, Herriage was drafted by the A's and spent the 1956 season in the major leagues. He had allowed 16 runs in just 14 innings going into his May 22 start against Washington, but he pitched a three-hitter to beat the Nationals, holding them to just one run. That would be the only win in the only season of Herriage's major league career. He finished with a record of 1–13, and his ERA aside from his one victory was 7.18. Herriage started 16 games; only two pitchers in major league history started more games in their career without recording more than one win, Nabors and Mike Thompson. (Thompson started 29 games from 1971–75 and finished with a 1–15 record; he didn't make my list of unlikeliest performances because he had another start that was nearly as good as his win.) Herriage's win was the only game in which he pitched more than five innings and allowed fewer than three runs.

9. CLARAL GILLENWATER, CHICAGO WHITE SOX, AUGUST 25, 1923

Gillenwater (whose first name sometimes appeared in print as Claude or Clyde) had a 10–1 record in the Class B Michigan-Ontario League when he was purchased by the White Sox in mid-August 1923. In his major league debut he was blasted for six runs in two innings of relief work. Five days later he made his first start and shut out the Red Sox on four hits. He pitched just three more games in the majors and lost all three, allowing nine runs in 10.1 innings. His career ERA aside from his one win was 9.49, and he struck out just two of the 96 batters he faced in his brief career. Gillenwater is the first of several pitchers on this list whose only major league win was a shutout.

8. MIKE MODAK, CINCINNATI REDS, SEPTEMBER 5, 1945

Under the eligibility rules of the time, Modak was able to play college baseball and football at Indiana University (where one of his teammates in both sports was future Reds star Ted Kluszewski) while playing minor league baseball during World War II. Modak joined the Reds after finishing the school year at IU in June 1945 and was used primarily out of the bullpen, allowing five runs in three innings in his first start. When he got the starting nod again on September 5 his ERA was 5.72...which he promptly lowered by shutting out the Phillies. He made just one more start, getting knocked out in the third inning, and didn't pitch in the majors after that season. His ERA aside from his win was 7.29. I have him ahead of Gillenwater on this list because Gillenwater at least managed to go six innings in one of the starts he didn't win.

7. ED FALLENSTIN, BOSTON BRAVES, APRIL 30, 1933

Fallenstin (his last name sometimes misspelled as Fallenstein) pitched 24 games in relief as a 22-year-old rookie with the Phillies in 1931, posting a 7.13 ERA. He returned to the majors in 1933 with the Braves and in his first major league start shut out the Giants (who would go on to win the National League pennant) on three hits. After that, he made three more starts, and while he won one of them he allowed 12 runs in 16 innings. Fallenstein was sent to the minors in July and never pitched professionally after that season. Only Cadore and Oeschger had a greater difference between their two best game scores among pitchers who made at least four starts.

6. WALLY HOLBOROW, WASHINGTON NATIONALS, AUGUST 4, 1945

Holborow was one of the unlikely major leaguers who got a chance during World War II. (It's not a shock that three of the unlikeliest pitching performances ever came in 1945, when major league manpower was at its leanest due to the number of players in military service.) A native New Yorker, Holborow was pitching for a prominent semi-pro team, the Brooklyn Bushwicks, when he signed with the Nationals in 1944. His previous professional experience appears to have been limited to three games in the Class C Middle Atlantic League in 1935. Holborow made one relief appearance late in the 1944 season, throwing three scoreless innings, and spent the entire 1945 season in Washington. He wasn't used often that year, but he was effective, with an ERA of 2.08 through his first 11 appearances, all in relief.

Then on August 4, with the Nationals in second place in the American League, just three games behind Detroit, Nats manager Ossie Bluege called on Holborow to start the first game of a doubleheader against the Red Sox in Washington. Holborow "took the mound with the misgivings of the 13,035 fans," Shirley Povich reported in the next day's *Washington Post*, "and then delighted them with a masterful performance," shutting out the visitors on two hits.[7] (The Nationals were just two and a half games out of first after splitting that day's doubleheader but never did catch the Tigers and finished one game behind them.)

Holborow's shutout didn't earn him another starting opportunity; he made only three appearances the rest of the year, all in relief. After the season, with hundreds of players returning to the majors from the military, Holborow turned in his voluntary retirement papers and went back to the Bushwicks. But in late August 1948, A's owner/manager Connie Mack lured Holborow, then 34 years old (although newspaper reports of his signing said he was 31), to Philadelphia.[8]

After three relief appearances with the A's Holborow was called on to make his second career major league start on September 23 at Detroit. The A's staked him to a 7–2 lead in the fifth inning (Holborow knocked in three of the runs himself), but the Tigers rallied, and Sam Vico hit a two-run triple in the bottom of the ninth to give Detroit a 8–7 win. Mack left Holborow in to pitch to the bitter end, allowing him to face 43 batters and give up 16 hits. The difference in game scores between Holborow's two starts is the largest gap between any pitcher's two best starts.[9] Holborow made one last relief appearance for the A's before he was released after the 1948 season and returned to the Bushwicks, never again to play professional baseball.

5. MARK BROWNSON, COLORADO ROCKIES, JULY 21, 1998

Brownson faced a difficult task in his major league debut, pitching in Houston against an Astros team that would finish the season with 102 wins and an average of 5.4 runs per game. Brownson held the Astros hitless for the first five innings and finished with a four-hit shutout, an unexpected performance from a former 30th-round draft pick who had a 5.13 ERA in the Triple A Pacific Coast League when he was called up to the majors.[10] But Brownson's debut was not a harbinger of future success. Six days later he gave up seven runs in 4.1 innings and went back to the minors for the rest of the year; he started seven games for the Rockies in 1999 and won none of them. His only other major league win came in relief for the Phillies in 2000. Brownson's 6.94 career ERA (including his shutout) is the third highest for any pitcher who has ever thrown a shutout. (The higher ERAs belong to Hooks Iott and Carl Doyle, both of whom had at least one other reasonably good game in their careers to keep them off this list.)

4. BOB CLARK, CLEVELAND INDIANS, AUGUST 15, 1920

After leading the Class B New England League in wins in 1919, Clark spent the entire 1920 season on the Indians roster, but he did little more than pitch batting practice for the first several months. Aside from an appearance in which he pitched to one batter on May 26, he did not get into a game until August 1. He had less than 10 innings of major league experience when manager Tris Speaker tapped him to face the St. Louis Browns on August 15, with the Indians just a half-game out of first place. "Clark has as much stuff as any pitcher on my staff and I do not feel as if I were experimenting," Speaker said.[11]

Clark shut out St. Louis on four hits to move the Indians into first (they went on to win the American League pennant and World Series) and in the process he earned kudos from Browns first baseman George Sisler. "There was no fluke about Clark's victory," the future Hall of Famer said afterward. "He has the stuff and he had us puzzled. He will win a lot more games for Cleveland."[12] But Sisler was no Nostradamus. Clark never won another major league game, and in his only other start nine days later he was bombed for seven runs on 13 hits. His career ERA aside from his shutout was 6.59. Only Holborow and Cadore have a bigger difference between their two best game scores than Clark.

3. LARRY ANDERSON, MILWAUKEE BREWERS, SEPTEMBER 28, 1975

Not to be confused with his contemporary Larry Andersen, who had a long career as a major league relief pitcher, Anderson was the Brewers' second-round pick in the June 1971 draft out of a suburban Los Angeles high school. It was not a shining moment for the Brewers' scouting department; George Brett was taken two picks later, and Mike Schmidt was selected right after that. In his inauspicious professional debut in the short-season New York-Pennsylvania League, Anderson walked the first five batters he faced.[13]

Anderson showed enough in the Double A Texas League in 1974 that the Brewers wanted to take a closer look at their 21-year-old prospect, so they brought him to the major leagues in September and he made two scoreless relief appearances. But in 1975 he seemed to regress. Pitching for Sacramento, he walked 95 batters in 110 innings and led the Pacific Coast League in hit batsmen and wild pitches despite not spending the entire season there. Between his time in Sacramento and in the Texas League he threw 37 wild pitches that year.

That may not sound like a resumé begging for a major league call-up, but the Brewers felt otherwise and brought Anderson back to Milwaukee in September. It did not go well. He gave up five runs in three innings in his first appearance, five runs in three innings in his second, and four runs in 5.1 innings in his third, all in relief. In seven relief appearances in September he had a 7.17 ERA and a .344 batting average against.

Yet despite his lack of success, on the last day of the season Anderson got the ball for his first big league start and shut out the Tigers (finishing a woeful 57–102 season) on five hits, all singles.

Anderson never started another major league game. He spent the entire 1976 season in the Pacific Coast League, where he had a 6.14 ERA, walked 100 batters in 145 innings and threw a league-leading 25 wild pitches. Despite his poor numbers, Toronto selected him in the American League expansion draft. Two months later the Blue Jays traded him to the White Sox, and he pitched six games in relief for the White Sox in 1977, winning one of them. But he issued 11 unintentional walks and threw four wild pitches in just 8.2 innings and was sent back to the minors, where he continued to pitch until 1980 without returning to the big leagues.

Aside from his shutout, Anderson's career major league ERA was 7.24. He is one of only four pitchers to hurl a shutout in his only major league start. Don Fisher, introduced at the beginning of this piece, is another. The others are Luis Aloma, a successful relief pitcher for the White Sox in the early 1950s, and Frank Williams, who made 332 relief appearances in his six-year career and pitched a rain-shortened five-inning shutout when the Giants came up short of starting pitchers in 1984.

2. JOHN (JACK) McPHERSON, PHILADELPHIA PHILLIES, JUNE 22, 1904

McPherson made his major league debut with the Philadelphia A's at age 32 on July 12, 1901, giving up five runs in four innings in a loss to Boston. He didn't return to the majors until three years later, when he surfaced with the Phillies at age 35. The Phils finished in last place with a 52–100 record, and McPherson played his part with a 1–12 record and an ERA well above league average. But his one win was a dandy, a 13-inning shutout of Brooklyn on June 22 in which he allowed just six hits.[14] McPherson was back in the minors a month later and never pitched in the majors again. His 13 career losses are the most for a pitcher whose only career win was a shutout. His might seem to be the unlikeliest pitching performance ever: a pitcher with a 1–13 career record whose only win was a 13-inning shutout when he was 35 years old.

1. DON FISHER, NEW YORK GIANTS, SEPTEMBER 30, 1945

And yet I still think Fisher's gem is the unlikeliest of all. Fisher spent a brief time in professional baseball in his younger days, spending a month with Fargo-Moorhead of the Class D Northern League in 1938, but he made his name pitching in the adult sandlot leagues in his hometown of Cleveland while working as a "trouble shooter" for the city's electric company.[15] By 1944 he was with the powerhouse team sponsored by Bartunek Clothes and posted a 12–2 record that year as the Bartuneks won their fourth straight Class A city championship.[16] In September, he struck out 23 batters while pitching an 11-inning shutout in a National Baseball Federation tournament game.[17] His 1945 season went just as well, as he went 9–1, including a game in which he pitched a four-hit shutout, struck out 16, and hit a home run and two singles.[18,19]

The 29-year-old Fisher reportedly turned down several offers to sign with major league teams before finally coming to terms with the Giants in August.[20,21] A few days after joining the team he made his major league debut on August 25. He entered the game with the Giants trailing Brooklyn 9–0 and pitched the final five innings, giving up four runs (although he did contribute at the plate with an RBI double).

And that was the only major league action Fisher saw until manager Mel Ott sent him out to start the first game of a season-ending doubleheader at Boston. On a chilly afternoon, Fisher went the distance in a 13-inning game won by the Giants 1–0, as he scattered 10 hits and walked three. It would be his last major league appearance.

Fisher went to spring training with the Giants in 1946, but with players back from the war the Giants had plenty of more experienced pitchers from which to choose and sent him to their Jersey City farm club in the International League.[22] Fisher went 2–3 in nine games with Jersey City before he was released; he signed with Columbus of the American Association, where he had a 1–5 record in 21 games.

And that was the end of Fisher's professional baseball career. He returned to Cleveland and wound up spending 37 years working for the Cleveland Electric Illuminating Company before he died in 1973 at age 57.[23] I nominate his 13-inning shutout in his only major league start as the unlikeliest pitching performance ever. ■

Acknowledgments

Baseball-Reference.com's Play Index was invaluable in researching this article. I am also extremely grateful to B-R.com founder Sean Forman for providing me a list of the pitchers with the largest difference between their best and second-best game scores. Without that list it is likely I wouldn't have found Holborow, Fallenstin, or Lacey.

Notes

1. Box score is in the *Boston Sunday Herald*, September 2, 1906.
2. C. Paul Rogers III, "Jack Coombs," SABR Baseball Biography Project, http://sabr.org/bioproj/person/f64fded8.
3. Oeschger held Brooklyn scoreless for the final 21 innings of his duel with Cadore for the major league record for most consecutive scoreless innings in a game.
4. Bill Nowlin, "Joe Harris," SABR Baseball Biography Project, http://sabr.org/bioproj/person/2775e140.
5. "Game score" is determined as follows: Start with 50 points. Add 1 point for each out recorded (or 3 points per inning). Add 2 points for each inning completed after the 4th. Add 1 point for each strikeout. Subtract 2 points for each hit allowed. Subtract 4 points for each earned run allowed. Subtract 2 points for each unearned run allowed. Subtract 1 point for each walk. http://www.baseball-reference.com/about/pi_glossary.shtml.
6. The list of largest differences appears at https://prestonjg.wordpress.com/2015/02/07/a-few-final-maybe-thoughts-on-the-unlikeliest-pitching-performances-in-major-league-history/.
7. Shirley Povich, "Nats Win 7th Straight 4 to 0; Then Bow, 15–4," *Washington Post*, August 5, 1945.
8. "Holborow, Former Nat, Joins A's Slab Staff," *Washington Evening Star*, August 31, 1948.
9. His 1945 start had a game score of 84 while the 1948 start had a score of 18 for a difference of 66. Leon Cadore had the second-largest difference, 53, and his second-best score came in an 11-inning shutout.
10. Mike Klis, "Rookie dazzles in debut," *Denver Post*, July 23, 1998.
11. "Cleveland Indians on Last Invasion of East," *Cleveland Plain Dealer*, August 16, 1920.
12. Ibid.
13. "5 Leagues Begin Pennant Scramble," *The Sporting News*, July 10, 1971.
14. Box score is in *The New York Times*, June 23, 1904.
15. John Henehan, "Bartuneks' One-Two Punch Flattens Rivals," *Cleveland Plain Dealer*, July 12, 1945.
16. "Four Pilots Optimistic as 'A' Season Opens Today," *Cleveland Plain Dealer*, May 6, 1945.
17. "Dayton's Homers Oust Bartuneks From N.B.F. Tournament, 5–0," *Cleveland Plain Dealer*, September 13, 1944.
18. "Fisher Breaks In As Giants Drop 2," *Cleveland Plain Dealer*, August 26, 1945.
19. "Fisher Whiffs 16 As Bartuneks Win," *Cleveland Plain Dealer*, July 25, 1945.
20. John Henehan, "Bartuneks' One-Two Punch Flattens Rivals," *Cleveland Plain Dealer*, July 12, 1945.
21. John Drebinger, "Giants Pound Wyse and Rout Cubs, 9–3," *The New York Times*, August 21, 1945.
22. John Drebinger, "32 on Giant Squad as Ott Drops Nine," *The New York Times*, April 2, 1946.
23. "Donald R. Fisher," *Cleveland Plain Dealer*, August 2, 1973.

Switch-Hit Home Runs: 1920–60

Cort Vitty

Mickey Mantle posted a .353 batting average, slammed 52 homers, and drove in 130 runs in 1956. It was a breakout season for "The Mick" and a performance warranting American League Triple Crown honors. Mantle's remarkable season called attention to switch-hitting, affirmed his status as the premier switch-hitter in the game, and established a standard for future hitters with power from both sides of the plate.

Switch-hitting dates back to the earliest days of the game, when singles produced runs and homers were a rare occurrence. Good players found hitting from both sides provided an advantage against sidearm deliveries and tricky pitches, but in the early part of the twentieth century contributed little power. As Robert McConnell noted in the 1979 issue of the *Baseball Research Journal*, "Prior to Mantle's time, switch-hitters made little contribution in the home run, slugging and RBI departments."[1] Looking at 1920 as the first season after the Deadball era, the top career switch-hitting home run hitters through that year are listed below, career totals in parentheses:

Mantle was turned into a switch hitter when he was "barely old enough to walk." He remains the only switch-hitter in the history of the game to earn Triple Crown honors.

George Davis	72 HR	(.295 BA, .767 OPS, .405 SLG)	1890–1909
Walt Wilmot	58 HR	(.276 BA, .741 OPS, .404 SLG	1888–1909
Duke Farrell	51 HR	(.277 BA, .723 OPS, .385 SLG)	1888–1905
Tom Daly	49 HR	(.278 BA, .746 OPS, .386 SLG)	1884–1903
John Anderson	49 HR	(.290 BA, .734 OPS, .405 SLG)	1894–1908
Tommy Tucker	42 HR	(.290 BA, .737 OPS, .373 SLG)	1887–1899
Dan McGann	42 HR	(.284 BA, .744 OPS, .381 SLG)	1896–1908
Candy LaChance	39 HR	(.280 BA, .697 OPS, .379 SLG)	1893–1905
Cliff Carroll	31 HR	(.251 BA, .649 OPS, .329 SLG)	1882–1893
Max Carey	31 HR	(.275 BA, .713 OPS, .364 SLG)	1910–1929

The arrival of Babe Ruth changed everything. As Bill James writes, "The fans were galvanized by the Ruth phenomenon; his coming was unquestionably the biggest news story that baseball ever had."[2] Coinciding with the emergence of Ruth and the elimination of the spitball and other trick pitches, excited fans delighted in watching runs scored in bunches. Owners were happy to comply, while filling seats to capacity. Hitters started to copy the Ruthian swing, but few had significant power from both sides of the plate.

Indiana native Max Carey enjoyed a fine career as a switch-hitter with the Pittsburgh Pirates and Brooklyn Robins. His major league tenure (1910–29) bridged the transition from deadball to the modern era. Max reached double-digits in 1922, poking 10 home runs and commented: "Naturally, I was a right-handed hitter. But I forced myself to learn left-handed batting. Even now I can hit the ball harder right-handed, but the percentage in favor of the left-handed batter is too great to be ignored, especially where the batter wishes to capitalize his speed as I have done."[3] Carey ultimately finished his career with 70 lifetime home runs, moving him up to second on the all-time list, behind George Davis. (Frankie Frisch would surpass Carey.)

Washington, D.C. native Lu Blue served as an Army sergeant during World War I, and subsequently patrolled first base for the Tigers, Browns, White Sox, and Dodgers. Blue started switch-hitting in the minor leagues as an antidote to a prolonged slump; he enjoyed immediate success and continued to hit from both sides during his major league career. *The Sporting News* called the lefty thrower, "incomparable to any man in baseball as a fielding and throwing first baseman."[4] Blue's power was sufficient enough to poke 14 home runs in 1928. Lu and his ultra-selective batting eye retired with a lifetime on-base percentage of .402. He passed away in 1958 and is interred at Arlington National Cemetery.

New York native and future Hall-of-Famer Frankie Frisch segued from being a star athlete at Fordham University to signing with the New York Giants in 1919. He emerged as a prominent switch-hitter with power, hitting 12 home runs in 1923. A natural left-hand hitter, "Frisch batted cross-handed when he hit from the right-side, keeping his left hand above his right hand. Manager John McGraw worked with him, teaching fielding and sliding techniques, plus how to hold the bat properly."[5] Frisch would ultimately move on to become a player-manager with the St. Louis Cardinals, where his talented line-up included fellow switch-hitters Jack Rothrock and Ripper Collins.

The colorful Collins made his major league debut in 1931, hitting four home runs with the St. Louis Cardinals. His home run output rose to a healthy 21 dingers in 1932. By 1934, Ripper helped spark the "gashouse gang" to a world championship, by muscling an impressive 35 round trippers, tying him for the league lead with Mel Ott. Up to this point, Walt Wilmot of the Chicago Cubs was the only switch-hitter to lead the National League, smacking 13 home runs in 1890, and tying for the league lead with Oyster Burns and Mike Tiernan. Collins's 1934 performance became the single season standard for a switch-hitter until Mantle hit 37 in 1955. Did switch-hitting help the club win the 1934 World Series? "Yes," answered manager Frisch. "The more a team can keep its infield and outfield intact, the smoother its play is likely to be."[6]

Collins was a natural left-hander; his dad taught him to hit (and throw) both left and right-handed. Ripper kept a personal collection of discarded (game used) gloves and bats; from his huge cache he routinely carried a right-handed fielder's glove and practiced throwing right-handed. According to Collins, "Manager Frankie Frisch once considered inserting me into the lineup at third base, when he was short an

Frankie Frisch hit two homers as an All-Star, from the left side in 1933 and from the right side in 1934.

NATIONAL BASEBALL HALL OF FAME LIBRARY, COOPERSTOWN, NY

infielder; I would've been removed as a left-handed first baseman to play as a right-handed third baseman."[7] Ripper tied and surpassed George Davis on April 27, 1935, hitting career home runs number 72 and 73 off Pirates right-hander Jim Wilson. Retiring in 1941, Rip's 135 lifetime home runs placed him at the top of the all-time list, among career switch-hitters.

California native Buzz Arlett debuted with the Philadelphia Phillies on April 15, 1931, and proceeded to hit for a .313 batting average, with 18 round trippers. Despite those respectable numbers, his best years were spent in the Pacific Coast League and his skills were considerably diminished by the time he reached the major leagues. Originally a good hitting pitcher, Arlett won 29 games in 1920 before overuse ruined his pitching arm. The bad wing made swinging from his natural right side impossible, so Buzz was granted permission to practice hitting left-handed; he subsequently became a switch-hitting outfielder and went on to smack 432 minor league round trippers, before retiring in 1937.

Also of note in 1931 was the October 20 birth of Mickey Mantle in Spavinaw, Oklahoma. Mickey's dad Elvin "Mutt" Mantle was a huge baseball fan and likely took notice of switch-hitters Collins and Arlett arriving on the major league scene. "My dad always believed there would be platooning some day," Mantle said. "As a kid barely old enough to walk, Mantle was turned into a switch-hitter."[8]

Frankie Frisch had the honor of hitting left/right home runs in the first two (one in each) All-Star games. On Thursday July 6, 1933, at Chicago's Comiskey Park and batting left, Frankie victimized Alvin (General) Crowder in the sixth inning, though the National League fell, 4–2. The very next All-Star match was at the Polo Grounds in New York on July 10, 1934; this time Frisch went deep in the first inning while batting right-handed against Lefty Gomez. The American League went on to a 9–7 victory.

Versatile Augie Galan enjoyed a fine major league career spanning 1934 to 1949. As a child in California, Augie fell out of a tree and broke his right arm. Fearing retribution from his parents, he never told them about the accident. The arm didn't heal properly and he compensated by learning to throw using his shoulder muscles. Galan ultimately slugged 100 lifetime homers and on June 25, 1937, he had the distinction of becoming the first National League player to homer from both sides of the plate in a single game. Batting lefty, the Cubs outfielder took Brooklyn's Freddie Fitzsimmons deep in the fourth inning. Hitting right-handed against Ralph Birkofer, he homered again in the eighth. Roscoe McGowan of *The New York Times*

Augie Galen was first National League player to homer from both sides of the plate in a single game.

noted: "Galan was the first to profit by the new fence in left field, which brings the barrier twenty feet closer to the plate. His second home run just cleared the fence, which is the first bit of construction leading toward installation of new bleachers to increase park capacity by 5,000."[9] Augie turned into solely a left-hand batter from 1943 until 1949.

In the American League, Athletics catcher Wally Schang hit lefty/righty home runs on September 8, 1916, at Shibe Park in Philadelphia against the New York Yankees. Batting left, his first homer was served by right-hander Allen Russell, while his second was hit while batting right-handed versus lefty Slim Love; this one bounced over the fence and was recorded as a homer according to 1916 rules. The incident was not publicized at the time, due to an unusual circumstance. "So much rain fell that day that reporters, assuming the game could not possibly be played, did not go to the park. For scheduling purposes, Connie Mack insisted that the game be played in a late afternoon sea of water, in front of fewer than 100 people."[10]

Under modern rules, the first American Leaguer to actually muscle the ball over the fence from both sides was Johnny Lucadello of the St. Louis Browns, also while playing the Yankees. On September 16, 1940, he connected as a right-hand batter against lefty Marius Russo in the first inning; he next homered as a left-hand batter against Steve Sundra in the seventh. The Brownies went on to complete a 16–4 drubbing of the defending AL champs. Curiously, these were the only two home runs Lucadello hit all season, coming on the same day, from both sides of the plate. Johnny hit only five homers during a big league career from 1938 to 1947; albeit shortened by four prime years lost to military service during WWII.

Fayette City, Pennsylvania, native Jim Russell became the first major leaguer to hit lefty/righty homers in the same game twice in a career. Russell began switch-hitting as a youngster to compensate against his brother's tricky curve ball. Originally a Pittsburgh Pirate, Russell moved over to the pennant-bound Boston Braves in 1948. He connected from both sides against the Chicago Cubs on June 7, 1948, going deep against LHP Dutch McCall in the fifth and again versus RHP Ralph Hamner in the seventh. Moving over to the Brooklyn Dodgers in 1950, he enjoyed a second switch-hit homer day on July 26, against the St. Louis Cardinals. This time he drove one out one against lefty Harry Brecheen in the first inning, followed by taking right-hander Red Munger deep in the fifth. Russell was gone from the majors after the 1951 season; he posted a total of 67 career homers. His best single season mark was 12 homers in the last wartime season of 1945, back with the Pirates.

At the close of the 1940s, journeyman switch-hitter Roy Cullenbine had 110 career home runs, good enough to place him second to Ripper Collins on the all-time list. Roy grew up in Detroit and served as Tigers batboy in 1929–30. Invited to a tryout, he was signed by Detroit in 1933 as a right-handed hitter. In 1935, while playing for Springfield in the III league, he impetuously jumped over to the left batter's box, during batting practice. Manager Bob Coleman watched Cullenbine launch several pitches deep into the right-field stands, and announced, "Roy from now on you're a switch hitter."[11]

During a career spanning 1938 to 1947, Cullenbine made stops with the Dodgers, Tigers, Browns, Indians, Senators, and Yankees. Weight gain greatly affected his performance, and it was the slimmer version of Cullenbine acquired by the Yankees on August 31, 1942. The move was intended to fortify the outfield when Tommy Henrich enlisted in the Coast Guard. Roy hit .364 in 21 games and helped the Yankees cop the AL pennant. The Yankees assigned him uniform number 7, possibly warming it up for a future Yankee slugger with power from both sides of the plate. Roy's lifetime batting average was .276; however, his uncanny ability to draw 853 career walks, along with 1,072 hits, gave him an impressive on base average of .408 lifetime. Roy's top home run total was 24 as a Detroit Tiger in 1947, his final big league season.

The 1950s saw the arrival of a speedy switch-hitting center fielder—not yet Mickey Mantle, but Sam Jethroe, a successful Negro League star with the Cleveland Buckeyes. Jethroe, along with Jackie Robinson and Marvin Williams, was given a sham tryout in April 1945, by the Boston Red Sox. Afterwards, management summarily dismissed all three as not being up to big league standards. Later in 1945, Jethroe would go on to win the Negro American League batting title, hitting .393.[12]

Jethroe ultimately signed with the Dodgers. Dealt to the Braves, he earned 1950 rookie-of-the-year honors at the age of 32, hitting 18 round trippers for Boston, while leading both major leagues with 35 stolen bases. Buck O'Neill of the Kansas City Monarchs played against him and recalled his incredible speed, which led appropriately to "Jet" as his nickname. "When he came to bat, the infield would have to come in a few steps or you'd never throw him out."[13] Jethroe followed up with another 18-homer season in 1951, but his offensive numbers fell off sharply in 1952 and he was gone from the majors after a short trial with the Pirates in 1954. Lifetime, "Jet" smacked 49 round trippers.

The Chicago White Sox called up Dave Philley for a cup of coffee in 1941, just before he left to serve during World War II. Returning in 1946 and up for a full season in 1947, the speedy native of Paris, Texas, became a mainstay in the Chicago White Sox outfield. Possessing a strong right throwing arm, Philley led American league outfielders in assists three times dur-

ing his tenure. His career best was smacking 14 home runs for the 1950 White Sox.

Philley started switch-hitting as a youngster, when an arm injury prevented him from swinging left-handed, his natural side. By the late 1950s, his role changed from regular outfielder to pinch hitter extraordinaire. He pounded 18 hits off the bench for the Phillies in 1958, with eight hit consecutively to end the season. His streak was extended to nine when he added another pinch hit in his first appearance of 1959. He laced 24 pinch hits for the Baltimore Orioles in 1961 and ultimately posted 84 round trippers during his long career.

As a youngster in Illinois, Red Schoendienst injured his left eye repairing a fence while serving with the Depression-era Civilian Conservation Corps. An exercise program ultimately strengthened the injured eye, but while healing he learned to hit left-handed and became an adept switch-hitter. At the 1950 All-Star game in Chicago's Comiskey Park, his 14th-inning home run, served up by lefty Ted Gray, and provided the margin of the 4–3 victory for the National League; it was the first extra-inning summer classic.

On July 8, 1951, Schoendienst joined the switch-hit homer club by hammering one from each side of the plate against the Pittsburgh Pirates. He connected against right-hander Ted Wilks in the sixth inning, and then hit one out served by lefthander Paul LaPalme in the seventh. His top home-run production was 15, in both 1953 and 1957. His health would again be tested due to a serious bout of tuberculosis, sidelining the star second baseman virtually all of the 1959 season.

During batting practice in the minor leagues, Roy Cullenbine impetuously jumped into the left-handed batters box and hit several home runs, prompting manager Bob Coleman to make him a switch hitter.

A boyhood eye injury spurred Red Schoendienst to learn to hit left-handed and he carried the ability to switch hit into the major leagues.

Mantle first connected from both sides of the plate on May 13, 1955. He tied the Jim Russell mark (second time) on August 15, 1955 and on May 18, 1956, became the first major leaguer to homer from both sides of the plate for a third time. This dinger, served up by Dixie Howell of the Chicago White Sox, was career home-run number 136, placing Mantle into the top position on the all-time list, by passing Ripper Collins' 135 round-trippers. By the end of the decade, he'd up that total of same game, switch-hit homers to seven. During the 1956 season, he became the first switch-hitter to reach the 40- and then the 50-homer plateau in a single season. Mantle remarked, "1956 was a great year, the best I ever had in baseball. I would never again duplicate that season. I finally accomplished the things people had been predicting for me, especially Casey Stengel, and I felt good about that."[14]

At the start of the 1960 season, the ten players with the most career switch-hit home runs included:

Mickey Mantle	280
Ripper Collins	135
Roy Cullenbine	110
Frankie Frisch	105
Augie Galan	100
Dave Philley	81
Red Schoendienst	80
George Davis	73
Max Carey	70
Jim Russell	67[15]

Mantle ultimately went on to smack 536 blasts during his storied career, ending in 1968. He remains the only switch-hitter in the history of the game to earn Triple Crown honors. Lifetime, his OPS was .977, while he posted a career slugging percentage of .557. Players on the above list, still active after 1960, included both Philley and Schoendienst; each would finish their respective careers with a total of 84 home runs. Players capable of hitting with power from both sides of the plate will continue to come and go, but Mantle's strength, talent and influence certainly remains the standard. ∎

Sources

Allen, Lee. Hot Stove League. A.S. Barnes & Co. New York, 1955, 35.

Daley, Arthur. "The Idle First Baseman." The New York Times, January 20, 1957.

Goldstein, Richard. "Sam Jethroe is Dead at 83." The New York Times, January 19, 2001.

James, Bill. Historical Baseball Abstract. Villard Books: New York, 1988, 125.

Lane, F.C. Batting. University of Nebraska Press: Lincoln, NE, 2001, 53.

Mantle, M. & Pepe, Phil. My Favorite Summer 1956. Doubleday: New York, 2001, 241.

Vincent, David. Home Run: The Definitive History. Potomac Books, Washington D.C., 2007.

The Baseball Encyclopedia. Ed. Joseph Reichler. MacMillan: New York, 1982.

The Home Run Encyclopedia. Ed. Robert McConnell & David Vincent. MacMillan: New York, 1996.

The SABR Baseball List & Record Book. Ed. Lyle Spatz. Scribner: New York 2007.

McGowan, Roscoe. "Cubs Quickly Route Fitzsimmons." The New York Times, June 26, 1937.

Shirley, Bill. "The Art of Switch-Hitting." Los Angeles Times, March 24, 1985.

Karst, Gene. "Frisch Credits Cardinals' Success to "Turn" Batters." The Sporting News, January 24, 1935.

Vincent, David. Home Run lists contained in this article.

Newspapers

Chicago Tribune
Los Angeles Times
The New York Times
The Sporting News
Washington Post

Websites

Baseball Almanac
Baseball-Reference.com
Retrosheet
SABR Baseball Biography Project

Notes

1. Robert McConnell, "Mantle is Baseball's Top Switch Hitter," The Baseball Research Journal (1979): 1.

2. Bill James, Historical Baseball Abstract, Villard Books: New York, 1988, 125.

3. F.C. Lane, Batting, University of Nebraska Press: Lincoln, NE, 2001, 53.

4. The Sporting News, April 9, 1925.

5. Fred Stein, SABR BioProject.

6. The Sporting News, January 24, 1935.

7. Arthur Daley, "The Idle First Baseman," The New York Times, January 20, 1957.

8. Bill Shirley, "The Art of Switch-Hitting," Los Angeles Times, March 24, 1985.

9. Roscoe McGowan, "Cubs Quickly Route Fitzsimmons," The New York Times, June 26, 1937.

10. Robert McConnell, "Searching Out The Switch Hitters," The Baseball Research Journal (1973): 1.

11. The Sporting News, September 10, 1942.

12. Richard Goldstein, "Sam Jethroe Is Dead at 83," The New York Times, June 19, 2001, 21.

13. Bob Ajemian, "$100,000 Jethroe May Be Flop in Outfield," The Sporting News, March 29, 1950.

14. Mickey Mantle & Phil Pepe, My Favorite Summer 1956, Doubleday: New York, 2001, 241.

15. Home Run List(s) courtesy David Vincent.

"That Record Will Never Be Broken!"

How Many "Unbreakable" Records Are There?

Douglas Jordan

Baseball aficionados often argue that certain records will never be broken. A classic example is Cal Ripken's 2,632 consecutive-games-played streak. However, for the most part, the arguments given to support an assertion that a particular record will never be broken are subjective and not analytically rigorous. The primary purpose of this paper is to examine some baseball records closely in order to increase awareness of the greatness of these feats, and to make a less subjective judgment of any claim that a particular record will never be broken. A secondary purpose is to make fans aware that there are probably more than just one or two baseball records that may never be broken.

Before we look at the records, we must first define what we mean by "never be broken." Never is a long time. A lot of things we currently think impossible (in baseball and in general) may not be not quite so impossible given eternity as a timeframe. For example, in 2003 it didn't look like anyone would ever make more than 257 hits in a season since it had been over 80 years since that record was set. But Ichiro Suzuki made 262 in 2004. In 1981 it looked very unlikely that anyone would ever steal more than 118 bases in a season, but Ricky Henderson stole 130 the next season. In addition, the unstated assumption buttressing the "never be broken" argument is that the game of baseball will remain as we know it today. For example, if the mound is lowered again (as *Sports Illustrated* baseball analyst Tom Verducci suggested in a May 2014 column) in an effort to increase offense, increase attendance, and reduce injuries to pitchers, it will increase the probability of offensive records being broken and decrease the probability of breaking pitching records. Therefore, for purposes of this paper, "never be broken" will be taken to mean the record will not be broken over the next 110 baseball seasons played under rules similar to today's rules. The time period of 110 years is chosen because the first World Series where the American League and National League as we know them today met was played roughly 110 years ago and because some of the records discussed herein only use data from 1903 on. All of the data used to do this analysis were taken from the web site Baseball-Reference.com with the exception of the information included in the endnotes.

BASELINE RECORDS ANALYSIS

The main point of this article is to examine the "breakability" of various major league single-season and career records. The primary technique used in the analysis will be to compare the records against a standard (and each other) on four separate dimensions.

Although this analysis technique does not yield an actual probability that a record will be broken, it does quantify the discussion of records that are claimed to be unbreakable by allowing records to be ranked on the four dimensions.

In order to do the ranking it is necessary to have baseline numbers in each of the dimensions for comparison. Therefore, Cal Ripken's record of 2,632 consecutive games played will be used as the standard against which other records are compared when examining the likelihood of other records being broken. This record is chosen as the standard because it represents over 16 seasons of baseball without missing a game. Although it is possible to play more games consecutively, the probability of any player doing so is so small that there is little question that this record deserves the never-be-broken tag. The numbers associated with the discussion of Ripken's record in the next paragraph are shown in the sixth line of Table 2. The following observations can be made based on the calculations associated with Ripken's record. Records that will be difficult to break are likely to be roughly 20 percent better than the next highest record, and will be two to three times better than the 11th best record or the average of the next ten records. Such records are also likely to be four standard deviations or more from the average of the next ten records. Cal Ripken also set a related record that is not as widely known as his consecutive games played record. Table 2 shows that Ripken also holds the record of 8,264 consecutive innings played. It took him most of seven straight seasons to play in the 904 games during this streak. This record is just as impressive (and as unlikely to be broken) as his consecutive games played record even if not as widely disseminated. Thanks to Trent McCotter for making me aware of this record in his interesting article in the Fall 2012 *Baseball Research Journal*, "Ripken's Record for Consecutive Innings Played."[1]

Both single-season and career records will be examined. The records that have been analyzed were subjectively chosen as records that a priori seemed difficult to break. These lists are not intended to be an examination of every possible baseball record. Some of the single-season records only include data from 1903 on. That year was subjectively chosen as the year of the first World Series[2], with the pre-1903 data being excluded, because in some respects the game of baseball prior to 1903 is not really comparable to the post-1902 game. For example, according to Baseball-Reference.com, there are 104 pitchers on the single-season innings pitched record list from the 1800s before the first post-1902 pitcher is listed. All of those pitchers threw more than 465 innings during a season, with Will White topping the list with a whopping 680 innings thrown in 1879. The game has changed significantly enough since then that those records are simply not comparable to the post-1902 game and are therefore excluded from the analysis.

SINGLE-SEASON RECORDS DISCUSSION: Offense

A careful and thoughtful look at the single-season records in Table 1 reveals that they are all impressive feats. Let's look at some of them in detail starting with my personal favorite, Rickey Henderson's incredible 130 stolen bases. Henderson was 23 in 1982 when he set this record. That season he played in 149 games, batted .267 with a .398 on-base-percentage, had 143 hits, and walked a league-leading 116 times. Most of

his steals (94) were of second base but he also stole third base 34 times (for perspective, the Kansas City Royals led the majors in steals—153—and steals of third—29—in 2014) and stole home twice. He stole three bases in six games and had three amazing games in which he stole four bases—impressive even if short of the post-1902 record of six in a game done twice by Eddie Collins in 1912 and tied by Otis Nixon (1991), Eric Young (1996), and Carl Crawford (2009).[3] He also stole between 22 and 27 bases every month of the season except September and stole 84 bases over the first 88 games of that season.

Why is this a record that's not likely to be broken? It's 12 steals more and about 10 percent better than the next highest total of 118 bases that Lou Brock stole in 1974 when he was 35(!) years old. In comparison, the recent high for stolen bases is 78 set by Jose Reyes in 2007. Henderson's record is more impressive on a games-played-per-stolen-base basis. For Henderson, Brock, and Reyes these three ratios are 1.15, 1.30, and 2.05 respectively. That means that Henderson needed just over one game for each of his stolen bases (or almost a stolen base per game on average) while the best base stealer in recent times took over two games for each base stolen. An additional consideration is that given how expensive star players are in today's game, it is unlikely that a team will allow a star player like Mike Trout, for instance, who led the league with 49 steals in 2012, to take the physical pounding that stealing that many bases would require. Conclusion:

Table 1. Single-Season Record Analysis

Category	Record holder (age) (year) + means HoF	Record	Next highest record	Fraction above next highest record	Fraction above 11th highest record	Fraction above average of the next 10 records	Standard deviations above the average of the next 10 records
Triples*	John "Chief" Wilson (28) (1912)	36	26	1.38	1.57	1.46	9.74
Walks	Barry Bonds (39) (2004)	232	170***	1.36	1.57	1.49	10.30
Consecutive game hitting streak	Joe DiMaggio +(1941)	56	45	1.24	1.6	1.41	5.82
Walks	Barry Bonds (39) (2004)	232	198**	1.17	1.55	1.42	4.60
Stolen Bases*	Rickey Henderson+(23) (1982)	130	118	1.10	1.35	1.24	3.50
Runs Scored*	Babe Ruth+ (26) (1921)	177	167	1.06	1.16	1.12	3.84
Doubles	Earl Webb (33) (1931)	67	64	1.05	1.18	1.11	2.47
HR	Barry Bonds (36) (2001)	73	70	1.04	1.26	1.17	2.70
RBI	Hack Wilson+ (30) (1930)	191	185	1.03	1.14	1.10	2.99
Wins *	Jack Chesbro+ (30) (1904)	41	40	1.03	1.32	1.20	2.40
Hits	Ichiro Suzuki (30) (2004)	262	257	1.02	1.09	1.05	2.36
Innings Pitched *	Ed Walsh+ (27) (1908)	464	454.2	1.02	1.20	1.14	2.50
Strikeouts *	Nolan Ryan+ (26) (1973)	383	382	1.00	1.16	1.08	1.72

* Data from 1903 on only.
** Barry Bonds holds this record too.
*** Bonds's record compared to the first non-Bonds player; Babe Ruth who drew 170 walks in 1923

Table 2. Career Record Analysis

Category	Record holder (length of career) + means HoF	Record	Next highest record	Fraction above next highest record	Fraction above 11th highest record	Fraction above average of the next 10 records	Standard deviations above the average of the next 10 records
Steals of Home	Ty Cobb+ (24)	54	33	1.64	3.00	2.34	6.38
Years Managing	Connie Mack+	53	33	1.61	2.21	1.9	7.72
Consecutive innings played*	Cal Ripken+	8264	5152	1.60	2.89	2.27	6.00
Stolen Bases	Rickey Henderson+ (25)	1406	938	1.50	2.04	1.77	6.82
Wins Managing	Connie Mack+	3731	2763	1.35	1.96	1.64	4.87
Consecutive games played	Cal Ripken+	2632	2130	1.24	3.29	2.51	3.81
Wins	Cy Young+ (22)	511	417	1.23	1.55	1.41	6.36
Walks	Barry Bonds (22)	2558	2190	1.17	1.58	1.39	3.76
Strikeouts	Nolan Ryan+ (27)	5714	4875	1.17	1.71	1.49	3.46
At Bats	Pete Rose (24)	14053	12364	1.14	1.28	1.23	5.43
Plate Appearances	Pete Rose (24)	15890	13992	1.14	1.27	1.22	5.15
Wins **	Walter Johnson+ (21)	417	373	1.12	1.33	1.23	3.83
Saves	Mariano Rivera (19)	652	601	1.08	1.87	1.57	3.01
RBI	Hank Aaron+ (23)	2297	2214	1.04	1.22	1.16	3.23
Hits	Pete Rose (24)	4256	4189	1.02	1.3	1.2	2.65
Runs Scored	Rickey Henderson+ (25)	2295	2246	1.02	1.22	1.1	1.64
HR	Barry Bonds (22)	762	755	1.01	1.33	1.19	2.09

* Statistics for this record are taken from McCotter: "Ripken's Record for Consecutive Innings Played," *BRJ* Fall 2012
** With Cy Young removed since he played roughly half his career prior to 1903.

it is highly unlikely anyone will ever steal 130 bases again.

What about the hits record? The number is easy to remember; it's exactly 100 hits more than the number of games in a season, 262. Could that possibly be true? Did Ichiro Suzuki really make 100 more hits than there are games in a season in 2004? Incredibly, he did, but given that he did it only about ten years ago, you might think it's absurd to consider it a record that might never be broken. But a closer look at Ichiro's numbers that season will show just how extraordinary getting 262 hits is and why it will be a very difficult record to break even if set relatively recently.

Suzuki broke George Sisler's 1920 record of 257 hits and Sisler broke Ty Cobb's 1911 record of 248 hits. The only modern players with at least 240 hits (besides Suzuki) are Wade Boggs and Darin Erstad, who each had 240 hits in one season. These data show that even after adding eight games to the schedule in 1961 (AL) and 1962 (NL) it's still very difficult to get more than 240 hits in a season. The only modern player to do it is Suzuki, who did it twice (he also had 242 hits in 2001). Sisler's record had stood for over 80 years before Suzuki broke it.

Why did 257 hits stand so long? Because to accumulate that total Sisler had to play in 154 games, make 692 plate appearances, strike out only 19 times, walk only 46 times, and bat .407 for the season. He made four hits in 12 games, three hits in 29 games, two hits in 33 games, and a single hit in 56 games. He played in only 24 games that season in which he failed to get a hit. In comparison, Adrian Beltre, who led the league in hits in 2013 with 199, had 41 games in which he failed to get a hit.

These numbers show that in order to challenge the hits record, a player has to play in virtually every game of the season, make a very high number of plate appearances, hit for high average, and not walk very much. High average by itself will not get it done. For example, even with the 56-game hitting streak in 1941 and a .357 batting average that year, Joe DiMaggio had only(?) 193 hits that season. Ted Williams only(?) had 185 hits that same year when he batted .406. DiMaggio's and Williams's career best hit totals are 215 and 194 respectively.

What are Suzuki's numbers for 2004? He played in all but one of the Mariners games (161), led the league in plate appearances (762) and batting average (.372), and struck out just 63 times. The 762 plate appearances are eighth on the all-time list, which is topped by Jimmy Rollins's 778 appearances in 2007. Suzuki had four games in which he made five hits, six games

Cal Ripken's record of 2,632 consecutive games played also gives him the record for consecutive innings played at 8,264.

with four hits, 24 games with three hits, 46 games with two hits, 54 games with a single hit, and he failed to get a hit in only 27 games that season. In spite of having such a tremendous season, Suzuki had 251 hits after playing in the same number of games as Sisler (154) and reached that total only because he had a five-hit game and a four-hit game a few games earlier. In subsequent games he made 1, 2, 1, 1, 3 (October 1, the day he broke the record), 1, and 2 hits to get to his total of 262. He made at least one hit in each of the last 13 games of the season for a total of 26. If Suzuki had made only(?) 20 hits in those last 13 games, he would not have broken the record.

The fact that George Sisler's record of 257 hits stood for over 80 years is a testament to how great his 1920 season was. Ichiro Suzuki needed an equally extraordinary season to break that record. Anything is possible, but a player will have to play in almost every game and have a simply superb season to exceed either of these hit totals. It's not likely to be done anytime soon, and quite possibly will never be done again.

Hack Wilson's amazing record of 191 RBIs in 1930 will be examined next. The record is just six better or about three percent higher than the 185 runs that Lou Gehrig drove in in 1931. But it is 26 RBIs better than the modern high of 165 by Manny Ramirez in 1999, so I'm going to compare Wilson's record to Ramirez's

rather than Gehrig's. Ramirez played in 147 games, made 174 hits, hit 44 home runs, batted .333, and slugged a league-leading .663. He had eight RBIs in one game and five in another. He had five games with four RBIs, 12 games with three, 30 games with two, and 36 games with one. He failed to drive in a run in just 62 games. Those are superb RBI numbers for single season.

What numbers did Wilson put up in 1930? He played in 155 games, made 709 plate appearances, had 208 hits, batted .356, and led the league in home runs (56), RBIs (191), and slugging (.723, which is 22nd on the all-time list). He had two games with six RBIs, three games with five RBIs, seven games with four RBIs, 15 games with three RBIs, 26 games with two RBIs, 39 games with a single RBI, and 63 games with none. He drove in nine runs in the last three games of the season and 12 runs in the last five games. These are amazing RBI totals. In order to generate that many, he had to have men on base to drive in. Woody English and Kiki Cuyler batted in front of Wilson that season and had OBAs of .430 and .428 respectively. It's rare to have a pair of teammates with OBAs that high. Wilson's 191 RBIs in 1930 is an astounding record that will most likely never be broken. (Zach Rymer wrote an interesting article about Wilson's record in 2013 for *Bleacher Report*.[4])

The next two players on the RBI list are Lou Gehrig and Hank Greenberg. Historically, Gehrig had been credited with 184 in 1931 and Greenberg with 183 in 1937. But research by Herm Krabbenhoft corrected Greenberg's total to 184 (*BRJ* Spring 2012)[5] and Gehrig's to 185 (*BRJ* Fall 2012).[6]

Space considerations preclude a detailed discussion of all the single-season hitting records in Table 1, but a couple other records deserve to be mentioned. Taking the numbers at face value (setting aside the discussion of how steroids should or should not be considered with respect to records) means that Barry Bonds's astounding 232 walks in 2004 is very unlikely to ever be broken. The next highest total on the walks list is 170 by Babe Ruth in 1923. The only player to exceed 170 is Bonds, who did it three times between 2001 and 2004. The next highest total is 162 set by Mark McGwire (1998) and Ted Williams (1947 and 1949). Since no player but Bonds has ever exceeded 170, Bonds's 232 walks is likely to stand a very long time. The same is true of John "Chief" Wilson's record 36 triples in 1912. That record is 38 percent better than the next highest post-1902 total (26) and 46 percent better than the average of the next ten. The modern high for triples is Curtis Granderson's 23 in 2007, with most years having a high well under 20 triples. The Pirates home ballpark in 1912, Forbes Field, probably had something to do with Wilson's total. With an incredible 462 feet to the center field wall, the 1912 Pirates hit the most triples (129) since 1902.[7] Wilson said of his record, "A three-base hit may usually be made only by driving the ball clear to the fence, particularly toward center field on most grounds."[8] Whatever the cause of Wilson's outburst, nobody is likely to hit 36 triples again anytime soon.

SINGLE-SEASON RECORDS ANALYSIS: Pitching

Before discussing specific pitching records, it is appropriate to examine changes in pitching in general over the last century or so. Changes such as going from a four-man rotation to a five-man rotation in the mid-1970s and the increased use of relief pitchers since the 1980s have resulted in a general trend of using more pitchers who pitch fewer innings over time. These changes have substantially reduced the number of innings pitched by starting pitchers, which in turn has reduced the number of decisions awarded to starting pitchers. This makes it highly unlikely that pitching records set in the early 1900s will ever be broken unless the use of pitchers changes substantially in the future.

The arguments in the previous paragraph apply to both the innings pitched and wins records in Table 1. Ed Walsh pitched an incredible 464 innings in 1908 and Jack Chesbro had an amazing 41 wins in 1904. To achieve that innings pitched total, Walsh started 49 games and completed an astonishing 42 of them while compiling a 40–15 overall record. He appeared in 66 games and had six saves. Chesbro started 51(!) games and had 48(!) complete games on his way to a 41–12 season and a total of 454 innings pitched. All of these totals are impossible to achieve in today's game, since starting pitchers have a maximum of about 35 starts during a season.

But what about a pitching record that is only about 40 years old rather than 100 years old? Does the same logic apply? For example, Nolan Ryan struck out an astonishing 383 batters in 1973. This total is just one strikeout more than the second highest total (Sandy Koufax's 382 in 1965) but is 16 percent higher than the 11th highest record. Ryan started 39 games, completed 26 of them, pitched 326 innings, and had a 2.87 ERA. He finished with a record of 21–16 and also walked a league-leading 162 batters. He averaged 10.6 strikeouts per nine innings over the course of the season. He struck out 17 batters in one game and 16 in another. He also had an incredible total of 23 games with double-digit strikeouts.

Since both Ryan and Kofax pitched in a very different pitching era from today, it might be tempting to say this is a record that will never be broken. But the third-place record on the list is just 11 strikeouts fewer than Ryan's total and was put up a little over a decade ago. Who did it? Randy Johnson. The Big Unit struck out an amazing 372 batters in 2001 when he went 21–6 with a 2.49 ERA. It's interesting to note that he threw 249 innings and had a 2.49 ERA that season. He threw three complete games in 34 starts. How did he accumulate almost as many strikeouts in about 80 fewer innings? Johnson struck out an incredible 13.4 batters per nine innings that season (the best-ever ratio for strikeouts per nine innings; he holds six of the top eight in that category). He struck out 20 batters in one game and 16 batters in three other games. Like Ryan, he had double-digit strikeouts in 23 of his starts. With strikeout numbers like that, it is not surprising he approached Ryan's record that season.

So does Johnson's accomplishment mean that Ryan's record does not belong in the never-be-broken category since Johnson approached it relatively recently? In spite of Johnson's heroic efforts, it is very unlikely that anyone will exceed 383 strikeouts in a season. Johnson had a season for the ages in terms of strikeouts in 2001 and still did not break the record. The next two recent pitchers on the season strikeout list (who are not Ryan, Koufax, or Johnson) are Sam McDowell, who struck out 325 in 1965, and Curt Schilling, who struck out 319 in 1997. Those still impressive strikeout totals are a far cry from 383. The numbers show that Ryan, Koufax, and Johnson were very special pitchers in terms of strikeouts. Even in the current era with batters striking out at historic rates, it will take an extraordinary effort over the course of a season to exceed either Johnson's or Ryan's total. So in spite of how recent Johnson's effort is, as with Ichiro Suzuki's recent 262 hits in a season, 383 strikeouts may never be broken.

What about Joe DiMaggio's record 56-game hitting streak? This record enjoys iconic status and the numbers in Table 1 associated with this record are similar to the numbers associated with Chief Wilson's record 36 triples. The similarities of the numbers for the two records implies that the hitting streak record deserves its iconic status. However, Wayne Winston in his 2009 book Mathletics argues that the breakability of this record is primarily a function of the overall baseball batting average.[9] He argues that as league batting averages move upward, the probability of a 56-game hitting streak increases. To be specific, Winston finds that there is a 2.4% probability of a 56-game hitting streak over 107 seasons. He concludes, "Our calculations show that given all the opportunities for a 56-game hitting streak to occur, such a streak is highly unlikely, but certainly not impossible."

CAREER RECORDS DISCUSSION: Offense

Career records are analyzed in the same manner as the single-season records. The results are shown in Table 2.

A thoughtful examination of the records in Table 2 can elicit only one response: wow! All of the career records are amazing! With the sole exception of the saves record, every one of them required over 20 years of sustained, superior performance. Given the magnitude of the accomplishments in Table 2, it's not unreasonable to consider that none of the career records may ever be broken. Let's look at some of them in detail, starting again with stolen bases.

Rickey Henderson's career total of 1,406 stolen bases is simply incredible. It is 468 stolen bases and 50% better than Lou Brock's second place (and still impressive) total of 938. Just how big is that difference? There are only 45 players on the career stolen base list who have more than 468 stolen bases (however a stolen base is defined) in their whole career. Henderson has that many more than Brock. The top mark for players who are currently playing is Ichiro Suzuki's 498 (as of this writing) career total. Recent season highs for stolen bases have been around 70. That total would have to be achieved for 20 years in order to get to Henderson's total. Is that possible? Yes. Is it likely? No.

How did Henderson do it? He needed extraordinary longevity, durability, and performance. During his 25-year career (an amazing career length given how stealing bases punishes the body and can result in injury) he led the league in steals 12 times, stole over 100 bases three times, stole between 77 and 93 bases four times, and between 41 and 66 bases nine times. He played in over 100 games in all but five of his seasons while maintaining a career .279 batting average and a .401 career OBP. Henderson achieved such a high career OBP by walking a lot. In fact, as Table 2 shows, his 2,190 career walks is second only to Barry Bonds's 2,558. In comparison, Lou Brock, who played for 19 years, led the league in steals eight times, had a single season with over 100 steals, and just two other seasons with 70 or more steals. He batted .293 lifetime and had a career OBP of .343. Those are impressive numbers but a far cry from Henderson's. Brock's record may be broken, Henderson's is virtually unreachable.

Table 2 also shows that Henderson leads the career list for runs scored with 2,295. Although this total is just two percent above the 2,246 put up by Ty Cobb, it is still a very impressive total. Henderson's seasonal runs scored numbers need to be considered in the context of recent performances to be fully appreciated. The recent high for runs is the 152 put up by Jeff Bagwell in 2000. The seasonal high has been in the 120–140 runs scored range recently. What did Henderson do? He scored more than 100 runs 13 times with his high being 146 in 1985, and scored at least 118 runs in four other seasons. He scored at least 40 runs every other season except for his shortened last season. How likely is this record to be broken? The next players on the career runs scored list after Cobb are Barry Bonds with 2,227 and Hank Aaron with 2,174. If they couldn't do it with their outstanding careers, it's going to be very difficult for anybody else to break this record.

Arguably, the numbers 714 and 755 are the most famous figures in baseball history. Even casual baseball fans are likely to know that these are Babe Ruth's and Hank Aaron's career home run totals. It is also widely known to current baseball fans that Barry Bonds broke Aaron's record in 2007 and amassed a total of 762 home runs in his career. Baseball fans tend to throw these numbers around casually, but it must be understood that for anybody to hit more than 700 home runs in a career is incredible. It takes 14 seasons with 50 home runs or 17.5 seasons of 40 home runs to reach 700. Hitting 50 home runs in a season is quite an achievement; only 27 different players have done it a total of 43 times. Even at the height of the steroid era there were only two years (1998 and 2001) where four players hit 50 or more home runs. In that same era there were only seven years where the top ten totals for home runs were at least 40. So 40 home runs, even in a hitter's era, is still a special achievement. That means all three of the men who have hit over 700 career home runs had very rare careers.

I'm going to focus on Hank Aaron's career because of sentiment like the following. I heard Bob Costas on a national TV broadcast in August 2014 say something like, "Everybody knows Hank Aaron holds the true career home run record." Bonds needed to hit his very controversial 73 home runs in 2001 to even have a chance at 755. Aaron's stellar career numbers are untainted. Hammerin' Hank's career home run numbers over the course of his 23-year career are nothing short of awe-inspiring. Even though he never hit 50 home runs in a season, he hit 40 or more home runs eight times, with a career high 47 in 1971, 39 home runs in two other seasons, and 38 in another. In four other seasons he hit 30 or more, and 20 or more in five other seasons. That means he hit 20 or more home runs in all but three of his seasons, the first and last two (13,12,10 home runs respectively) being the exception. He was able to hit that many because of his incredible durability. He played in at least 120 games in all but two of those 23 seasons, which resulted in 13,941 plate appearances (third on the career list) and 12,364 at bats (second on the career list).

Aaron's numbers are impressive (and I believe generally underappreciated) but it would be inappropriate to discuss the career home run record without at least mentioning Babe Ruth. Ruth's career high of 60 home runs in 1927 is fairly well known. But what may be less widely recognized is how far ahead of his peers Ruth was in terms of home run production. In his first season with the Yankees, 1920, Ruth hit 54 home runs. This total is almost triple the next highest of 19 that George Sisler hit that season and is more home runs than every other team except the Philadelphia Phillies hit that year. The following season Ruth hit 59 with the next highest total being 24. In addition to those three stellar seasons Ruth had a fourth 50-plus home run season in 1928 when he hit 54 again. Only two other players, Mark McGwire (70, 65, 58, 52) and Sammy Sosa (66, 64, 63, 50) have had four 50 or more home run seasons. Ruth also hit 40-plus home runs in seven other seasons and had between 22 and 35 home runs in five additional seasons. The fact that his career total of 714 has been exceeded does not diminish the magnitude of his home run accomplishments. It should also be noted that his career total would likely be higher had he not started out as a (very good) pitcher.

Two more points about the home run record. Willie Mays hit 660 home runs lifetime. But he missed most of 1952 and the entire 1953 season due to military service. He hit 41 and 51 home runs during the 1954 and 1955 seasons respectively. It is not unreasonable to argue that he could have exceeded 700 if he had not missed the majority of those two seasons. Finally, are there any current players who can challenge Bonds's total of 762? As of this writing Albert Pujols is 35 years old and has 554 home runs. He needs 208 more home runs to tie the record. Assuming he plays until he's 41 (six more seasons) he would need to hit about 35 home runs per season to get to 762. The last six seasons he's hit 42, 37, 30, 17, 28, and 34 (to date in 2015) home runs. Given these totals for the last six years, it appears he has an outside chance to hit 762 if he can stay healthy and continue to perform at the highest level. He's probably not going to get there but it's not impossible. Alex Rodriguez has an impressive 682 home runs lifetime (to date in 2015). He needs to hit another 80 home runs to tie the

Bobby Cox won 2,504 games in a 29-year managerial career, but is only fourth on the all-time list behind Tony LaRussa (2,728), John McGraw (2,763), and Connie Mack (3,731).

record. But he turned 40 during the 2015 season and even having a noteworthy comeback season in 2015 has 28 home runs (to date). He needs to have three more seasons of that type of production to approach the record. If he plays another season or two he will probably exceed 700 career home runs, but it's not very likely he'll get to 762.

Let's move on to the career RBI record. It's an interesting coincidence that Rickey Henderson's career total of 2,295 runs scored is almost the same number as the record 2,297 career RBIs set by Henry Aaron. This total is about four percent higher than Babe Ruth's second-place total of 2,214. Perhaps it's not surprising that the men with the highest career home run totals are also the men with the highest career RBI totals (Barry Bonds is fourth on the list with 1,996) but that fact doesn't diminish these accomplishments. Aaron's RBI numbers are a model of consistent superior performance. He reached 118 or more RBIs in nine seasons with a career high of 132 in 1957. He had two other seasons with over 100 and seven other seasons with between 86 and 97. To put these numbers in perspective, during the recent hitter's era, there were just six years (1996-2001) where the tenth highest RBI total for the season exceeded 118. In every other season since 1936 Aaron's 118 (at least) RBIs would have been in the top ten in the league. The inevitable conclusion: this is another record that will be very difficult to break.

As an aside, research for this article has led me to conclude that Hank Aaron is underappreciated historically. Discussions about the best players from his era tend to focus on Willie Mays and Mickey Mantle. Aaron's career accomplishments exceed both of those great players. He is first on the career RBI and total bases list, second on the career home run and at-bats list, third on the career hits, plate appearances, and games played list, and fourth on the career runs scored list. Mays is third on the career total bases list, fourth on the career home run list and seventh on the career runs scored list. To be fair, Mays missed an entire season (1953) in his prime due to military service and Mantle's career numbers were reduced due to injury. Even so, I believe Hank Aaron does not get the recognition he deserves for his all-around outstanding abilities.

The number 4,256 is another famous baseball number. It's the record number of hits that Pete Rose had in his stellar career. This is another figure that gets thrown around a lot without being fully appreciated. To amass a total of 4,000 hits a player has to make 200 hits a year for 20 years! And even though 200 hits is a long way from the 262 that Ichiro Suzuki had in 2004, a player who makes 200 hits is always recognized as having had a great season. To emphasize how rare it is, the last season with the top ten players all making more than 200 hits was 1937. There are some seasons where no player gets 200 hits. This is why there are only two players who have more than 4,000 career hits, Rose and Ty Cobb with 4,189. Ichiro Suzuki's career total for hits is 4,201 if you add the 1,278 hits he had during his first nine seasons in Japan to the 2,923 hits (to date in 2015) he has in the U.S. This impressive total is just more evidence that he's one of the best hitters to ever play the game, even if the Japanese hits are discounted slightly due to weaker pitching.

How did Charlie Hustle do it? First, he had a 24-year career with extraordinary durability. He played in at least 148 games in all but five of those seasons. This durability combined with a career .303 batting average resulted in ten seasons with more than 200 hits and a high of 230 hits in 1973. He batted at least .311 in all ten of those seasons. He had three other seasons where he made more than 190 hits and seven additional seasons with between 139 and 185 hits. Since he started his career in 1963, he achieved these totals while playing at least part of his career in what is recognized as a pitchers' era. The magnitude of Cobb's achievement of 4,189 hits can be seen by the fact that Rose needed almost every one of his hits to break Cobb's record. Rose broke the record on September 8, 1985, on his way to a 107-hit season, and

had just 52 hits in his last season of 1986. It's arguable that Rose would not have gotten so many hits if he had not had Cobb's record to shoot at.[10] This is another record that is virtually unbreakable. For example, as great as Derek Jeter's 20-year career was, his 3,465 career hits are almost 800 shy of the record.

Rose's extraordinary durability and longevity puts him at the top of career lists in three other categories. He played in the most games (3,562), made the most plate appearances (15,890), and had the most at bats (14,053) of any player. All three of these numbers are extraordinary and could be analyzed in a manner similar to the hits record, but I'm going to do a brief analysis of just the plate appearances record to make the point. The 15,890 plate appearances in 24 years are astounding. This is an average of about 636 plate appearances for 25 years or roughly 795 plate appearances for 20 years. How many plate appearances did Mike Trout (arguably the best young player in the game today) have in his first three full seasons? He had 639, 716, and 705 in 2012–14. Trout will have to put up similar numbers for another 20 years to get close to the record. Is that possible? Yes. But injuries could easily lower season totals or shorten his career, making it very unlikely that he (or anybody else) will reach Rose's total. One last point about Pete Rose. His lifetime ban from baseball for gambling does not diminish the magnitude of his on-field accomplishments.

CAREER RECORDS DISCUSSION: Pitching and Managing

Now let's look at the career strikeout record. Nolan Ryan pitched for 27 years (how is that possible!) and accumulated an astounding total of 5,714 strikeouts. No one else even has 5,000 career strikeouts. Second place is held by Randy Johnson with 4,875. Ryan's record is an amazing 17 percent better than Johnson's total. How did he get to 5,714? Ryan struck out over 300 batters in six separate seasons with his three highest totals being 383, 367, and 341. He struck out at least 200 batters in nine other seasons. And in addition to those years, he had nine other seasons with at least 125 strikeouts. Those are simply incredible strikeout totals. Johnson also struck out 300 batters in six seasons but comparing Ryan to the third place pitcher on the career list will put Ryan's accomplishments in better perspective.

Roger Clemens retired in 2007 after 24 seasons. Clemens won the Cy Young award seven times and was known for being a strikeout pitcher. He led the league in strikeouts five times and is third on the career list with 4,672 strikeouts. How do his seasonal totals compare to Ryan's? Clemens did strike out at least 200 batters in 12 seasons (a very impressive statistic) but his best two totals were 292 and 291. The third best strikeout pitcher in history never had a 300 strikeout season but Ryan (and Johnson) did it six times. Here's another way to look at it. A total of 5,714 strikeouts requires an average of about 229 strikeouts per year for 25 years or about 286 strikeouts per year for 20 years. To put those numbers in recent perspective, the 2013 league leader was Yu Darvish with 277 strikeouts (Ryan exceeded that strikeout total six times), and only three pitchers had more than 228 strikeouts (Ryan exceeded that strikeout total 10 times) in 2013. Can Darvish strike out 280 men each year for the next 20 years? Unlikely, and maybe impossible. For example, Darvish was injured in 2014 and struck out 182 men that season. Ryan's career strikeout total is another record that is virtually unattainable.

What about the career record for wins? Here's a number that can be said with certainty to not be breakable without drastic changes in how pitchers are currently utilized or changes to how wins are awarded. The numbers associated with Cy Young's 511 wins and the 417 wins that Walter Johnson put up in the purely post-1902 era are almost inconceivable by today's standards. Young got his total by winning over 30 games in five seasons and over 20 games in 10 more seasons. He started 40 or more games in 11 of those seasons. Johnson won over 30 games twice and at least 20 games in 10 other seasons. He started at least 36 games in nine seasons with two seasons of 40 and 42 starts. All of these numbers are impossible to reach today. The best that modern pitchers have managed to do in terms of wins is the still very impressive 355 that Greg Maddox won during his 23-year career and the controversial 354 wins put up by Roger Clemens. To get to 400 wins a pitcher would have to win 20 games a year for 20 years. That's virtually impossible with just 35 starts per year. Young's record will never be broken.

I'd bet that most baseball fans have at least heard of Connie Mack. But if they're like me (before the research for this article) they probably don't know why he's famous. All Mack did is manage for 53 years and win 3,731 games in the process! Second on both lists is John McGraw who managed for 33 years and won 2,763 games. Mack also holds the record for games managed (7,755) and for losses (3,948). This is not the appropriate venue for a complete biography of Mr. Mack. But in brief; he managed the Philadelphia Athletics for 50 years from 1901 until the end of the 1950 season. His teams won five World Series titles and nine American League pennants. He was elected to the Hall of Fame in 1937.

Even in a hitter's era, 40 home runs in a season is an accomplishment. Henry Aaron did it eight times.

What is germane to this article is the fact that it is highly unlikely that any of Mack's records will ever be broken. The second longest tenure is 20 years shorter and the second most wins is almost 1,000 fewer. It should be noted however, that some of the longest lasting and winningest managers in baseball history have been active recently. Tony La Russa managed for 33 years and won 2,728 games. Bobby Cox had 2,504 wins in 29 years, and Joe Torre won 2,326 games during his 29-year career. These three men are third, fourth, and fifth on the career wins list. Here is one final (and astounding) non-playing field related statistic. Vin Scully has been (and continues to as of this writing) broadcasting Dodger baseball since 1950 when he was 22 years old. Do the arithmetic yourself. Scully's broadcasting tenure is another incredible record that will be almost impossible to break.

CONCLUSION

This paper was written to convey three main points. The first is simply to make the reader more aware of some of the incredible feats performed in baseball history. The second is to look at the stock phrase "never be broken" in a more serious manner. It is easy to make such a claim in casual conversation, but do the data support any such assertion? The third is to make baseball fans aware of just how difficult it will be to break the records listed in Tables 1 and 2.

So what is the answer to the title subheading? How many records will never be broken? The answer: probably lots of them! It's arguable that some of the single season records are more likely to be broken than the career records since a player "only" needs a single outstanding season to do so. In spite of that rationale, I'd bet that Henderson's stolen base record (130), Wilson's triples record (36), and Bonds's walk record (232) will not be broken in the next 110 years. Hack Wilson's 191 RBIs and Ichiro Suzuki's 262 hits are also very unlikely to be exceeded. Current trends in pitching mean that the post-1902 innings pitched record (464) and wins record (41) will not be broken. Since Randy Johnson recently came within 11 strikeouts of Nolan Ryan's season strikeout record of 383, I suppose it's possible for another pitcher to break Ryan's strikeout record. But I doubt it will happen. What about the career records? Frankly, it's hard to imagine any of the records in Table 2 being broken. It's possible that Alex Rodriguez or Albert Pujols could break the career home run record of 762 but it's very unlikely. A similar argument can be made for the rest of the career records. The final conclusion: many existing baseball records may never be broken. ∎

Acknowledgments

I sincerely thank three anonymous peer reviewers for their insightful comments and suggestions. Their input resulted in a much better paper. I also need to thank Clifford Blau for his meticulous fact checking. The paper is more accurate because of his rigorous attention to detail.

Notes

1. Trent McCotter, "Ripken's Record for Consecutive Innings Played," *Baseball Research Journal*, 41 (Fall 2012): 7–9.
2. Postseason play prior to 1903 is not considered in this paper.
3. These stolen base records are taken from the Baseball Almanac web site: http://www.baseball-almanac.com/recbooks/rb_stba.shtml.
4. Bleacher Report, http://bleacherreport.com/articles/1645610-why-hack-wilsons-rbi-record-is-impossible-to-break-in-todays-mlb.
5. Herm Krabbenhoft, "Hank Greenberg's American League RBI Record," *Baseball Research Journal*, 41 (Spring 2012): 20–27.
6. Herm Krabbenhoft, "Lou Gehrig's RBI Record: 1923–1939," *Baseball Research Journal*, 41 (Fall 2012): 10–13.
7. The Wikipedia entry for Forbes Field contains the following: Barney Dreyfuss (owner of the Pirates) "hated cheap home runs and vowed he'd have none in his park," which led him to design a large playing field for Forbes Field. The original distances to the outfield fence in left, center, and right field were 360 feet (110 m), 462 feet (141 m) and 376 feet (115 m), respectively. The web site is: https://en.wikipedia.org/wiki/Forbes_Field.
8. Quoted from Mark Armour's article on Wilson in the SABR Baseball Biography Project: The specific web site is: http://sabr.org/bioproj/person/ed5711f8.
9. Wayne L. Winston, *Mathletics: How Gamblers, Managers, and Sports Enthusiasts Use Mathematics in Baseball, Basketball, and Football* (Princeton, New Jersey: Princeton University Press, 2009).
10. His career hit total was also likely increased because he was filling out the lineup card as player/manager for the Reds in 1985 and 1986.

Examining Stolen Base Trends by Decade from the Deadball Era through the 1970s

John McMurray

In 1976, for the first time in thirty-three seasons, total stolen bases exceeded total home runs in Major League Baseball.[1] A consistent turn towards more frequent basestealing had already become evident on the field, as teams collectively stole over 1,000 more bases in 1976 than they did only three years earlier. This sea change invites consideration of the factors that led to the spate of stolen bases which characterized baseball in the mid-1970s.

If it is true that baseball trends run in cycles, the Deadball Era was when the stolen base was paramount; the 1920s was a time of transition, when home runs gained on stolen bases before overtaking them by the end of the decade; the 1930s and 1940s were decades of relative stability between home runs and steals; the 1950s were the low point in major league history for stolen bases; and the 1960s brought a renewed use of the stolen base, culminating in the extremely high totals of the 1970s and beyond. Considering each of these time periods will help to explain why stolen bases increased so dramatically during the 1970s and will underscore how substantial the shift towards stealing bases became during that decade.

THE EARLY TWENTIETH CENTURY: Basestealing as a Primary Focus

Perhaps the most telling statistic in all of base-stealing history is that major league teams from 1906 through 1909 averaged more than 10 stolen bases for every home run hit, with a peak of 11.8 steals per home run in 1909. This single-minded focus on stolen bases captures a core characteristic of the Deadball Era, where scoring was low and stolen bases, with the frequent complementary use of bunting and hit-and-run plays, were high. That teams in the American League from 1910 through 1914 and teams in the National League in 1905 and 1911 averaged at least 200 stolen bases per season—an enormous feat, never approached since—plays into this image.

But the Deadball Era was not about all stolen bases. Following the 1916 season, stolen bases declined in every season through 1919 in the American League and plunged similarly in the National League, albeit with an uptick in 1919. By the end of the Deadball Era in 1919, stolen base totals had fallen by nearly 40 percent from their peak roughly a decade earlier.

Indeed, the 1919 season was a sign of things to come, as total home runs in major league baseball nearly doubled from the year prior. While it is reasonable to see baseball as a game driven by stolen bases, particularly during the first sixteen years of the twentieth century, the philosophical shift toward employing fewer stolen bases, likely shaped by changes in managerial philosophy stemming from offensive woes derived from pitchers scuffing the baseball, began in 1916.[2] From a stolen base perspective, it is quite reasonable to consider the last three years of the Deadball Era as being stylistically removed from the first 16 years. The introduction of the livelier baseball in the next decade would mean that fans would never again see the stolen base as the primary driver of baseball offensive success.

THE 1920s: Home Runs Overtake Stolen Bases

The plunge in stolen bases during the next decade is made evident by two statistics: after 1920, no player in the major leagues stole as many as 60 bases during the rest of the decade, and only twice in either league from 1921 through 1929 (the National League in 1921 and 1923) did teams collectively average more than 100 stolen bases. A 1922 article in *The Literary Digest* noted the pronounced decline, commenting that "the last few seasons have seen a falling-off in base-stealing so pronounced as to prove alarming to any one who wishes to see baseball preserved as a well-rounded game in every department."[3]

The change in style of play was striking. The same article in *The Literary Digest* bemoaned the loss of stolen bases at the expense of the livelier ball, saying: "Is it not time that this most interesting, most thrilling of baseball plays should be rescued from the slow-moving but iron-bound tendencies of the modern game which are crushing out its very existence?"[4] Further, the author cited the loss of unpredictability in the game as stolen bases diminished: "The stolen base is the most perfect example in baseball of the unexpected. In attack it is the farthest removed from the established rule. It injects an element of uncertainty into the game very welcome in these days of crystallized baseball methods. It allows scope for human initiative which is also very welcome."[5]

In 1922, teams collectively hit more than 1,000 home runs (1,055) for the first time in major league history. Still, there is a frequent misconception that, with the introduction of the livelier ball, teams immediately eschewed the stolen base. In fact, total stolen bases exceeded total home runs in major league baseball in every season until 1929. Moreover, even the 1929 season was only a slight point of inflection, as teams collectively hit only 15 more home runs than they stole bases. Even so, with stolen bases in decline in most seasons during the 1920s after 1923, it was clear that the offensive winds were shifting.

THE 1930s AND 40s: Establishing a New Normal

What would become a steep decline in stolen bases first became evident in the National League, as from 1931 through 1945, no NL player stole as many as 30 bases in a season. League-leading totals were also often paltry: Stan Hack stole 16 and 17 bases, respectively, in 1938 and 1939, winning the National League stolen base title in '38 and tying for the league lead in '39. Even though American League teams routinely averaged about 10 more stolen bases in each season than National League teams during this 15-year period, low stolen base totals increasingly became more commonplace across major league baseball. In 1945, for instance, the Cleveland Indians, Philadelphia Athletics, and St. Louis Browns each stole fewer than 30 bases as a team.

The overall ratio of stolen bases per home run remained relatively stable during the 1930s, with teams, for the most part, hitting roughly 1.5 home runs for each stolen base. With the exception of 1943, when total stolen bases actually exceeded home runs once again since comparatively few power hitters were active during World War II and because of the lifeless balata ball that used, the same general balance held true. Moreover, suggested writer Lew King, the falloff in steals was not due to a lack of players who could run. Writing in 1947, King said: "The major leagues boast as many fast men as years ago. But the modern style of play, dictated by the lively ball, has a sedentary effect on all but a few of the speed boys."[6]

John Drebinger, writing in *Sportfolio* in 1947, suggested that the downturn in stolen bases during the late 1940s was a result of managers becoming risk averse on the bases, given the superabundance of power hitters. Drebinger cited Joe Cronin, who as manager of the Boston Red Sox, mused "Why risk an out simply to gain a base, when most any batter on your club, if he connects properly, can smack it over the fence?"[7] At the same time, Drebinger notes that teams in the 1940s were likely to promote "clever" baserunning in lieu of stolen bases.[8] Mentioning Billy Southworth as a proponent of this approach, Drebinger said: "Though modern managers are still loathe (sic) to risk signaling for a stolen base, unless gifted with one of those modern rarities like George Case, Pete Reiser, or George Stirnweiss, several have stressed the value of alert, heads-up base running where players are instructed to keep on their toes, take advantage of every slip and at all times be prepared to grab that extra base on a hit."[9]

Further, a May 1948 article titled "Is Base-Stealing Becoming a Lost Art?" offered a perspective on why both stolen bases and home runs were higher in the American League than in the National League during this period: "A…logical explanation seems to be that the outstanding basestealers, such as (Ben) Chapman and (Bill) Werber, are in the American League and the tendency always is for teammates and Leaguemates to emulate such examples. Similarly, the prowess of home-run hitters such as Ruth and Gehrig and Foxx in the American League has been the incentive which has steadily increased the rate of home runs in that League."[10]

It was in the latter half of the 1940s when stolen bases began to decline most precipitously and home runs began to rise to then-historic heights. In 1949, only six years after stolen bases had exceeded home runs, there were only 730 total steals in major league baseball, while 1,704 home runs were hit. More of the same was to come.

THE 1950s: The Nadir of Stolen Bases

With teams collectively compiling only 650 steals, the 1950 season was the low point for stolen bases in major league history. Dom DiMaggio led the American League with a mere fifteen steals. Eight of the sixteen major league teams stole 40 or fewer bases in 1950, and the St. Louis Browns, Detroit Tigers, and Chicago White Sox each accumulated more outs caught stealing than they did stolen bases.[11] In 1950, home runs also outpaced stolen bases by more than one-thousand (1,453) for the first time, a gap which would have been hard to imagine only a decade prior.

During the 1950s, some teams did steal bases with regularity. The 1953 Brooklyn Dodgers stole 90, while the 1957–59 Chicago White Sox stole more than 100 bases in each season. The 1959 White Sox, a team bereft of power hitters, won the pennant while stealing more bases than they hit home runs. Such examples, though, were exceptions to the rule.

It is reasonable to infer that the individual philosophies of stolen-base-minded managers in the 1950s, such as Paul Richards and Charlie Dressen, led to their respective teams making more stolen base attempts than others. The same was true in reverse for, say, the Yankees under Casey Stengel or Milwaukee Braves under Fred Haney. The New York Yankees teams of the 1950s surely were slow-footed, but that power-laden team also rarely attempted to steal bases (Billy Martin, for example, was the only player on the 1953 Yankees who attempted as many as 13 stolen bases, stealing only six that season).

Of course, it made sense for teams to eschew stolen bases considering the array of power hitters in the game at the time. In 1956, when teams hit a combined 2,294 home runs—the highest total of the decade—every team in the major leagues other than the Baltimore Orioles hit more than 100 home runs. Clearly, at a time when Ted Williams, Gil Hodges, Duke Snider, Ernie Banks, Larry Doby, Frank Robinson, Vic Wertz, Al Kaline, Eddie Mathews, Hank Aaron, Willie Mays, Mickey Mantle, Yogi Berra, Harmon Killebrew, Stan Musial, and Roy Sievers, were all playing, there was little need for most teams to take an extra base.

Billy Evans, then a retired umpire, suggested also that umpires' refusal to enforce recently-enacted rules requiring pitchers to hold the set position for a full second was another reason why stolen bases fell so substantially in the 1950s. "Unquestionably, this is a good rule if properly enforced," wrote Evans in 1953. "During the first few weeks of a season a few years ago, the umpires did enforce the rule and chaos resulted. The drastic pitching change apparently came too quickly. Soon the pitchers were back in the old rut—doing just about as they pleased and getting away

Luis Aparicio won the American League stolen base title in nine straight seasons, 1956–64.

with it."[12] Hence, without the rule being stringently enforced, Evans implied that runners were held more closely to first base, thus limiting stolen bases.

But, over and above the explanations, the downturn in stolen bases was huge. In 1950, 1953, and from 1955 through 1958, approximately three home runs were hit for every base stolen, a ratio never seen before or since. In the last five years of the decade, more than 2,200 home runs were hit in every season, while teams stole more than 800 bases in only one of those seasons (853 in 1959). Though it was in the direction of home runs rather than stolen bases, it is reasonable to say that the 1950s offered as single-minded a style of play as did the Deadball Era.

THE 1960s: A Discernable Upswing

As stolen bases began to rise again in 1959, it spoke in part to the influence of White Sox shortstop Luis Aparicio, who won the American League stolen base title in nine straight seasons, from 1956 though 1964. As Bob Broeg noted: "Not until Luis Aparicio of the White Sox stole 56 in 1959 was there a noteworthy league-leading total over in the A.L. (during the 1950s)."[13] After leading the league while stealing fewer than 30 bases during each of his first three seasons, Aparicio, like the rest of baseball's prominent base stealers, soon began running more.

Aparicio helped to best bridge the gap between the predominantly power-hitting game of the 1950s to the one of the 1960s, where players stealing bases took their place alongside home run hitters. Willie Mays also contributed significantly in that regard. Ultimately, the stolen base landscape of the 1960s was most prominently characterized by four players who together won the stolen base title in every season but one during that decade: Aparicio, Bert Campaneris, Maury Wills, and Lou Brock.[14]

With his then-record 104 stolen bases in 1962, Wills' influence on reviving the stolen base as an offensive tool was enormous. According to Leonard Koppett: "when Wills began doing it regularly, the idea of reviving the weapon—not as a special case, but as a regular part of the baseball arsenal—started to grow in other baseball minds."[15] Change was not immediate, as stolen bases did decrease in 1963 and 1964, but Wills laid the groundwork for the emphasis on stolen bases that was to come.

Wills's achievement of stealing 104 bases in a season was even more staggering given that Aparicio's American League-leading total from the same year was a mere 31. "How many people realize," asked Koppett, "that when Wills stole 104 bases in 1962, breaking the record

Lou Brock's frequent success kept awareness of stolen bases at the forefront of managerial strategy. Brock won seven stolen base titles before breaking Wills's record in 1974.

set by Ty Cobb in 1915, Maury's total was higher than any of the other 19 teams in both leagues?"[16]

Noting that Babe Ruth's home run greatness was assured by how far he outdistanced his contemporaries, Koppett also points out that "in 1962, no other player in either league even stole one-third as many bases as Wills…In the 41 years before Wills exploded with the 1962 Dodgers, not a single National League player even stole even half as many bases as Wills did that year. And during the same span, only four American Leaguers did it—barely. Ben Chapman (1931) and George Case (1943) reached 61. George Stirnweiss (1944) had 55 and Aparicio had 56."[17]

In 1961, a year before Wills's record-breaking feat, stolen bases in the major leagues exceeded 1,000 (1,046) for the first time since 1943. They surged to 1,348 in 1962 and stayed high throughout the decade, topping at 1,850 in 1969. But an increased emphasis on stolen bases did not lead to a corresponding fall in home runs. Instead, given the vast collection of power-hitting talent already in baseball, home run totals in the 1960s grew overall throughout the decade.[18]

The result was a game which, for the first time, employed power and speed with roughly equal effectiveness. Though players would cumulatively steal even more bases and hit more home runs in subsequent decades, the style of play adopted during the 1960s, emphasizing both facets, was the closest approximation to date of baseball as it has been played in more recent decades.

THE 1970s: Why Did Stolen Bases Surge in the Middle of the Decade?

While stolen base levels from 1970 through 1973 were, for the most part, in line with 1960s totals, baseball's emphasis on the stolen base began to increase markedly in 1974. The shift was dramatic: during the

1974 season, teams collectively stole more than 400 bases more than they did during the year prior. Just two years later, in 1976, players would steal more than 3,000 bases, a total last achieved in 1915. With the exception of 1900 through 1903, this three-year period from 1974 through 1976 represented the largest year-by-year increase in stolen bases in major league history.[19]

Stolen base totals rose in every year but one from 1971 through 1977 (declining only slightly in 1977), before again reaching new modern-era heights in both 1980 and 1983, as well as a modern high in 1987. This sudden flood represented the largest consistent output of stolen bases since the Deadball Era. Once teams broke the 2,000 stolen base threshold in 1973, so began a stretch which has continued unbroken to the present, where teams collectively accumulate at least that many stolen bases in a season. Stolen bases became such a priority that the Oakland A's, as is well known, provided a roster spot to speedster Herb Washington, whose only role was to steal bases as a pinch runner.

Although home runs did decline a bit in several seasons during this stolen-base surge (most notably, in 1974 and 1976), power numbers were mostly robust throughout the 1970s. Though buoyed in absolute terms by expansion in both the 1960s and 1970s, of course, teams still hit more than 3,000 home runs in four seasons during the decade, occasionally exceeding home run levels which would be reached during the 1990s. With stolen bases and power both being high, steals and home runs were once again generally in a one-to-one ratio during the latter half of the decade, a balance last seen in the 1940s.

The unprecedented emphasis on both stolen bases and home runs during the 1970s raises the question of why stolen bases rose so dramatically after power-hitting had been established for several decades. Considering that each prior era emphasized either home runs or stolen bases, but never both to this degree, it is important to understand the complementary factors which explain why this period in the 1970s broke with convention and ushered in a new style of play.

FOUR REASONS FOR THE CHANGES IN STYLE OF PLAY DURING THE 1970s

(1) A Shift in Thinking: Wills, Brock, and Baseball's Unwritten Rules

In much the way that Ruth provided an example to other players of how they might hit, it is reasonable to infer that Wills' 1962 performance laid the groundwork for the spate of steals to come in the 1970s. "The answer," wrote Broeg in 1977, "was probably in the so-called book, that unwritten tome of percentages, of disciplinary do's and don'ts of the diamond. For instance, you DON'T run when your team is way ahead, players were told. You DON'T run when you're a couple or more runs behind. Then, along came Wills, who studied the art form and increased his percentage of successes."[20]

The upshot, according to Koppett, is that, in time, managers adjusted their approaches accordingly, maximizing stolen bases. "When Wills began (stealing bases) regularly, the idea of reviving the weapon—not as a special case, but as a regular part of the baseball arsenal—started to grow in other baseball minds."[21] Koppett notes that 1970s managers Billy Martin, Chuck Tanner, and Whitey Herzog were all inspired by Wills to expand their base-stealing strategies, saying: "They didn't get it from Wills; they applied their own ideas to new circumstances that had arisen from Wills's example."[22]

If Wills provided the spark for the stolen base revolution, Lou Brock's influence kept stolen bases at the forefront. Having already won seven stolen base titles before breaking the all-time single-season record, set by Wills, in 1974, Brock's example "opened everyone's eyes to the possibilities" of stealing bases with great frequency.[23] In contrast to the more elaborate sliding styles of both Ty Cobb and Maury Wills, Brock also helped to promote a more economical approach to sliding, thus making success at stealing bases easier: "Cobb took a long lead and favored the hook slide, or fadeaway. Brock takes a short lead and goes straight into the bag with a quick pop-up, hardly a slide at all."[24]

The circumstantial evidence linking Wills, in particular, to a change in contemporary managerial philosophy is strong. As Koppett noted in 1986: "Before Wills, only two players in 40 years had reached

Bert Campaneris was the AL stolen base leader six times, beginning in 1965 when he broke Aparicio's string of nine stolen base crowns in a row. Campaneris would lead the league four consecutive years, 1965–68, then again in 1970 and 1972.

60 stolen bases in a season; once each. Since 1965, in addition to Wills, 11 other players have done it a total of 24 times (including Lou Brock's record 118 in 1974)."[25] It is no coincidence that many of the most successful teams of the 1970s included players who stole bases with the dedication and determination of both Wills and Brock.

(2) A New Trend: Players Who Could Both Hit for Power and Steal Bases

Up to this point, few players in baseball history were capable both of hitting home runs and stealing bases in quantity. More often than not, home runs hitters had been in the mold of Ted Williams, Ted Kluszewski, or Duke Snider—sizeable players who rarely attempted to steal a base—while basestealers resembled Nellie Fox or Max Carey, namely diminutive players who posed little threat of hitting a home run. Though a few players were capable of doing both (Minnie Minoso, Willie Mays, Jackie Robinson, and Chuck Klein among others), it was relatively rare for it to happen in practice.

In contrast, the 1970s style of play, supported by managers who promoted both hitting for power and stealing bases, brought multi-talented players to the forefront, including Don Baylor, Reggie Jackson, and Joe Morgan. Also prominent were speedsters with some consistent power, such as Ron LeFlore, Bill North, Amos Otis, Phil Garner, and Roy White. Never before did baseball have so many active players who could excel at both stealing bases and hitting home runs, albeit in varying degrees.

Contributing to the stolen base surge was the reality that there were fewer pure power hitters than in the decades immediately prior. As Koppett pointed out, "the super-sluggers, of whom Hank Aaron is the last current example, have not been as plentiful as they were a generation ago."[26] Perhaps only George Foster, Greg Luzinski, Willie Stargell, and Tony Perez from the 1970s could be considered to have been in the same mold as the most notable power hitters of the 1950s.

Consequently, a wider range of players was stealing bases than ever before, resulting in many players with a modest number of stolen bases contributing to the high league-wide totals. An American League press release issued on August 2, 1976, noted that "thirty-eight players have already stolen ten bases," a statistic which comports with most fans' impressions of the style of play in the 1970s.[27] In fact, eight different players won the stolen base title during the 1970s in the American League.

With the exception of 1901 through 1910, when nine different players led or tied for the league lead in stolen bases during those seasons, repeat winners of the stolen base crown were the norm until the 1970s. Then, a wider range came to prominence. In the National League alone, Joe Morgan, Larry Bowa, Dave Concepcion, Davey Lopes, Frank Taveras, and Omar Moreno were only a few of the players other than Lou Brock in the 1970s who contributed significantly to the lofty aggregate stolen base totals. For the first time since the early 1900s, most teams fielded lineups where the majority of players were capable of—and encouraged to—steal bases.

(3) The Development of the 'Science' of Basestealing

As basestealing became an integral facet of baseball offenses in the 1970s, with it came more attention to the study of how to steal bases more efficiently. The aforementioned American League press release trumpeted not only the depth of the basestealing pool but also the success rate of basestealers, noting A.L. players as of August 1976 had stolen 68.2 percent of the bases they attempted and that many teams were stealing bases at a better than 70 percent success rate.[28] (Ultimately, players would steal 66.4 percent of the bases they attempted in 1976). Part of those successes, which are representative of much of the 1970s stolen base picture, surely stems from better practices.

The Kansas City Royals, a team without much power in the 1970s, worked to increase their stolen base totals by using a stopwatch to gauge which players were getting the best jumps. The result was a more methodical approach to stealing bases, which allowed even slower runners the chance to steal bases effectively when the situation allowed: "We've got guys like (George) Brett, (Hal) McRae and Joe Zdeb who aren't pure baserunners and are the type most clubs wouldn't give free reign (sic) to," said Kansas City first base coach Steve Boros in 1977. "But we let them go here because our base running is such a science."[29] Boros noted: "We may not be leading the league in stolen bases, but we've got the best ratio," citing another philosophical trend of the time.[30]

It is not that players of prior years did not study pitchers' tendencies when electing when to steal; as Dick Kaegel notes: "The brainy Cobb was the first of the modern players to study and mentally catalogue the movements of pitchers, searching for that one little flaw that would give him the edge."[31] Rather, it was an emphasis on studying combined with modern techniques that made stealing bases profitable: "Years later," Kaegel continued, "Brock was doing the same thing, adding such refinements as filming pitchers and clocking their motions with a stopwatch."[32]

In 1962, Maury Wills's achievement of stealing 104 bases in a season was staggering, given that Aparicio's AL-leading total from the same year was a mere 31.

Of course, stolen base strategists had to stay one step ahead of the competition. Melvin Durslag noted in 1977 that basestealers were vexed by opposing management trying to water the infield to slow runners up; pitchers stretching the rules to hold runners on; shortstops leaning towards second base to thwart basestealing attempts; and first basemen relentlessly chatting with baserunners in order to break the latter's concentration.[33] With these impediments, both teams and defenses were strategizing constantly about stolen bases—and how to prevent them. It was a noteworthy change of focus that helped basestealers to proper in the 1970s.

(4) A Decline in Batting Average, and Ballpark Effects

From 1965 through 1972, batting averages were generally lower than they were during the late 1940s and 1950s. The overall major league's batting average ranged from .237 (in 1968, during the so-called Year of the Pitcher) to .254 in 1970. While teams had generally enjoyed batting averages in the .260's between 1945 and 1955 and in the .250's between 1955 and 1964, the decline in batting average from the mid-1960s into the '70s obviously made scoring runs more difficult.

With batting averages falling to .244 in 1972, teams sought new ways to score runs. As Koppett said: "In short, it's no secret that home run totals and batting averages have been much, much lower over the past decade than for the 40 years before that. And the response has been renewed interest in the value of stealing a base."[34] The urgency of taking steps to advance runners, Koppett implies, required a shift in approach: "And as batting averages have dropped, the chance of getting two singles with a man on first has become less, so it has become that much more important to get your man to second so that one single can score him."[35]

With the opening of several large stadiums in the early 1970s—including Riverfront Stadium in Cincinnati, Three Rivers Stadium in Pittsburgh, and Veterans Stadium in Philadelphia—it is easy to see why teams emphasized speed over home-run hitting power. Further, the attraction of scoring runners from second base on singles hit on Astroturf surely influenced teams to place an additional premium on fast players. One example of an owner who did so was Charlie Finley, owner of the Oakland A's, who, according to writer Ron Bergman, had "an obsession with speed."[36]

The combination of a dearth of high-average hitters along with spacious ballparks makes the 1970s unique. Although teams continued to hit home runs at a steady rate, they also adopted aspects of Deadball-Era style play when necessary. Yet, beyond that, players in the 1970s were much more able to provide both power and speed whenever necessary, leading the way for Rickey Henderson in the 1980s and foreshadowing a type of player which has become comparatively frequent today.

SUMMARY

The conditions that led to the superabundance of stolen bases in the 1970s were unique, jointly caused by the influence of two prominent basestealers, Maury Wills and Lou Brock; players who were encouraged to use multiple talents; a heightened emphasis on the strategy of basestealing; and circumstances involving batting average and ballpark configuration that made adopting a new strategy imperative. Rarely—if ever—have so many conditions conspired to shift baseball's style of play. Once baseball players and managers rediscovered the stolen base in the 1970s, it again became a fundamental part of all teams' offensive approach, rarely flagging even when great sluggers abounded, especially during the two decades to follow. The success that basestealers enjoyed during the 1970s represented a significant and consequential change for the way baseball was played relative to prior decades. ∎

Acknowledgments

With thanks to the Baseball Hall of Fame for providing clippings of vintage articles cited in this piece.

Notes

1. Year-by-year data on stolen bases and home runs used in this article is courtesy of Baseball-Reference.com. In comparing stolen bases over time, it is important to recognize that the definition of what a stolen base is has changed multiple times. One well-known modification to the stolen base rule took place in 1920, when a stolen base would no longer be permitted when there was defensive indifference. When comparing stolen base totals between eras, the differing rules about what a stolen base was at the time obviously impact data comparisons.
2. Referring to the American League and National League only, not including the Federal League. The drop in stolen bases was greater between 1913 and 1915 than it was between 1916 and 1918, but I am referring to when there was an overall change in base-stealing philosophy.
3. "Base-Stealing's Sensational Decline," *The Literary Digest*, April 19, 1922.
4. Ibid.
5. Ibid.
6. Lew King, "The Fleet-Feet Boys," *Baseball Magazine*, 1947, 419.
7. John Drebinger, *Sportfolio*, 1947.
8. Ibid.
9. Ibid.
10. "Is Base-Stealing Becoming a Lost Art?," National Baseball Hall of Fame Clippings File, publication unknown, May 1948.
11. Strikingly, Detroit players were caught stealing 40 times in 1950 while stealing only 23 bases.
12. Billy Evans, "Base Stealing a Lost Art: Help Needed to Revive It," National Baseball Hall of Fame Clippings File, publication unknown, March 5, 1953.
13. Bob Broeg, "Wills Triggered a New Steal Era: Few Thefts Before Maury," *The Sporting News*, October 15, 1977, 8.
14. The exception was in 1969 in the American League, when Tommy Harper led the league.
15. Leonard Koppett, "Wills Prompted Running Revolution," *The Sporting News*, August 30, 1980, 17.
16. Ibid. Koppett credits Wills with breaking Cobb's record, though Cobb played under a different definition of stolen base. Hugh Nichol still has the most single-season stolen bases, with 138 in 1887.
17. Ibid. It is worth noting that Wally Moses also stole 56 bases for the Chicago White Sox in 1943.
18. Total home runs fell between 1966 and 1968, from 2,743 in 1966 to 2,299 in 1967 to 1,995 in 1968, before rising again in 1969, when baseball expanded.
19. Since stolen bases were not recorded in all seasons, this comment considers only those seasons in which stolen bases were officially recorded. The increase from 1900 to 1903 was slightly greater, as the number of teams doubled.
20. Broeg, 8.
21. Koppett, "Wills Prompted Running Revolution."
22. Ibid. Koppett wrote that "stealing a lot of bases is a characteristic that runs in 'families,'" meaning groups of managers. See Leonard Koppett, "Old Orioles Spread Base Theft Gospel," *The Sporting News*, August 13, 1976.
23. Leonard Koppett, "Base-Stealing Art Zooming to a Peak," *The New York Times*, July 7, 1976, 30.
24. Dick Kaegel, "Fiery Cobb, Cool Brock Got Same Results," *The Sporting News*, September 10, 1977, 3–4.
25. Koppett, "Wills Prompted Running Revolution."
26. Leonard Koppett, "New Era for Base Burglars," *The Sporting News*, October 12, 1974.
27. American League press release, "American League Stealing Bases at Blinding Pace," August 2, 1976.
28. Ibid.
29. UPI, "Stealing's a Science in Kansas City," *New York Daily News*, July 24, 1977, 33C.
30. Ibid.
31. Kaegel, "Fiery Cobb, Cool Brock Got Same Results."
32. Ibid.
33. Melvin Durslag, "Silence Golden to Base Thieves: Lopes Wants No Lip," *The Sporting News*, April 9, 1977, 26.
34. Koppett, "New Era for Base Burglars."
35. Ibid.
36. Ron Bergman, "Jury Still Out in Case of A's Hustling Herb," National Baseball Hall of Fame Clippings File, Publication Unknown (but likely *San Jose Mercury News*) December 7, 1974.

Measuring Franchise Success in the Postseason

Stuart Shapiro

Baseball is unique in that its postseason has existed for over 110 years, enough time for teams to have many ups and many downs. This produces a vast trove of data with which to examine franchise success and failure. The history is deep enough that every team that has won a World Series can lay a claim to some period, however brief, when it was king of the hill in Major League Baseball. I will hereby examine the ebbs and flows of baseball and franchise success.

METHODOLOGY

I derived the method of analysis from one that Jason Kubatko used to compare basketball dynasties across eras.[1] The basic idea is that the goal of a season is to win the World Series and doing so gives you a perfect score for the season of 100 points. All other point totals are derived from how close the team came to winning. The World Series loser gets 50 points because the highest level that they achieved was a 50 percent chance of winning the title. League Championship series losers receive 25 points for being one of the final four teams alive. LDS losers are assigned 12.5 points because they were among the final eight World Series contenders. Finally in 2012 and in 2013, the wild card game losers received 6.25 points because they had a 50 percent chance of reaching the round of eight.

The remainder of the teams are given a number of points equal to 100 divided by the number of major league teams active in that season. In other words, they get the number of points reflecting their probability at the beginning of the season of winning the World Series. With 30 teams currently in the Major Leagues, each non-playoff team get 3.33 points reflecting the 3.33 percent chance that each team had to win the World Series when the season opened. This number increases in earlier seasons when there were fewer teams in the major leagues. The nine cases when a one- or three-game playoff was used to determine playoff eligibility are a special situation. In these cases, teams that lost these playoffs received half the worth of the lowest postseason value described above that was available in the season of the playoff. The points are outlined in Table 1.

Table 1. Postseason Point Totals

Accomplishment	Points Earned
World Series winner	100
World Series loser	50
League Championship Series Losers	25
League Division Series Losers	12.5
Wild Card game losers (2012–present)	6.25
Do Not Make Playoffs	100 divided by number of teams in league

This system uses postseason success (including making the playoffs) as the sole barometer of success. The 40-win 1962 Mets receive the same credit as the 103-win 1993 Giants who missed the playoffs by one game.[2] One could simply use franchise wins as an alternative measure of success. As discussed below, this leads to very different rankings. Ideally, one may want to combine wins with postseason success in order to come up with a complete system but that is a subject for another article.

POSTSEASON SUCCESS

I used the system described above to calculate total postseason success points for each of the thirty major league franchises through 2014. Not surprisingly, the New York Yankees dominate the field with nearly twice the number of points as the second place team. The St. Louis Cardinals hold second by more than 200 points (two World Series victories) over the third place team. The Dodgers, Giants, and A's are in a tight race for third (with the Giants pulling ahead in 2014) followed by the Boston Red Sox. There is then a significant dropoff between 6th and 7th place. The totals for each of the sixteen franchises in existence at the time of the 1903 World Series are listed in Table 2. Surprisingly the least successful of these is not the much-maligned Chicago Cubs, but rather the Cleveland Indians.

Using total points makes it impossible to compare the oldest franchises with the expansion teams. By the time of the first expansion since the establishment of the World Series in 1961, the oldest teams had been accumulating postseason points for 58 seasons. That gave even the Indians enough of a head start to make it impossible for expansion teams to catch them in postseason points. However we can use a metric of postseason points per season in existence. For the original teams this would involve dividing their total points by 111, the number of seasons between 1903 and 2014 (excluding 1994 when there was no postseason).[3] The results in Table 2 are in order of postseason points/season.

Even this is not a terribly fair comparison for the expansion teams, which are typically awful for a number of years after their creation.[4] This will lower their per season averages compared to more established franchises. Still, despite this handicap, the Diamondbacks, Marlins, Mets, Blue Jays, and Royals did manage to achieve per-season postseason point totals that exceeded a number of the original sixteen. Eight of the expansion teams have never won the World Series and they lag even the Cleveland Indians (as do the Los Angeles Angels with one World Series win). At the extreme end of futility the Nationals (née the Montreal Expos) would need three straight World Series triumphs to catch even the Indians.

POSTSEASON SUCCESS COMPARED WITH REGULAR SEASON SUCCESS
Table 2 also contains the number of regular season wins and wins/season for each franchise. As one might expect, postseason points for each franchise have a much higher variance than wins. The comparison between wins and postseason points is interesting. Eliminating the Yankees who are outliers in both variables, wins per season range from 83.93 (the New York/San Francisco Giants) to 72.47 (the Phillies) with a standard deviation of 2.75.[5] Postseason points/season range from 18.94 (the St. Louis Cardinals) to 4.46 (the Washington Nationals/Montreal Expos) with a standard deviation of 3.83. The standard deviation divided by the mean is nearly ten times as large for postseason points as it is for wins.

Comparing postseason points/season with wins/season allows us to see which teams have been postseason disappointments and which ones have particularly capitalized on their comparatively few opportunities in October.

LUCKY TEAMS THAT HAVE GOTTEN THE MOST BANG FOR THE BUCK IN THE POSTSEASON
The Athletics: The Athletics, on their journey from Philadelphia to Kansas City to Oakland, have given baseball fans some of the most memorable teams in baseball history. Before the current Moneyball era, when the A's were good, they won championships. They had dynasties in the early 1910s, the late 1920s, and the 1970s.[6] When they were bad they were awful, losing games in bunches. All this adds up to a team with a lot of postseason points despite a poor overall winning percentage.

The Marlins: The Marlins rank eighth in postseason points/season, best for any expansion team and better than a majority of original teams. The origin of this is simple; they have been in existence for 21 years and have won the World Series twice. Of course they also dismantled these World Series winning teams more quickly than they built them, leading to a losing overall record despite their postseason success.

Table 2. Total Postseason Points: Original 16 Franchises

Franchise	Total Points	Points/ Season	Wins	Wins/ Season
New York Yankees	3853	34.4	9913	88.51
St. Louis Cardinals	2121	18.94	9093	81.19
San Francisco/New York Giants	1974	17.63	9406	83.93
Los Angeles/Brooklyn Dodgers	1891	16.88	9121	81.44
Oakland/Kansas City/Philadelphia A's	1808	16.15	8465	75.58
Boston Red Sox	1723	15.39	8990	80.27
Detroit Tigers	1357	12.11	8885	79.93
Miami/Florida Marlins	264	11.99	1643	74.68
Atlanta/Milwaukee/Boston Braves	1340	11.96	8475	75.67
Arizona Diamondbacks	202	11.91	1355	79.71
Cincinnati Reds	1311	11.71	8795	78.53
Pittsburgh Pirates	1288	11.50	8794	78.52
Chicago Cubs	1198	10.70	8770	78.30
New York Mets	550	10.37	4038	76.19
Baltimore Orioles/St. Louis Browns	1152	10.29	8296	74.07
Toronto Blue Jays	389	10.22	2985	78.55
Minnesota Twins/Washington Senators	1100	9.82	8375	74.78
Philadelphia Phillies	1092	9.75	8117	72.47
Kansas City Royals	439	9.55	3528	76.70
Chicago White Sox	1002	8.94	8771	78.31
Cleveland Indians	967	8.63	8893	79.40
Los Angeles/Anaheim/California Angels	444	8.22	4318	79.96
Tampa Bay Rays	131	7.69	1272	74.82
Houston Astros	345	6.5	4120	77.74
San Diego Padres	289	6.28	3398	73.87
Colorado Rockies	136	6.17	1641	74.59
Texas Rangers/Washington Senators	331	6.14	4094	75.81
Seattle Mariners	206	5.42	2822	74.26
Milwaukee Brewers/Seattle Pilots	243	5.28	3501	76.11
Washington Nationals/Montreal Expos	205	4.46	3527	76.67

UNLUCKY TEAMS WITH SUCCESS THROUGH SEPTEMBER BUT HEARTBREAK IN OCTOBER

The Indians: They rank eighth in wins/season but are the worst original franchise in postseason points/season. That's what happens when you make the World Series five times in 111 seasons and win it only twice. That's also what happens when your greatest success comes at a time when baseball's dominant franchise is winning AL pennant after AL pennant in the 1950s. Finally, that's what happens when you win 111 games in a season and then lose in the World Series as the Indians did in 1954.

The Angels: The Los Angeles Angels have made the playoffs frequently in the expansion era. But the 2014 season was an all too typical outcome for them. They led the American League in wins and then proceeded to lose in the first round of the playoffs to the Royals. Again and again (except in 2002), the Angels have followed wonderful regular seasons with disappointment in October.

DOMINATING A TIME PERIOD

This tool can also be used to provide an answer for questions of which team achieved the most over a given period of time. As each decade concludes, debate often takes place over which team deserves the title, "Team of the Decade." Table 3 shows the Team of the Decade using this system in each of the eleven completed decades for both the American and National Leagues since 1903. The team with the most postseason points in the majors is highlighted in bold text.

Table 3. Teams of the Decade (Overall winner in bold)

Decade	AL	NL
2000s	**Yankees**	Cardinals
1990s	Yankees	**Braves**
1980s	A's/Royals	**Dodgers**
1970s	**A's**	Reds
1960s	**Yankees**	Dodgers
1950s	**Yankees**	Dodgers
1940s	**Yankees**	Cardinals
1930s	**Yankees**	Cardinals
1920s	**Yankees**	Giants
1910s	**Red Sox**	Giants
1900s	Tigers	**Cubs**

Again the Yankees dominate these titles garnering the most postseason points in the major leagues in six of the eleven decades and winning the American League (but surprisingly not the major leagues) in the 1990s. Other franchises to "win" a decade include the Atlanta Braves in the 1990s, the Los Angeles Dodgers in the 1980s, the Oakland A's in the 1970s, the Boston Red Sox in the 1910's and the Chicago Cubs in the 1900s. The Cubs obviously followed their decade win with a bit of an off century.

But ten-year periods don't all start in years ending in zero. Since 1903, there have been 103 decades in baseball history (1903–12, 1904–13, 1905–14, etc.). Again the Yankees, dominate the list of decades won but a broader array of franchises can claim to have been the most accomplished postseason performers for at least one decade. Table 4 lists the teams that have led the major leagues for at least one decade in postseason points and the number of decades of glory for these teams.

Table 4. Decades "Won"

Yankees	58
A's	13
Cardinals	6
Red Sox	6
Dodgers	4
Braves	4
Orioles	4
Giants	3
Blue Jays	2
Twins	2
Cubs	1

Ten of the original sixteen franchises have won a decade, as has one expansion team (the Toronto Blue Jays which won the decades beginning in 1984 and 1985). Not to pick on the Chicago Cubs, but they won the first complete decade of twentieth-century World Series history (1903–12) with two World Series titles and two other National League pennants and then never won another one. Still one win is more than six of the other original franchises.

What if we shorten the admittedly arbitrary time period from ten years? What if we lengthen it? Has each franchise had its time period in the sun? A time period when it can say, "We were the best?" As a final exercise, I looked at each team and found the longest period over which it had more postseason points than any other team in the majors. Teams that never won the World Series (Expos/Nats, Mariners, Rangers/Senators, Astros, Rays, Brewers, Rockies, and Padres) have no such period. Here are the longest times when every other team could claim it was the best in the sport:

Arizona Diamondbacks: 2001–03. With a World Series win in 2001 and a playoff appearance in 2002 the Diamondbacks were the best for this brief three year run. The other two World Series winners in this period did not make the playoffs either of the other two years.

Atlanta/Milwaukee/Boston Braves: 1982–99. It should surprise no one that the Braves' best era was quite recent, as their three pitching aces and manager from this period have been recently inducted into the Hall of Fame.

Baltimore Orioles/St. Louis Browns: 1965–80. This represents the peak of the Earl Weaver "Orioles Way" era and includes two World Series titles, three additional pennants, and two more division titles.

Boston Red Sox: 1903–22. As great as the Red Sox have been recently, their longest period of dominance was the first 19 years of World Series play. With five titles in a 19-year span, they were one of the first MLB powerhouses.

Chicago Cubs: 1903–12. But if we truncate the beginning of baseball history a bit, the Cubs get to claim the mantle of greatest team. Winning the World Series in 1907 and 1908 and pennants in 1906 and 1910 is enough to give them the title for baseball's first decade.

Chicago White Sox: 1917–20. Yes, the White Sox's greatest era contains the Black Sox team of 1919. This is the only time the White Sox have appeared in more than one World Series in less than forty years.

Cincinnati Reds: 1973–77. It is a short period but a dominant one. With a division title in 1973 followed by World Series wins in 1975 and 1976, the Big Red Machine won't be soon forgotten.

Cleveland Indians: 1920, 1948. Ah the Indians. They are one of only two original franchises that does not have a multi-year period in which it can claim supremacy. They have to settle for their two World Series winning years.

Detroit Tigers: 1932–35. The Tigers have had a number of great teams but few that were grouped together. Their best team includes the World Series winners of 1935 and pennant winners of 1934.

Kansas City Royals: 1979–85. The Royals of George Brett were a constant postseason presence in this era winning three divisions (and a half division in the 1981 split season), two pennants, and the 1985 World Series.

Los Angeles/Anaheim/California Angels: 2002. Like the Indians, the Los Angeles Angels have no multi-year period in which they were dominant.

Los Angeles/Brooklyn Dodgers: 1962–97. This is the second-longest dominant period of any franchise. It carries through the Koufax era, the great Dodger teams of the 1970s, and the Orel Hershiser/Kirk Gibson team of 1988. Surprisingly it does not include the great Brooklyn teams of the 1950s because they only won the one World Series in 1955 and this era was dominated by the Yankees.

Miami/Florida Marlins: 1997, 2003. See the discussion above for the reason the Marlins have no multi year periods in which they were the best team.

Minnesota Twins/Washington Senators: 1982–92. The Twins are the only team to win two World Series in this period which is enough to give them the title for this eleven-year era.

New York Mets: 1986–88. Ah, what could have been? A team that many forecast to dominate for years had a brief but well documented three-year run at the top of the heap.

New York Yankees: 1903–2014. Some team has to be the best of all time, and it isn't close. For this to change, the Cardinals would have to win 18 World Series in a row while the Yankees never make the playoffs. Mystique and aura can rest easy.

Oakland/Kansas City/Philadelphia Athletics: 1965–98. The great A's teams of the 1970s coupled with the Bash Brothers of the 1980s, give the A's the win over a period largely overlapping with and almost as long as the Dodgers. Interestingly the A's also have a 29-year period of postseason success from 1904–32 spanning Connie Mack's two great teams.

Philadelphia Phillies: 2007–11. One of the oldest franchises has recently had its peak. With its five consecutive division titles and 2008 World Series win, it's been the best time in history to be a Phillies fan.

Pittsburgh Pirates: 1909, 1925, 1960, 1971, 1979. The oddest result of all the teams in my view. The Pirates have won five World Series but have never had the most postseason points for any period longer than one year (they do tie with the Yankees from 1925–27 and the A's from 1971–72).

San Francisco/New York Giants: 1903–37. This is the fourth franchise whose dominant period starts at the beginning of the World Series era. Their stretch goes on significantly longer than those of the Red Sox or Cubs and largely spans John McGraw's career. For all periods from 1903 to years later than 1937, the Yankees have the most postseason points.

St. Louis Cardinals: 2000–14. For a team with such a storied history, I was surprised to see we are currently in their best stretch. But over the past 15 seasons, the Cardinals have won two World Series and been in the postseason a remarkable 11 out of 15 years.

Toronto Blue Jays: 1979–95. The Blue Jays have been away from the postseason longer than any other team. However they also have the longest stretch of superiority of any expansion team. It is easy to forget how they regularly contended for and won AL East titles in the 1980s before breaking through as World Series champions in 1992 and 1993. ■

Notes

1. Kubatko's method is described by Neil Paine on ESPN.com: http://insider.espn.go.com/nba/story/_/id/8831674/nba-which-team-lakers-spurs-heat-had-most-playoff-success-2005.
2. Actually the Mets get more credit, there were only 20 major league teams in 1962 but there were 28 in 1993.
3. I did give the New York Giants and Boston Red Sox 50 points each for winning their respective league pennants in 1904. There was no World Series played that year.
4. The expansion era has provided more opportunities for postseason points with expanded playoffs. However, these points are dwarfed by the 100 points for a World Series victory and 50 points for a World Series loss leaving the expansion teams at a disadvantage.
5. The standard deviation is a statistical measure of the variation in a set of data. It is calculated using the average difference between data and the mean of the data set.
6. Rob Neyer and Eddie Epstein, *Baseball Dynasties*, New York: W.W. Norton & Co, 2000.

The First Televised Baseball Interview

Robert D. Warrington

Baseball's relationship with the media can be traced back to the earliest days of the game. It started with newspapers in the nineteenth century, broadened to radio in the early twentieth century, then expanded to television by mid-century. While the innumerable, pervasive connections that bind baseball and the media today bear little resemblance to their modest beginnings, each linkage had to start somewhere. For baseball and television, that somewhere was in an experimental television station in Philadelphia in 1937, when an interview featuring Philadelphia Athletics manager Connie Mack was broadcast to demonstrate a qualitative leap forward in television technology.

THE EMERGENCE OF TELEVISION

Television was not invented by one person, nor was the invention created in one place. Multiple enterprises located in the United States and abroad contributed to the development of television over decades of work starting in the nineteenth century.[1] Television's feasibility as a mass consumer product depended on overcoming technological challenges. The greatest of these was improving the image definition of an analog television screen so that its quality approximated what moviegoers saw in theaters.[2] By the mid-1930s, significant progress had been made in creating greater television picture detail and stability by increasing the number of horizontal lines that together comprise the picture on an analog television screen.[3] Additional refinements in screen image quality were inevitable, but by whom, when, and how much?

PHILCO AND THE 441-LINE BREAKTHROUGH

Founded in the late nineteenth century, the Philadelphia Storage Battery Company—Philco—expanded its product line in the late 1920s to include radios. The move was a highly profitable one for the company; with an eye fixed on the future of home entertainment, Philco was an early leader in the effort to transform television into a marketable commodity.[4] The company was granted permission by the Federal Communications Commission (FCC) in 1932 to operate an experimental television station—one of the first in the country—in

its plant in Philadelphia.[5] Philco engineers strove to improve screen resolution quality.

In mid-1936, the Radio Corporation of America (RCA)—a rival of Philco's in television development—held the initial public demonstration of its new 343-horizontal-line screen technology, a substantial advancement over the previous 240-line standard.[6] Unbeknownst to RCA, however, Philco engineers had achieved an even more dramatic breakthrough in screen image quality—a 441-line picture definition.[7] Eager to unveil this achievement with maximum publicity, Philco invited 150 media, publishing, and communications industry representatives—along with FCC executives—from around the country to join senior company officials in witnessing the first public transmission of a 441-line television screen image.[8]

Still, a critical question faced company leaders: "What program would be shown on the screen to the audience?" Star power was the answer, and Philco brought together for the occasion two of the most famous personalities residing in the city: Connie Mack and Boake Carter.

CONNIE MACK

Readers of the *BRJ* should know the name Connie Mack. In his thirty-seventh year of managing the Philadelphia Athletics, Mack was by 1937 an iconic figure in major league baseball and a sports luminary in Philadelphia. His A's teams had won nine American League pennants and five World Series titles. Mack was selected to manage the American League squad in the first All-Star Game in 1933. The following year he led an impressive roster of major leaguers to play a series of exhibition games in Japan, China, and the Philippines. The City of Philadelphia acknowledged Mack's esteemed status as one of its leading citizens by presenting the Philadelphia Award to him in 1929—the first sports personality recognized with this highly prestigious honor.[9]

In January 1937, the Philadelphia Athletics Board of Directors elected Mack to be the franchise president, adding that position to his already-existing jobs as club manager and treasurer. The year also saw Mack voted into the National Baseball Hall of Fame.[10] To these laurels would be added the role of serving as the guest on the first televised baseball interview.

BOAKE CARTER

British-born Harold Thomas Henry "Boake" Carter was a journalist and foreign correspondent who by 1930 had migrated to Philadelphia, working as a reporter and commentator at radio station WCAU, a CBS affiliate broadcasting in the city.[11] Carter's big break came in 1935 when he covered the trial of Bruno Richard Hauptmann, the man charged with kidnapping the infant son of famed aviator Charles A. Lindbergh. His narratives describing the lurid details of the crime that more discreet reporters believed should not be broadcast across the country made Carter an instant celebrity.[12] Once the trial ended, Philco sponsored him to host a national radio news program on CBS, and Carter's voice could be heard coast to coast from the WCAU studio. He became one of the most influential commentators of his time, and given Philco's determination to attract the utmost public attention to the unveiling of its 441-line definitional television screen, he was as obvious a choice to conduct the interview as Connie Mack was to be interviewed.[13]

THE DEMONSTRATION

The date selected for the demonstration and accompanying luncheon was February 11, 1937, and the ballroom of the Germantown Cricket Club in Philadelphia was chosen as the place to hold it.[14] The television screen on which the interview was to be shown measured 12 inches in diameter,[15] and Philco placed several television sets in the ballroom so people could have an up-close look at the picture being broadcast.[16] The program lasted one hour.[17]

The Mack-Carter interview took place at Philco's experimental television station, located at C & Tioga Streets in Philadelphia and bearing the call letters W3XE. The television station and cricket club were approximately three miles apart.[18]

Reporting on the demonstration indicates that Philco earned the positive reviews it sought in displaying the 441-line screen image resolution. A reporter from *Etude Music Magazine* who attended the event provided a description of what he witnessed:

We have recently attended a private demonstration in which the Philco Company presented to publishers and editors from all parts of the United States the "last word" in the advancement of television. The program lasted one hour and was given in the ballroom of the Germantown Cricket Club. The pictures were reproduced in what is known as 441 lines, a big advance over the 335 [sic] lines previously possible. One of the striking pictures was a television interview

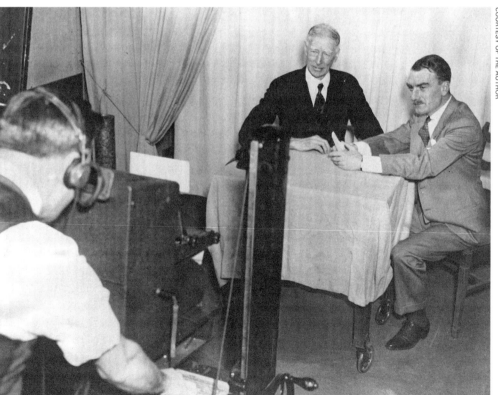

Publicity photo issued by Philco. Connie Mack (center) and Boake Carter (right) are shown conducting the interview. Note the television camera and how primitive it is by today's standards.

COURTESY OF THE AUTHOR

between Boake Carter and "Connie" Mack, well known news commentator and famous baseball manager, who were televised three miles away from the receiving set.

From the standpoint of sound, the transmission is no different from that of an ordinary radio. The pictures show the individuals televised (in black and white) at almost the same relative size as that seen in the full page illustrations in a magazine. The pictures came in with surprisingly little flicker and light variation, but they are not yet as steady in this respect as the ordinary good movie. That they are as good as they are is so marvelous that one continuously feels a desire to pinch himself to realize that it is all actually happening.[19]

As part of the campaign to publicize its improved television screen technology, Philco distributed a photo of Mack and Carter taken during the interview. The caption that accompanied the photo illustrates the company's eagerness to promote the groundbreaking nature of the demonstration:

America's No. 1 News Commentator Interviews America's No 1 Base Ball Manager... Connie Mack (left) engaged in first Televised sports interview with Boake Carter, famous Philco news commentator, in Philco Television Demonstration at Philadelphia, February 11th, 1937.

Cleverly, Philco switched the screen image quality between 441 lines and the previous horizontal line standard during the demonstration. By highlighting the comparison, as one observer stated, "The improvement was obvious." This same commentator also noted presciently when evaluating the remarks made by Philco's vice president Sayre Ramsdell, "Mr. Ramsdell definitely spiked the impression that has gotten around to the effect that television would supersede sound broadcasting."[20]

The demonstration did not go entirely uncriticized, however. A reporter from *The New York Times* who attended the event wrote: "The greenish tint that has characterized television pictures in the majority of past demonstrations has been overcome. Black and white advances television closer to the cinema, but television has a long way to go to equal the movies in clarity."[21]

Improving picture clarity and stability was only one of the challenges Philco had to overcome to make television a marketable commodity. The opinion of another attendee at the demonstration illustrates this point:

I'd like to have one of those sets in my home, and so would lots of other people. However, I understand that the first television sets may cost four or five hundred dollars. That's too much money to spend for any radio set, with or without pictures. But if they can get the cost down to, say, two hundred, it's my guess that the average person would feel that he had his money's worth with entertainment such as that given here.[22]

A HISTORIC MOMENT, BUT NOT FOR SPORTS

Any significance Philco attempted to attach to Mack and Carter engaging in the "first Televised sports interview" went completely unnoticed in contemporary accounts of the demonstration. While the unprecedented nature of the interview was noted in the caption accompanying the photograph of the men distributed by the company, none of the sports sections of newspapers in Philadelphia and New York touched upon it, nor was the interview ever mentioned in *The Sporting News*. It is not surprising, however, that the interview was overlooked at the time as an epochal event in sports, and that the potential of a future relationship between baseball and television went unrecognized.

In 1937, television still was in its infancy, judged by many to be nothing more than an exotic toy for the rich. It was far from certain television would ever equal—let alone supplant—radio as the primary home entertainment medium nationwide. Satisfactory screen quality and an affordable purchase price were still daunting hurdles to be overcome.

In addition, the demonstration was intended to promote Philco's breakthrough in television picture definition and stability. Mack and Carter were included on the program because their celebrity status helped publicize the event, and because the interview broadcast illustrated the magnitude of the qualitative improvement in screen image resolution. Attendees were drawn to the event to witness a major leap forward in television technology, not to experience the novelty of the "first Televised sports interview." That is why the demonstration was covered by entertainment reporters, not sports reporters.

The fact that the interview's purpose was confined to supporting the demonstration is further evidenced by the fact that no video or audio recording of it is known to survive. If Philco hoped the demonstration would be historic, it was based on the marvel a great advance in television technology would inspire, not on the curiosity the first televised sports interview would trigger. It is highly unlikely anyone at the company considered the greater significance for baseball and the media of including a sports interview as part of the program shown to attendees. The role television could play in bringing baseball into the homes of American families was an intriguing question, but one too soon to ask in 1937. The development of television had not reached the point where such a relationship could be realistically envisioned. That would come later.

BEYOND THE INTERVIEW

Despite Philco's claim that the 441-line definitional image was the "last word" in the advancement of television screen quality, its status at the forefront of picture technology lasted only a brief period. The company itself recognized that its 441-line image would not stand the test of time, and in 1940, Philco engineers increased the resolution of its television screen picture to 525 lines.[23] The need to fight and win World War II interrupted the emergence of television as a mass consumer product, although research to improve it as a marketable commodity continued.[24] Once the war ended, television's popularity skyrocketed.[25]

Baseball's relationship with television matured as additional "firsts" occurred in the aftermath of the Mack-Carter interview. The first televised baseball game took place on May 17, 1939, between Princeton University and Columbia University at the latter's Baker Field. Princeton won, 2–1. It was shown on W2XBS, an experimental station in New York. The first professional baseball game ever to be aired on television took place several months later on August 26, 1939, when W2XBS, using one camera near the visitors' dugout along the third base line and one in the second tier behind home plate, showed a doubleheader between the Brooklyn Dodgers and Cincinnati Reds at Ebbets Field. The first batter to appear on television: Reds third baseman Bill Werber. The first pitch was thrown by Luke Hamlin. The Reds took the first game, 5–2, while the Dodgers came back and captured the nightcap, 6–1. Although the start of scheduled broadcasts of major league baseball games as part of regular commercial television programming was delayed by World War II, it followed rapidly once the war concluded.[26]

TELEVISED GAMES AT SHIBE PARK

In 1947, just ten years after the Mack-Carter pioneering broadcast in a small experimental studio in a city

COURTESY OF THE AUTHOR

An extremely rare photo of the television cage that hung below the upper deck behind home plate at Shibe Park. The presence of the cage in the image is fortuitous since the photographer's subject was the two boys climbing the protective screen to retrieve a foul ball that had become lodged in the wire mesh. The photo was taken during a doubleheader between the Athletics and Red Sox on September 7, 1947—the first year games at Shibe Park were televised.

that could count televisions in only 100–150 homes,[27] televised broadcasts of Philadelphia Athletics games (and Philadelphia Phillies games) began.[28] Coverage of games at Shibe Park was rudimentary by today's standards. A single camera was used, and it was located in a small cage under the sloping tier of the upper-deck seats, first level, behind home plate. People watching at home could see only the infield.[29] By 1950, two more cameras were added—one each in the photographers' boxes along the first and third base lines—which provided multiple views of the infield and coverage of the outfield.[30]

Technicians manning television cameras at the ballpark worked under primitive and dangerous conditions. Don Paine, a cameraman at Shibe Park, remembered:

> You worked in this little cage behind home plate that hung down from the upper deck. To get to it, you had to climb down a ladder. My back was right up against the screen. The lens in the camera pointed out through an opening about 18 inches wide in the cage. A foul ball could go through there and knock the camera out. One time, a cameraman got knocked out when a ball hit him right in the head.[31]

A photograph that accompanies this article shows two boys climbing up the protective screen behind home plate at Shibe Park to retrieve a foul ball that had become lodged in the screen's wire mesh.[32] The photo provides an excellent view of the television camera cage. The opening cut in the screen for the camera to shoot through is visible, and the photo also reveals that a shade was present on the front of the screen that could be pulled down to cover the opening when the camera was not shooting through it. This presumably was done to provide protection for the camera and crew during batting practice, and to cover the opening when games were not being played at Shibe Park.

THE INTERVIEW IN HISTORICAL PERSPECTIVE

The Mack-Carter interview introduced baseball to television, although it is highly doubtful either man understood or even imagined how remarkable the moment was. It is only in retrospect that we can recognize the occasion's importance in the evolution and confluence of baseball and television. The significance of the interview as a milestone in baseball's relationship with the media is that it happened, not what was said or the circumstances under which it took place. Despite Philco's best efforts to etch its technological achievement in the annals of time, the 441-line analog

screen image is consigned to the past, while sports interviews have flourished on television and are now as much a part of the baseball viewing experience as the games themselves. The Mack-Carter interview heralded symbolically what swiftly became a paramount realization by baseball and television of the benefits both could reap by a close and continuing affiliation.

While early television coverage of baseball was hardly comprehensive or elegant, it changed the relationship that existed between baseball and its fans, and it forced baseball to redefine its understanding of the role of mass media in that relationship.[33] For the first time, a person could "see" a game without leaving home. In generating revenue through broadcast rights, promoting ticket sales, publicizing upcoming games, expanding the fan base through advertising, and marketing teams beyond the confines of a ballpark, the prospect for financial gain offered by television broadcasts of baseball games was enormous. In this fundamental and important way, television contributed significantly to baseball's transformation from a game being played to a commodity being merchandised. ∎

Notes

1. Two of the best books describing the invention and history of television are: Erik Barnouw, *Tube of Plenty: The Evolution of American Television*, Second edition (New York: Oxford University Press, 1990), and David E. and Marshall J. Fisher, *Tube: The Invention of the Television*, (Boston: Mariner Books, 1997).

2. An analog television operates by having optical images sent from the transmitting equipment converted from images to electrical signals by a camera tube. The signals are transmitted by UHF or VHF radio waves or by cable and reconverted into optical images by means of a television tube inside a television set. http://dictionary.reverso.net/english-definition/television%20set.

3. The first all-electronic television had 120 lines in 1932. The number doubled the next year to 240. Despite this remarkable improvement, the technological hurdle of increasing horizontal line density was difficult to overcome. Research was costly and progress uneven. Additional information on early improvements in analog screen image resolution can be found in "Television," http://www.clemenson.edu/caaah/history/FacultyPages/ PamMack/lec1., and in "Television systems before 1940," http://en.wikipedia.org/ wiki/Television_systems_before_1940. For a more general treatment of the horizontal line density technological hurdle within the overall context of the invention of television, see, Samidha Verma, "Invention of Television," http://engineersgarage.com/invention-stories/history-of-telev.

4. A chronological history of Philco is provided in, "The History of Philco," http://www.philcoradio.com/history/htm.

5. "Channel 3's History: The Early Years," http://www.broadcastpioneers.com/bpl/3history.html. The FCC was called the Federal Radio Commission in 1932. It became the Federal Communications Commission in 1934 in recognition that its jurisdiction over communications mediums would transcend just radio.

6. RCA's demonstration of its new screen technology is noted at http://www.tvhistory.tv/1936%20QF.htm.

7. A description of the 441-line screen resolution image breakthrough achieved by Philco engineers is contained in Chapter 3 of "The History of Philco." The company was also the first to employ interlacing to improve definitional screen imaging. "By interlacing and scanning at a faster

rate of 30 frames (or 30 complete scans of both odd and even lines), all noticeable flicker is removed." Nat Pendleton, "The Dawn of Modern, Electronic Television," http://www.earlytelevision.org/pendelton_paper.html.

8. "441-Line Television," *Radio Engineering*, February, 1937.

9. Frederick G. Lieb, *Connie Mack: Grand Old Man of Baseball* (New York: G.P. Putnam's Sons, 1945), 231, 251, 253–54.

10. Ibid., 263, 268

11. Carter's initial broadcast assignment was as the announcer for a rugby game. WCAU covered the game, and Carter was the only person at the station who was familiar with the sport. http://en.wikipedia.org/wiki/Boake_Carter.

12. http://www.otr.com/bcarter.html.

13. http://en.metapedia.org/wiki/Boake_Carter and http://en.wikipedia.org/wiki/Boake_Carter. Despite his overall popularity, Carter's star began to dim when he became increasingly vitriolic in his criticism of President Franklin Roosevelt and his "New Deal" and foreign policies. Philco did not renew Carter's contract in 1938, and he migrated the next year to the Mutual Broadcasting System. Carter never returned to the prominence he had previously enjoyed, however, and he died in 1944 of a heart attack. Readers interested in learning more about Carter can read, David H. Culbert, *News for Everyman: Radio and Foreign Affairs in Thirties America*, Reprint edition (Santa Barbara: Praeger Publishers, 1976).

14. *Radio Engineering*, February, 1937. The irony of the first televised baseball interview being shown at a cricket club should not be lost on readers. Cricket is one of the antecedents from which the game of baseball is derived, organized and structured. See, Fred Lieb, *The Baseball Story* (New York: G.P. Putnam's Sons, 1950), 3–8.

15. The dimensions of the actual image were 7½ by 10 inches. A black border around the picture covered the rest of the screen. "Television, When?," *Etude Music Magazine*, June, 1937.

16. A history of Philco provides more technical details on the transmission-receiver set-up as arranged for the demonstration. "The company's prototype TV sets on display at the demonstration were housed in leftover 1936 Model 116PX radio-phonograph cabinets, with no dial or controls on the front panels. When the lid of a set was lifted, instead of a phonograph, the television screen and controls were revealed. A mirror under the lid allowed normal television viewing from across the room to take place. Each of the sets used twenty-six tubes." "The History of Philco." Details can be found in Chapter 3, "Leadership in Radio." http://www.philcoradio.com/history/indix/htm. For readers wishing to immerse themselves even more deeply into the technical details of the demonstration, Philco's transmitter used for the broadcast had a peak power of four kilowatts and operated on a frequency of 49 megacycles. Sound transmission was over a separate channel (54 megacycles). *Radio Engineering*, February, 1937.

17. The program consisted of interviews, newsreels and a fashion show, and it was preceded by remarks from James M. Skinner, president of Philco, Sayre M. Ramsdell, vice-president, and Albert F. Murray, engineer in charge of the company's television work. *Radio Engineering*, February, 1937. The highlight of the demonstration, nevertheless, was the Mack-Carter interview, which is the only segment of the program mentioned specifically by reviewers. *Etude Music Magazine*, June, 1937.

18. "Channel 3's History."

19. *Etude Music Magazine*, June 1937. The number of horizontal lines in an analog television screen picture prior to the 441 perfected by Philco was actually 343—shown by RCA in mid-1936—not the 335 lines stated in the article.

20. *Radio Engineering*, February, 1937.

21. Orrin E. Dunlap Jr., "Television Show Reveals Current State of the Art," *The New York Times*, February 21, 1937.

22. *Radio Engineering*, February, 1937. Price continued to be a drag on sales despite advancements in screen quality. RCA initially marketed its line of TV sets in New York City in 1939 with poor results. The company then reduced the price and met with better, albeit still tepid, success. America was not yet ready to embrace television as a mass consumer product. See, "Early Electronic Television," http://www.earlytelevision.org/prewar.html.

23. "The History of Philco." More information about Philco's efforts to improve definitional screen image quality beyond 441 lines can be found in Chapter 4, "Diversification and War." http://www.philcoradio.com/history/hist4.htm. On May 3, 1941, the FCC authorized a 525-line definitional image, and it became the industry standard for analog television screens thereafter. In September, 1941, Philco's experimental television station became one of the first in the country to be granted a commercial broadcasting license by the FCC. The station's call letters were changed from W3XE to WPTZ. "Channel 3's History." http://www.broadcastpioneers.com/bpl/3history.html. Analog television technology became obsolete in 2009 when television stations stopped broadcasting in that format and switched to digital transmission. http://www.fcc.gov/digital-television.

24. Mitchell Stephens, "History of Television," http://www.nyu.edu/classes/stephens/History.

25. Although large-scale production of TV sets started in the United States in 1946, by the end of that year, only 44,000 homes in the country had a TV set. By 1953, 50% of American homes had television. http://www.earlytelevision.org/american_postwar.html.

26. The Dodgers-Reds games at Ebbets Field were broadcast by an experimental television station and were not part of commercial programming. Indeed, in 1939, there were less than 2,000 homes with televisions in New York. More people saw the Dodgers-Reds doubleheader at the ballpark than at home. "Baseball broadcasting firsts," http://en.wikipedia.org/wiki/Baseball_broadcasting_firsts. Also see, "75 years ago today, the first MLB game was televised," http://wapc.mlb.com/cutfour/2014/08/25/91371436/75-years-ago-tl.

27. "Early Television Stations," http://www.earlytelevision.org/w3xe.html and "Channel 3's History." http://www.broadcastpioneers.com/bpl/3history.html.

28. Bruce Kuklick, *To Every Thing A Season: Shibe Park and Urban Philadelphia, 1909–1976* (Princeton: Princeton University Press, 1991), 104.

29. Ibid.

30. Rich Westcott, *Philadelphia's Old Ballparks* (Philadelphia: Temple University Press, 1996), 180–81

31. Ibid., 181.

32. The photograph was taken at Shibe Park on September 7, 1947 during a doubleheader between the Philadelphia Athletics and the Boston Red Sox. The Mackmen won both ends of the twin bill 7–4 and 4–3. http://www.baseball-almanac.com/teamsrars/schedule.php?y=1947t=PHA.

33. For a more extensive treatment of baseball's relationship with radio and television, see, Eldon L. Ham, *Broadcasting Baseball: A History of the National Pastime on Radio and Television* (Jefferson, NC: McFarland & Company, 2011).

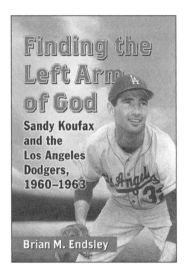

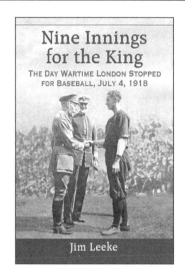

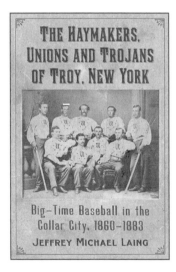
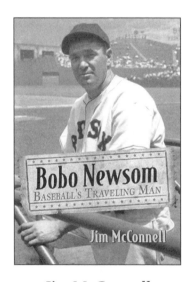

The New York Mets in Popular Culture

David Krell

METS MUSIC

When the New York Mets debuted in 1962, so did a song. More than a sonic icon, "Meet the Mets" is a member of the pantheon of Mets hallmarks occupied by Shea Stadium, Mr. Met, and the mantra "Ya Gotta Believe!" As any devotee of the blue and orange will tell you, "Meet the Mets" attracts Mets fans with a title reflecting the power of alliteration, lyrics infusing the feeling of community, and a horn section blaring the fanfare of excitement. "Meet the Mets" endures in popular culture, demonstrated notably in an episode of *Everybody Loves Raymond*, an impromptu performance by Bob Costas on *Sports Illustrated*'s webcast "Jump the Q," and a revised version in the 1980s.

When the nascent New York Mets set out to fill the National League void created by the migration of the Brooklyn Dodgers and the New York Giants to California after the 1957 season, they faced a Herculean task: to excite, inspire, and motivate baseball fans mourning the loss of two baseball mainstays while creating a unique identity. Rather than ignore the rich National League legacy of New York's departed teams, the Mets honored it by using Dodger Blue and Giant Orange for their team colors.

When the team announced that it was looking for a theme song, it received 20 submissions. One, called "Meet the Mets," was the work of the songwriting team of Ruth Roberts and Bill Katz, whose portfolio included "It's A Beautiful Day for a Ball Game," "I Love Mickey," and "Mr. Touchdown, U.S.A." They actually submitted two versions of the song. According to *New York Times* sportswriter Leonard Koppett, the entries fell under the scrutiny of Mets president George Weiss, promotion director Julie Adler, and executives of the J. Walter Thompson Advertising Agency. "They submitted one version of 'Meet the Mets' to Adler in November in 1961," wrote Koppett. "Subsequently, they submitted another version to the ad agency. The agency was impressed and called Adler, who was still mulling over some of the other candidates, but was leaning toward the original Roberts-Katz piece.

"Then the agency and Adler compared notes, so to speak, and out of the two versions grew the now familiar work."[1]

Glenn Osser created an original arrangement and his orchestra recorded "Meet the Mets" on March 1, 1963. Three years later, "Meet the Mets" entered the musical mainstream when children's television icon Soupy Sales hosted *Hullabaloo*, a television show catering to the teenage demographic by showcasing rock and roll groups *à la American Bandstand*.[2]

Sales's sons, Tony and Hunt, performed on the April 4, 1966, broadcast of *Hullabaloo* with their rock and roll band, Tony and the Tigers. The two sons then joined their father in singing "Meet the Mets" to mark the opening of the 1966 baseball season. It was a curious choice. The song is brassy, like a march. It does not fit into the rock and roll genre, but the Sales family made it work. The Hullabaloo Dancers complemented the Sales men, joining them halfway through the performance.

Additional lyrics reflect the lovable though hapless play of the Mets teams in the early to mid-1960s, describing the Mets as irresponsible, unreliable, and undependable.

Ray Romano used the song as a literary device in the March 1, 1999, episode "Big Shots" of his show *Everybody Loves Raymond*. Romano's character, *Newsday* sports writer Ray Barone, takes his brother Robert to the Baseball Hall of Fame for an event honoring players from the Mets' 1969 World Series championship team. A devoted Mets fan, Robert names his dog after Art Shamsky. On the car ride to Cooperstown, he points out that Shamsky homered in his first time at bat.

When an announcer introduces the Mets against the backdrop of an instrumental version of "Meet the Mets," Ray refuses to wait on line to meet Tommie Agee, Jerry Grote, Bud Harrelson, Cleon Jones, Ed Kranepool, Tug McGraw, Ron Swoboda, and Shamsky. He tries to use his journalist's credentials to avoid the wait. Frustrated by Ray's arrogance, the Hall of Fame security guards kick out the Barone brothers.

Robert takes the disappointment in stride, but Ray feels shame, anger, and embarrassment because his *Newsday* affiliation amounted to nil. Ray orders "No talking" on the car trip back to Long Island. Robert acquiesces, humming "Meet the Mets" instead.

44

Eventually, silence pervades the car. When a local cop stops Ray for speeding, Robert violates the ban on talking by explaining his credentials as a member of the NYPD. It is ineffective—the cop ignores Robert's status as a fellow law enforcement officer, prompting Robert to experience the same feelings that Ray had endured at the Hall of Fame.

"Meet the Mets" heals the rift. Ray begins singing the Mets' anthem. Robert joins him, first reluctantly and then joyfully. The scene signifies an unbreakable link among Mets fans, one that has the power to dissolve family tension by instantly recalling a common bond dating back to childhood.

In the mid-1980s, a jazzier version of the Mets' theme song expanded with new lyrics highlighting the diversity of the geography of Mets fans, mentioning Long Island, New Jersey, Queens, and Brooklyn. Obviously, the song excludes the Bronx—the home of the Yankees has no place in a song about the Mets. A 1990s rap interpretation offered another adaptation.

Koppett decried the lack of traditional arrangement in the song. "There is little in the score of interest to a mid-20th-century audience," he wrote. "The harmony is traditional; no influences of atonality or polytonality can be found. In fact, it's sort of un-tonal.

"The melody avoids being square, but is uninspired. The incorporation of folk material ('*East Side, West Side*') in bars 25–28 of the published score is appropriate enough, but not original.

"Nevertheless, if Miss Roberts and Katz have not produced a total success artistically, they should not be blamed nor shown disrespect. The subject is simply too vast. It could be treated with justice only by the mature Mozart, the Mozart of *Don Giovanni* and the *Marriage of Figaro*."[3]

METS MOVIES

One of the Mets' greatest achievements took place on June 27, 1967—a triple play. Unfortunately, it was fictional. "The triple play, filmed just before the start of the regularly scheduled Mets-Pirates game, was staged for a scene in Paramount Pictures' *The Odd Couple*, the film adaptation of Mr. [Neil] Simon's Broadway comedy about a couple of grass widowers,"[4] explained Vincent Canby in the June 28, 1967, edition of *The New York Times*.

Simon added the Shea Stadium scene and others to give the film version of *The Odd Couple* an authentic New York City flavor. It highlights the differences between the mismatched roommates, sportswriter Oscar and news writer Felix. During the top of the ninth inning of a Mets-Pirates game, the Pirates trail

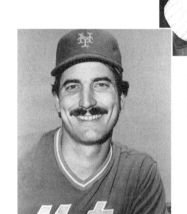

Marv Throneberry and Keith Hernandez are part of Mets popular culture lore.

the Mets by one run with the bases loaded and Bill Mazeroski at bat. Felix calls Oscar in the press box instructions to avoid eating frankfurters as he will be making franks and beans for dinner. During the phone call, Oscar misses Mazeroski hitting into a 5–4–3 triple play.

Canby added, "Before the filming, there was some tension among the Hollywood people, because after setting up their cameras, they had only 35 minutes in which to complete the shot before the start of the game."[5] (The actual Mets-Pirates game that took place on June 27, 1967, resulted in a 5–2 Mets victory.)

When *The Odd Couple* became a television series, Oscar sometimes wore a Mets cap.

The '69 Mets formed a plot point in the 2000 movie *Frequency*, which focuses on an NYPD detective in the present talking to his firefighter dad in 1969. John Sullivan convinces his father, Frank, that their communication is real by explaining certain events of the 1969 World Series.

In a review of the movie for the *Los Angeles Times*, Michael X. Ferraro explained the inevitability of the Mets' appearance in movies. "Of course it's the Mets," wrote Ferraro. "Who else could it be? It's no secret that baseball has a certain je ne say hey that Hollywood strives to appropriate whenever possible. But more specifically, when it comes to movie and TV references to the major leagues, the '69 Mets are the team to use when you're trying to invoke a sense of wonderment."

Ferrarro added, "Blessed by the baseball gods, and certainly bolstered by a cadre of New York-born writers and executives, many of whom came of age during the miraculous summer of '69, the Mets seem destined to live on in the annals of popular entertainment."[6]

Characters in the movies *The Flamingo Kid* and *City Slickers* wear Mets caps. Similarly, *Keeping the Faith* and *Trainwreck* offer homages to the Mets. In the 2005 movie *Fever Pitch*, Jimmy Fallon plays a Boston Red Sox fanatic who furthers his depression after a romantic breakup by watching the iconic play of Mookie Wilson's ground ball going through Bill Buckner's legs in Game Six of the 1986 World Series. As the title "character" in the 1977 movie *Oh, God!*, George Burns declares, "The last miracle I did was the 1969 Mets. Before that, I think you have to go back to the Red Sea."[7]

METS TELEVISION

Several episodes of *Seinfeld* incorporated the Mets into story lines, a result of Jerry Seinfeld being a Mets fan; Seinfeld's appears in the pilot episode, when the comedic icon declares, "If you know what happened in the Mets game, don't say anything. I taped it."[8] Keith Hernandez, a key member of the Mets' 1986 World Series championship team, plays himself in a two-part episode of *Seinfeld*.[9] When Kramer informs Jerry that the Mets play 75 games available only on cable television during the season, Jerry agrees to get illegal cable installed.[10] George Costanza pursues an executive position with the Mets, despite having a good front office job with the Yankees.[11]

Seinfeld co-creator Larry David also created the HBO series *Curb Your Enthusiasm*, a platform for portraying the misadventures of a fictional Larry David. In the episode "Mister Softee," Bill Buckner guest stars as himself, being a good sport regarding the legendary error in Game Six of the 1986 World Series. Accompanying Larry to a shiva call—a mourning process for Jews—Buckner gets promptly thrown out because one of the mourners is a Red Sox fan who holds a grudge against Buckner.

Buckner becomes a hero when he uses his baseball skills to save a baby. During an apartment building fire, a mother drops her baby from an open window toward the tarpaulin set up by firemen. As the baby bounces from the tarp over the crowd of horrified onlookers, Buckner judges the baby's trajectory as he would a fly ball and races to protect the baby from hitting the pavement.

A Mets pennant adorns a wall of Lane Pryce's office on *Mad Men*. When Pryce hangs himself, Don Draper appropriates the pennant. *Who's the Boss?* uses a baseball signed by the 1962 Mets as the focus of a story about the true value of things. Tony Micelli, played by Tony Danza, sells the ball to finance a ski trip for his daughter, Samantha, played by Alyssa Milano. Samantha refuses to let a family heirloom be sold, so she buys the ball back, thanks to some wealthy friends.[12]

Miller Lite's popular "Great Taste, Less Filling" television commercials in the 1970s benefit from Mets player "Marvelous" Marv Throneberry, who the Mets acquired on May 9, 1962, and whose mediocrity influences the commercial's humor: "If I do for Lite what I did for baseball, I'm afraid their sales will go down." A career .237 hitter beloved by Mets fans, Throneberry played in 116 games for the '62 Mets, achieved a .244 batting average and notched 87 hits; his career ended the following season, when he played 14 games for the Mets.

Ability, or lack thereof, endeared Throneberry to the denizens of the Polo Grounds in the Mets' first two seasons, before Shea Stadium's debut in 1964: "Marv Throneberry, legend has it, was once crestfallen to discover that his birthday cake had been devoured by his Mets teammates before he got a piece—to which Casey Stengel cracked that 'we wuz gonna give you a piece, Marv, but we wuz afraid you would drop it.'"[13]

As with Throneberry, it is endearment rather than excellence on the field that has made the Mets endure as a pop culture touchstone. ∎

Notes

1. Leonard Koppett, "For Mets' Fans: Music to Root By," *The New York Times*, May 14, 1963.
2. *American Bandstand* and *Shindig* attracted the same audience. *Shindig* and *Hullabaloo* each lasted about a year-and-a-half in the mid-1960s, indicative of popular music during the heart of the five-year gap between the Beatles' American debut on *The Ed Sullivan Show* in 1964 triggering a British invasion of music (e.g., Chad & Jeremy, The Rolling Stones) and the Woodstock concert that emblemized counterculture in 1969. *Hullabaloo* aired from New York City, alternating between studios in Brooklyn and Manhattan.
3. Ibid.
4. Vincent Canby, "Mazeroski Hits Into Triple Play in 'Odd Couple Filming at Shea," *The New York Times*, June 28, 1967.
5. Ibid.
6. Michael X. Ferraro, "The New York Mets, in the Movies with Startling 'Frequency,'" *Los Angeles Times*, May 6, 2000, http://articles.latimes.com/2000/may/06/entertainment/ca-27034.
7. *Oh, God!*, Warner Brothers, 1977.
8. Pilot, *The Seinfeld Chronicles*, NBC, July 5, 1989.
9. "The Boyfriend," *Seinfeld*, NBC, February 12, 1992.
10. "The Baby Shower," *Seinfeld*, NBC, May 16, 1991.
11. "The Millennium," *Seinfeld*, NBC, May 1, 1997.
12. "Keeping Up With the Marcis," *Who's the Boss?*, ABC, April 9, 1985.
13. Jason Fry, "Happy Birthday, Jake!," *Faith and Fear in Flushing*, June 20, 2015, http://www.faithandfearinflushing.com/2015/06/20/happy-birthday-jake.

Jury Nullification and the Not Guilty Verdicts in the Black Sox Case

William Lamb

With a near-century now having elapsed, it is difficult to determine which event post–World War I baseball fans found more improbable: the Cincinnati Reds defeat of the highly touted Chicago White Sox in the 1919 World Series, or the acquittal of the Sox players accused of dumping the Series at the ensuing criminal trial. The pretrial confessions of guilt made by four of the accused—Eddie Cicotte, Joe Jackson, Lefty Williams, and Happy Felsch—had rendered conviction a foregone conclusion to many. Thus, the not guilty verdicts rendered by the jury were unexpected, and in some quarters unfathomable.

Although much has been written about the Black Sox scandal, until quite recently comparatively little attention has been paid to its legal proceedings. For the most part, those commenting on courtroom events have been handicapped by misapprehension of what actually went on in and about the Cook County Courthouse, and by a lack of understanding of Illinois criminal law. Often, the trial has been summed up with the assertion that the prosecution's case foundered on the disappearance of the player confessions in the run-up to trial—an erroneous but enduring notion in Black Sox lore. In truth, the confessions of Cicotte, Jackson, and Williams were available at trial, and read at length to the jury. But to no avail. The defendants, even those who had confessed their guilt, were all acquitted.

Because the deliberations of a criminal case jury are conducted in private, and because jurors are not thereafter obliged to explain the reasoning behind their verdict, the grounds for the Black Sox acquittals are unknowable. It is, of course, possible that the prosecution failed because its proofs did not satisfy the jury of the defendants' guilt. But that seems unlikely in the case of Eddie Cicotte, Joe Jackson, and Lefty Williams, and arguably that of Chick Gandil, Swede Risberg, and the gambler defendant David Zelcer, as well. Against these defendants, if not the others, the government presented ample proof of guilt. It is also conceivable that the jury verdict may have been corrupted by defense-friendly outside forces. But this, too, seems unlikely, as no evidence of jury tampering has ever surfaced. This article will assay another possible basis for the not guilty verdicts, one heretofore little discussed in the Black Sox canon: jury nullification.

Jury nullification is an unpredictable but mercifully rare courthouse phenomenon. It involves the jurors' knowing and deliberate rejection of evidence and/or their refusal to apply the law against a criminal defendant, in violation of the oath taken by all jury members at the outset of trial. This dereliction of duty may be precipitated by an overriding desire to send some kind of message to the community at large. Or because the result commanded by the evidence and the law runs contrary to the jurors' personal sense of justice, morality, or fairness.[1] Whatever its cause, prosecutors dread jury nullification and court decisions have condemned it.[2] But the power of nullification exists nonetheless, and by virtue of the Double Jeopardy Clause of the Fifth Amendment, no recourse against those wrongfully acquitted is available to the government. In the writer's view, jury nullification presents an eminently plausible explanation for the acquittal of the six most seemingly guilty defendants in the Black Sox criminal case. Argument of the point is premised on the following matters of fact and law.

A. THE UNRAVELING OF THE 1919 WORLD SERIES FIX

An exhaustive account of the Black Sox scandal is beyond the scope of this article. Suffice to say that a reasonable reading of the historical record supports the proposition that eight members of the 1919 American League pennant-winning Chicago White Sox agreed to lose the World Series against the Cincinnati Reds. In return, the players expected $100,000 payoffs from at least two separate gambler contingents. The existence of a player-gambler conspiracy is established beyond peradventure by the in- and out-of-court admissions of Sox stars Eddie Cicotte, Joe Jackson, Lefty Williams, and Happy Felsch, as well as those of gamblers Bill Burns and Billy Maharg. Other matters—such as the duration of the conspiracy; the extent of player effort to lose Series games; the identity of some of the gambler conspirators; who exactly received payoffs, when, and for how much—remain indistinct and controversial. Whatever these particular circumstances, when the conspiracy unraveled in September 1920, at least three Series fix-related meetings were exposed: a players-only discussion at the Ansonia Hotel in New York; a subsequent parley at the Warner Hotel in Chicago between up to five corruptible players and gamblers identified as Sport Sullivan and Rachael Brown, and finally, an eve-of-Game One meeting at the Sinton Hotel in Cincinnati involving all the fix-agreeable players, save Jackson, and the gambler quartet of Bill Burns, Billy Maharg, Abe Attell, and someone called "Bennett," later identified as Des Moines gambler David Zelcer. The record also pretty well documents that payments were later made to all of the White Sox players who agreed to the Series fix, except perhaps Buck Weaver.[3]

Despite rumblings about the bona fides of the Series outcome, no action was taken to investigate the matter until mid-September 1920. Then, a Cook County (Chicago) grand jury inquiry into allegations that a meaningless late-August 1920 game between the Cubs and Phillies had been fixed unexpectedly morphed into a probe of the previous fall's World Series. Within days, complete disregard of the mandate that grand jury proceedings remain secret resulted in often-verbatim newspaper accounts of the proceedings. In short order, baseball fans nationwide were apprised that the 1919 Series had been corrupted and that eight White Sox players—Eddie Cicotte, Joe Jackson, Lefty Williams, Chick Gandil, Swede Risberg, Happy Felsch, Fred McMullin, and Buck Weaver—were targeted for indictment on fraud-related charges.[4] The lid was then completely blown off the Series scandal by fix insider Billy Maharg. In an article first published in Philadelphia and quickly reprinted in newspapers across the country, Maharg alleged that Game One, Game Two, and Game Eight had been deliberately lost by Sox players acting at gamblers' behest.[5]

From there, events unfolded rapidly. On September 28, 1920, an uneasy Eddie Cicotte was summoned to the office of attorney Alfred Austrian, legal counsel for the White Sox. Confronted by Austrian and Assistant State's Attorney Hartley Replogle, Cicotte broke down and admitted complicity in the fix of the 1919 Series. Whisked before the grand jury, Cicotte repeated his confession. But unlike the stories printed in the newspapers, the Cicotte testimony contained no admission that he had lobbed hittable pitches to Reds batsmen or committed deliberate misplays in the field. To the contrary, Cicotte admitted only accepting $10,000 to join the fix, and maintained that once he had hit Game One leadoff man Morrie Rath with a pitch, he had undergone a change of heart and tried his best thereafter to beat the Reds.[6]

Later in the day, this exercise repeated itself with Joe Jackson. In the Austrian office, Jackson denied attending any of the pre-Series fix meetings. Rather, he had been propositioned privately by Chick Gandil, and had agreed to join the conspiracy in return for $20,000 to be paid in installments as the Series progressed. Jackson then repeated this confession of fix complicity to the grand jury.[7] As was the case with Cicotte, newspaper accounts of the Jackson testimony were grossly distorted. Before the grand jury, Joe made no admissions of deliberate poor play. Despite accepting a $5,000 fix payment after Game Four, Jackson insisted that he had done nothing to earn his money. He had played to win at all times.[8]

The third fix conspirator to appear before the grand jury was Lefty Williams. After interrogation and breakdown at the Austrian office on the morning of September 29, Williams recounted his own involvement in the Series fix to the grand jury. Like Cicotte and Jackson, Williams maintained that he had actually played honest ball, damning appearances like his first-inning nightmare in Game Eight notwithstanding. But unlike the other two, Lefty went further. He identified the gamblers present at the Warner Hotel (Sullivan and Brown) and Sinton Hotel (Burns, et al.) by name. He also stated for the record that the White Sox players agreeing to the Series fix were "Cicotte, Gandil, Weaver, Felsch, Risberg, McMullin, Jackson, and myself."[9] Meanwhile, Happy Felsch was unburdening himself to reporter Harry Reutlinger of the *Chicago Evening American*, stating that widely-published newspaper accounts of the Cicotte grand jury testimony were "true in every detail"[10] Felsch added, sadly, "I'm as guilty as the rest of them. We are all in it alike."[11]

The other implicated Sox players reacted indignantly to the news leaking from the grand jury. Chick Gandil, Swede Risberg, Fred McMullin, and particularly Buck Weaver publicly protested their innocence, with Weaver vowing to retain the best lawyer he could find to fight any charges.[12] Those charges would not be long in coming. On October 29, 1920, the Cook County Grand Jury returned indictments charging the eight targeted White Sox players, fix intermediary Hal Chase, and gamblers Joseph (Sport) Sullivan, Rachael Brown, Bill Burns, and Abe Attell with multiple counts of conspiracy to obtain money by false pretenses and/or by means of a confidence game.

B. THE GRAND JURY DO-OVER

In November 1920, a Republican Party electoral landslide swept an entirely new administration into the Cook County State's Attorney's Office. Upon taking office in December, these new prosecutors found the heralded Black Sox case in disarray. The investigation was incomplete, evidence was missing from the SAO vault, and the staff attorneys most familiar with the case had moved on to private law practice. Worse yet, the former prosecutors had anticipated that the defendants who had confessed before the grand jury (Eddie Cicotte, Joe Jackson, and Lefty Williams) would turn state's evidence and testify against their cohorts at trial. But with top-notch legal counsel now at their side, the three were standing firm with the other defendants. They were also seeking to have their confessions suppressed as evidence. Aside from unindicted co-conspirator Billy Maharg, this left the prosecution bereft of a fix insider whom it could build its case around. And employment of its crucial confession evidence was in jeopardy.

Then catastrophe struck. In February 1921, Judge William E. Dever unexpectedly denied a prosecution motion for an indefinite postponement of further proceedings and gave the Black Sox case a short trial date. With the case in no condition to move forward, State's Attorney Robert E. Crowe unilaterally dismissed the charges. Crowe, however, coupled this stunning development with a vow to re-present the charges to a newly impaneled grand jury. True to his word, Crowe had the matter back on the grand jury docket within a week, and in late March new indictments were returned in the Black Sox case. Now, the charges included substantive fraud counts, as well as the previous conspiracy ones. In addition to the original defendants, all of whom were re-indicted, the roster of those accused was expanded to include five new gamblers: Carl Zork and Benjamin Franklin of St. Louis, and a trio of Des Moines gamblers, David "Bennett" Zelcer and the Levi brothers, Ben and Lou. By re-presenting the matter, prosecutors had gained the breathing space needed to put their case in better order for trial. But the addition of these new defendants would come back to haunt the prosecution.

C. 1919 ILLINOIS CRIMINAL LAW

The criminal law of Illinois worked greatly to the prosecution's advantage in the Black Sox case. The indictment's core offense was conspiracy, an offense usually defined as an agreement between two or more persons to commit an unlawful act.[13] In most jurisdictions, conspiracy charges also require an overt act, namely, action by at least one of the conspirators that takes the conspiracy past the talking stage. But not in 1919 Illinois. Under both its statutory and common law definitions of the offense, a conspiracy in that state

was complete upon the mere agreement to commit the unlawful act.[14] As elsewhere, moreover, conspiracy was an offense separate and distinct from the crime that was the conspiracy's object. For example, conspiracy (agreement) to rob a bank is one crime, while the bank robbery itself is another—although conviction on the two offenses might later be combined for sentencing purposes.

In the trial of the Black Sox, this relieved the prosecution of proving that the players had actually dumped the World Series, or any particular game. Illinois law only required proof positive that the accused players and gamblers had agreed to do so. In his self-serving 1956 account of the scandal, Chick Gandil maintained that the Black Sox players had gotten cold feet and never went through with their agreement to throw Game 1 or any other Series game.[15] Under Illinois law, however, this purported abandonment of the fix would have provided no defense to the conspiracy charge in the indictment. That offense was committed the moment that the players and gamblers agreed to rig the Series outcome.

A trickier task for the state was establishing that the object of the conspiracy—the fix of the 1919 World Series—was itself an unlawful act. Here, the prosecution was hamstrung by the fact that Illinois did not have a statute that criminalized the corruption of sporting events. Like other states, Illinois adopted a specific sports corruption statute in the wake of the World Series scandal, but this new law could not be applied retroactively to the Black Sox.[16] This necessitated shoehorning the World Series fix charges into a conspiracy to commit some form of criminal fraud, such as obtaining money by false pretenses or via a confidence game. Ominously for the prosecution, a California court had recently rejected this gambit, dismissing an indictment returned against players and gamblers accused of fixing the 1919 pennant race in the Pacific Coast League.[17] The Black Sox defense would expend considerable effort on having this ruling applied to the instant charges, but in the end trial judge Hugo M. Friend denied indictment dismissal motions, determining that application of Illinois fraud statutes to the Series fix was legally permissible.

While matters of statutory construction went the prosecution way, application of the law was not all one-sided in the Black Sox case. Of particular benefit to the accused was the prohibition of hearsay evidence at a criminal trial. Generally speaking, hearsay is testimony about out-of-court statements made by someone other than the witness on the stand.[18] During grand jury proceedings, any form of evidence, including hearsay, can be utilized by prosecutors. But at a criminal trial, the rules are different. In particular, the Confrontation Clause of the Sixth Amendment guarantees the accused the right to confront and cross-examine the evidence offered against him. And obviously, inanimate objects like a grand jury transcript or a newspaper article cannot be cross-examined. To use such evidence, the prosecution must put the statement's author on the witness stand.

In the Black Sox case, the indictments returned against the non-confessing defendants had been grounded largely on the grand jury testimony of Eddie Cicotte, Joe Jackson, and Lefty Williams. At trial, those statements would be admissible against the individuals who had made them. But unless Cicotte, Jackson, or Williams took the stand as a prosecution witness, their grand jury testimony was hearsay and could not be used as evidence against Gandil, Weaver, or anyone else on trial. This left the prosecution in urgent need of cooperation from a fix insider who would be willing to take the witness stand and subject himself to defense cross-examination. On the eve of trial and in return for immunity, codefendant Bill Burns came to the prosecution's rescue.

D. THE CRIMINAL TRIAL OF THE BLACK SOX CASE.

Among the problems facing the prosecution was an elementary one: getting the defendants, almost all of whom lived outside of Illinois, into court. In the end, the problem was only partially overcome. The Sox players, hoping for vindication and a return to the game, appeared voluntarily. But Fred McMullin did not arrive from California until after jury selection had begun. This necessitated a severance and deferral of McMullin's trial to some future date. The gambler defendants were another matter entirely. Sport Sullivan

and Rachael Brown could not be found by authorities; Hal Chase and Abe Attell defeated attempts to extradite them to Illinois, and Ben Franklin was excused from the proceedings on grounds of illness. Thus, the only gamblers to stand trial were Carl Zork, David Zelcer, and the Levi brothers.

The jury selection process was arduous, its length protracted by defense counsel efforts to indoctrinate prospective panel members with bias favoring the defense point of view, and prosecution attempts to gauge juror receptivity to testimony by a cooperating former defendant. Finally, a jury of 12 white men, all reportedly non-baseball fans, was chosen. The Black Sox trial then began with an extended opening address by the lead prosecutor, Second Assistant State's Attorney George E. Gorman. In sometimes dramatic tones, Gorman delineated the Series fix roles played by both the defendants in court and absent confederates like the non-indicted Arnold Rothstein and the unavailable Abe Attell. When their turn came, defense lawyers waived opening speeches, preferring to maintain silence for the time being.

After the prosecution entered facts about the 1919 Series into the record, their star witness, Bill Burns, took the stand. Over the next three days, Burns provided a detailed account of the Series fix from his perspective, identifying defendant David Zelcer as the fix operative called "Bennett," and deeply implicating the accused Sox players, particularly player spokesman Chick Gandil and fix henchman Swede Risberg. The only player defendant left unscathed was Joe Jackson, with whom Burns had had no direct contact. Those who had assumed that Burns would personify his *Sleepy Bill* nickname were in for a shock. Quick-witted and unflappable, Burns proved more than a match for sneering defense lawyers, first to the amazement

Black Sox trial jurors.

CHICAGO TRIBUNE

and then to the delight of the Black Sox press corps. Except for some hedging on dates, his testimony was unshakeable. By the time Burns stepped down, his press reviews were glowing and prosecutors jubilant.[19]

Unfortunately for the prosecution, it was now obliged to pay the price of over-indicting the case. Court time and attention would now have to be devoted to Zork and the Levi brothers, the Midwestern gamblers added to the case in the superseding indictment. Here, prosecution testimony did little except make obvious the weak and amorphous nature of the proofs against these defendants. The appearance of White Sox club secretary Harry Grabiner also played into the defense's hands. Summoned by the prosecution to clarify player contract technicalities, Grabiner later testified to the soaring fan attendance and handsome profits that the franchise had enjoyed during the 1920 season—greatly undermining the claim that the White Sox had been injured by the corruption of the 1919 World Series.[20]

Seeking to regain momentum, the prosecution proffered the Cicotte, Jackson, and Williams grand jury testimony.[21] But before it could be read to the jury, Judge Friend had to rule on the defense's challenge to its admissibility. With the jury excused from the courtroom, Eddie Cicotte, Joe Jackson, and Lefty Williams testified that their grand jury confessions had been induced by off-the-record promises of leniency made by White Sox counsel Alfred Austrian and grand jury prosecutor Hartley Replogle.[22] Replogle and other prosecution witnesses denied it. Finding the prosecution account of disputed events the believable one, Judge Friend determined that the grand jury confessions had been voluntarily given and could therefore be presented to the jury—but only after the confessions had been edited to eliminate reference to non-confessing codefendants. While this process, called redaction, was being undertaken back at SAO offices, Judge Charles McDonald, the presiding justice of the Cook County criminal courts, testified before the jury. According to the judge, Cicotte, Jackson, and, to a lesser extent, Williams had each admitted his fix guilt in chambers prior to their grand jury appearances.

At the conclusion of the McDonald testimony, the State returned to the player confessions. But the redaction process had deleted the explicit mention of defendants Gandil, Risberg, Felsch, and Weaver that the grand jurors had heard. Each place where one of their names appeared in the grand jury transcripts, it was replaced with the anonym *Mr. Blank*. When presented to the jury by means of a dialogue between Special Prosecutor Edward A. Prindiville and grand jury ste-

nographer Walter Smith, the repeated references to *Mr. Blank* rendered substantial parts of the narrative unintelligible. Compounding this problem was the stifling heat in the non-air conditioned courtroom. Between the droning of the Prindiville/Smith duet and the oppressive courtroom heat, the jury may well have been anesthetized.

With its case again in need of reviving, the prosecution then summoned Billy Maharg. Like Bill Burns, Maharg provided a firsthand account of various aspects of the fix, identifying defendant Zelcer as "Bennett" and putting all the accused players, save Jackson, deeply into the plot. Like Burns, the affable and guileless Maharg cruised through cross-examination, with defense lawyers hardly laying a glove on the one-time Philadelphia club fighter.

Their case refreshed by the Maharg testimony, prosecutors then made a tactical decision to abbreviate their case. Jettisoning prospective witnesses like Browns second baseman Joe Gedeon and St. Louis gambler Joe Pesch who might have bolstered the flagging case against the Midwestern gambler defendants, the prosecution rested. In doing so, the state effectively abandoned the charges against Carl Zork and the Levi brothers. Viewed in retrospect, narrowing its focus to the case against the Sox players and David Zelcer was an unremarkable move, the kind of decision that prosecutors routinely have to make on the fly during a trial. And wrapping up the government's case on a seeming high note was a sound stratagem, given the circumstances. But what does not make any sense is the prosecution's failure to tighten the noose around Happy Felsch before it rested. This could have been accomplished by having *Chicago Evening American* reporter Harry Reutlinger inform the jury of the abject admissions of guilt that Felsch had made back in September 1920. Given that testimony by an objective, non-partisan witness like Reutlinger would have been brief, effective, and virtually unimpeachable, the prosecution's failure to call him as a witness is a mystery.

Predictably, Judge Friend dismissed the charges against the Levi brothers for lack of proof as soon as the state's case closed.[23] With reluctance, the judge allowed the charges against Carl Zork, Happy Felsch, and Buck Weaver to survive, but warned prosecutors that any convictions returned against them were in peril of post-verdict vacation by the court. In hindsight, prosecutors may have been better off with the charges dismissed against those defendants, as well. Evidentially, the prosecution's case against them was tenuous and likely to become a distraction during the final push to convict Cicotte, Jackson, Williams, Gandil, Risberg, and Zelcer. Moreover, the court's ruling meant that Zork defense counsel A. Morgan Frumberg and Henry Berger, perhaps the two most effective lawyers in the Black Sox camp, would remain on the job, bedeviling prosecutors to the end.[24]

When it came time for the defense to take the floor, the gamblers went first. Testifying on his own behalf, David Zelcer unequivocally denied acquaintance with Bill Burns and Billy Maharg, and denied any involvement whatsoever in the plot to fix the 1919 World Series. The Zelcer claims of innocence and his semi-alibi defense, however, were both undermined by effective cross-examination by Special Prosecutor Prindiville and by prosecution rebuttal evidence. The Zork defense wisely kept its client off the stand, confining its presentation to good character evidence, and four respectable fact witnesses who eviscerated the testimony of the government's lone witness against Zork, embittered East St. Louis theater owner/gambler Harry Redmon, a heavy betting loser on the 1919 Series.

Then it was the players' turn. The Gandil defense preceded promised testimony from Chick with a parade of witnesses intended to make a liar of Bill Burns, but with little apparent effect. Then, with the courtroom gallery poised for Chick to take the stand, the Gandil defense rested. The other player defendants promptly rested their cases, as well. Caught off-guard by defense maneuvers, prosecutors scrambled to collect rebuttal witnesses, including Harry Reutlinger. But given that little by way of a defense case had been offered, Judge Friend barred most of the proffered rebuttal, rightly scoring prosecutors for not using Reutlinger earlier. Shortly thereafter, the proof-taking portion of the Black Sox case closed.

E. THE TRIAL ENDGAME, VERDICT, AND AFTERMATH

Speaking first to the jury, Special Prosecutor Prindiville ignored the charges against defendants Zork, Felsch, and Weaver, and took only a passing swipe at Swede Risberg. Rather, he concentrated his fire on defendants Cicotte, Jackson, Williams, Gandil, and Zelcer, harping upon how the testimony of Bill Burns and Billy Maharg, and the confessions of Cicotte, Jackson, and Williams, corroborated each other. With rhetorical flourish, Prindiville ended by calling the accused "killers. They conspired to kill baseball, our greatest sport," and demanding that the jury return convictions with the maximum sentence: five years imprisonment and a $2,000 fine.[25]

Given ten hours to make their closing arguments, defense counsel went on the offensive. Berger led off with a denunciation of defense turncoat Bill Burns, while co-counsel Frumberg decried the prosecution's failure to pursue reputed fix financier Arnold Rothstein and his agents. Thomas Nash, lead attorney for defendants Risberg, Felsch, and Weaver, portrayed the proceedings as a legal sham, no more than a vehicle for the destruction of Charles Comiskey and his Chicago franchise by American League President Ban Johnson, once a Comiskey friend but now his bitter enemy. Nash then turned the podium over to co-counsel Michael Ahern to discredit the Billy Maharg testimony. Ban Johnson resumed the role of off-stage villain in the closing remarks of Benedict Short, chief counsel for Joe Jackson and Lefty Williams. According to Short, the government had indicted White Sox players solely to placate a wrathful Johnson. Over vehement prosecution objection, he concluded with the declaration that Judge Friend, defense counsel, and the jurors were the only persons in the courtroom "not under Ban Johnson's thumb."[26]

After instruction on the law by Judge Friend, the case was given to the jury early in the evening of August 2, 1921. After deliberations of only two hours and 47 minutes and the casting of a single ballot, the panel informed court bailiffs that it had reached a decision. At 11:22PM, the first verdict was announced by the court clerk: "We, the jury, find the defendant Claude Williams—Not Guilty." The several hundred defense supporters packing the courtroom erupted in joy. After order was restored, the verdict poll continued to the drumbeat of Not Guilty—as to all defendants on all charges. After the final acquittal was recorded, Judge Friend congratulated the jury, terming their verdict a just one. With that, all restraint in the courtroom dissolved. Eddie Cicotte ran over to shake the hand of jury foreman William Barry, while the other defendants warmly congratulated one another. Hats and papers soared through the air, with court attendants abandoning efforts to restore decorum upon noticing the smile on Judge Friend's face. They, too, then joined in the celebrations. For the next five minutes, "the courtroom was a love feast, as the jurors, lawyers and defendants clapped each other on the back and exchanged congratulations."[27] Jurors thereupon hoisted Jackson, Williams, and several other defendants onto their shoulders and paraded them around the courtroom, before the celebrants finally gathered on the courthouse steps for a smiling group photo.[28]

When queried by reporters, jurors declined to comment on their verdict. They then repaired to a nearby Italian restaurant to wind down. There, by some coincidence, the Sox players whom they had just acquitted had gathered for a party. Upon discovering each other, the two groups promptly united. Juror resolve to remain silent evaporated soon after. Opening up regarding the trial, one unidentified juror related, "We thought the State presented a weak case. It was dependent on Bill Burns and Burns did not make a favorable impression on us."[29] The panel was also displeased that the trial had been allowed to take so long. "We felt from the time that the State finished that we could not return any verdict but not guilty," the anonymous juror added.[30]

Juror bonding with the accused was reflected in the post-verdict sentiments of another unnamed panel member, who was quoted as telling Eddie Cicotte that "I know that every man on this jury hopes that the next time he sees you it will be at the center of the diamond putting over strikes."[31] "And we'll be there in a box cheering for you and the rest of these boys, Eddie," chimed in another juror.[32] Continued into the early morning hours, juror/defendant revelry reportedly ended with a chorus of "Hail, Hail, The Gang's All Here."[33]

The Black Sox joy was short-lived. Even before the verdict was fully digested, Commissioner Kenesaw Mountain Landis issued his famous edict permanently banning the acquitted players from Organized Baseball. And with that, Joe Jackson, Eddie Cicotte, Buck Weaver, and the others were consigned to the wilderness, playing out their careers in outlaw baseball.

F. JURY NULLIFICATION

As in most multi-defendant criminal matters, the proofs arrayed against the accused in the Black Sox case were uneven, strong against some defendants, weaker against others. Regarding the latter, Constitutional constraints and evidence rules had had significant effect, precluding the use at trial of incriminating evidence earlier presented to the grand jury. Critically, the bar on hearsay drained content from the grand jury confessions, and the trial jurors never got to hear Chick Gandil, Happy Felsch, Swede Risburg, Buck Weaver, and the absent Fred McMullin named as fix participants by Eddie Cicotte, Joe Jackson, and Lefty Williams. And inexplicably, the prosecution did not move to present Happy Felsch's self-incriminating newspaper interview until it was too late. Nevertheless, this does not satisfactorily explain the not guilty verdicts, at least those rendered upon some of the defendants. For the reasons which follow, it seems

This well-known Chicago Tribune *photo of Black Sox defendants, attorneys, jurors, and supporters shows them celebrating the not guilty verdicts on the steps of the Cook County Courthouse. A number of the celebrants have numbers inscribed on their images. These are as follows: (1) Chick Gandil; (2) Weaver/Risberg/Felsch co-counsel Michael Ahern; (3) Zelcer attorney Max Luster; (4) Gandil attorney James O'Brien; (5) Swede Risberg; (6) Lefty Williams; (7) Joe Jackson; (8) Zork co-counsel Henry Berger; (9) gambler defendant Carl Zork; (10) Zelcer co-counsel J.J. Cooke; (11) Weaver/Risberg/Felsch lead counsel Thomas Nash, and (12) Jackson/Williams attorney Benedict Short. The men in white shirtsleeves are members of the Black Sox jury.*

more than likely that the acquittals of Eddie Cicotte, Joe Jackson, and Lefty Williams, and perhaps those of Chick Gandil, Swede Risberg, and David Zelcer, as well, were the product of jury nullification.

The legal dictionary definition of jury nullification has already been provided. But in essence, jury nullification substitutes emotion for reason. To disregard their solemn promise to base their verdict on the evidence presented at trial and the law as explained by the court—and nothing else—jurors must be overcome by some powerful impulse. In certain instances, jurors may form an attachment to the accused. Or become consumed by dislike of prosecution witnesses. Or lack sympathy for the crime's victim. Whatever the basis, jury nullification is more likely to occur in highly-charged cases, like the Black Sox matter.

No arcane legal theory is needed to explain the outcome on Happy Felsch. As previously noted, he was the beneficiary of prosecution mishandling of his confession. The acquittals of Buck Weaver and Carl Zork were based on the thinness of the evidence presented against them. In Zork's case, his very indictment [and that of the excused Ben Franklin] had been a prosecutorial misjudgment. The placement of these two Midwestern tinhorns, and the Levi brothers, too, amidst a high-priced fix purportedly underwritten by New York City underworld kingpin Arnold Rothstein made little sense and only served to complicate the scenario proposed by prosecutors to the jury.[34]

The prosecution proofs against reputed fix enforcer Swede Risberg were respectable enough, provided that the testimony of Bill Burns and Billy Maharg was believed, a problematic matter for prosecutors. This was because in 1921, as today, criminal case jurors tend to disdain testimony by cooperating codefendants. Indeed, juror dislike of "rats" is almost reflexive, even though such witnesses may be as sharp on the stand as Burns or as affable as Maharg.[35] In a post-verdict disclosure, one anonymous Black Sox juror stated that Burns had not made a "favorable impression" on the panel. That, however, does not mean that the Burns [or Maharg] testimony was not worthy of belief, particularly given that its recitation of fix events seemed to coincide with the details of the Cicotte, Jackson, and Williams confessions.

The same holds true for David Zelcer, except in his case, he was not a popular hometown ballplayer like Swede Risberg, but an admitted Sinton Hotel roommate of the sinister, if missing, Abe Attell. Zelcer, moreover, had interposed a partial alibi defense—he claimed to have been in Chicago on the date that Burns and Maharg had him in attendance at a fix meeting in New York—that seemed to backfire. Hauled back to the stand as a government rebuttal witness, hotel clerk Harold Schwind recanted his earlier pro-Zelcer testimony, rendering the alibi a nullity, at best. The consequences here were dangerous for Zelcer, as criminal case juries usually convict defendants seemingly caught in a lie.

Stronger still was the prosecution case against Chick Gandil. Manifestly, the evidence against Gandil rested largely on the testimony of Burns and Maharg. But even without them, Gandil seemed, ineffably, to be involved in the fix. And the admonition of the court against speculation notwithstanding, it would have been difficult for jurors not to conclude that Gandil was one of the Mr. Blanks mentioned in the Cicotte, Jackson, and Williams confessions. Indeed, of all the Black Sox, Gandil was the most likely Mr. Blank to have been the fix ringleader.

But the argument for jury nullification becomes most persuasive when the not guilty verdicts returned in favor of Eddie Cicotte, Joe Jackson, and Lefty Williams are considered. Here, the evidence of guilt was so overwhelming that jury nullification appears to be the only rational explanation for their acquittal. The first and foremost indicator of jury nullification is the irreconcilability of these verdicts with Illinois conspiracy law. Remember, to convict the accused, the jury was not obliged to conclude that the Black Sox had thrown the 1919 World Series, or any particular

game of it. Indeed, the law of conspiracy did not even require them to try—although there was considerable evidence introduced at trial showing that the players had tried and succeeded in dumping at least the first two Series games. As a matter of Illinois law that the jurors were duty-bound to accept and apply, conviction on the conspiracy charges required no more than proof positive that the players had *agreed* to the plot to fix the Series. And given the completion of the conspiracy at the moment of such agreement, the crime could not thereafter be undone by a player's subsequent change of heart and abandonment of the plot, even if such a thing had happened.[36]

Regarding the question of whether the accused had entered such an agreement, the jury did not have to accept the testimony of a Bill Burns or a Billy Maharg. Or even that of the respected Judge McDonald. Conviction only required the jury to accept the word of Eddie Cicotte, Joe Jackson, and Lefty Williams himself, as each had confessed to agreeing to the fix of the 1919 World Series in his grand jury testimony.[37] And all three had admitted taking payment for the deed, besides. Once those confessions were admitted in evidence at trial, the guilt of Cicotte, Jackson, and Williams on the conspiracy charges was facially incontestable.

In attempting to explain an inexplicable verdict, one commentator has suggested that the acquittals may have been prompted by an aspect of Judge Friend's final instructions to the jury.[38] To convict on the charges, the court directed, the proofs had to show not only that the accused had agreed to fix the World Series, but that in doing so, their conscious intent had been to defraud the public and/or the other victims specified in the indictment (i.e., club owner Charles Comiskey, the White Sox corporation, fellow White Sox teammates, and Chisox bettors). But conscious intent to defraud was self-evident, as in-the-know gamblers like Sport Sullivan, Abe Attell, and Arnold Rothstein would have found it impossible to place their high-stakes bets without it—for who would have bet on the White Sox if the corruption of the Series outcome was public knowledge? Besides, post-verdict juror comments indicate that the panel had resolved to acquit the defendants as soon as the state rested its case, and well before it even heard the legal instructions of Judge Friend. In sum, the instructions-to-the-jury hypothesis is a non-starter.

In addition to providing the only comprehensible basis for the not guilty verdicts returned against at least some of the Black Sox defendants, jury nullification is betrayed in both the record and historical circumstance. Beginning with the jury selection process, defense counsel strove to have the mostly working class jury pool identify with the blue collar ballplayers. Even if their dubious disclaimers of much interest in baseball were credible, the jurors' post-verdict comments demonstrate that they had grown fond of the player defendants as the trial progressed, and wished them well. Not likely so with the victims, particularly White Sox owner Charles Comiskey. Old and ailing, Comiskey had been baited into a blustery self-righteous outburst by defense counsel Short in the early trial going, an incident that served defense purposes nicely. From the outset, the defense had attacked Comiskey's character, portraying him as an uncaring, skinflint owner and as a putative victim unworthy of juror sympathy. In fact, Comiskey was a decent man and a relatively generous employer. The 1919 Chicago White Sox had the second highest payroll in major league baseball, and a number of Sox players (with third baseman Weaver and pitcher Cicotte among them) were at or near the top of the pay scale for their respective positions.[39] But the jury did not know this, and the imbalance between the life stations of the well-heeled Charles Comiskey and his working class ballplayers (and the Black Sox jurors) was doubtless accentuated by testimony about the handsome profits made by the Chicago club during the 1920 season. The fix of the 1919 World Series had not grievously injured its leading victim. He was doing great. Throw in defense counsels' bristling summation argument that the accused players were also the innocent victims of some vague but malevolent scheme of American League President Ban Johnson, and all the ingredients for jury nullification were in place.

Those who acquitted the Black Sox went to their graves long ago, taking any explanation of their verdict with them. All that can be said for it is that Judge Friend, a fair-minded and able jurist, found their judgment a "just" one. And perhaps it was as to some of the defendants. But not when it came to Eddie Cicotte, Joe Jackson, and Lefty Williams, at a minimum. Regarding those three, the verdicts were inconsistent with the mandate of Illinois law on conspiracy and the overwhelming weight of the evidence presented at trial. In the final analysis, those particular verdicts may have been nothing more than the product of an indiscriminate acquittal stampede in the jury deliberation room. Or their verdicts may have been simply irrational, and thus inexplicable. But if the question why Eddie Cicotte, Joe Jackson, and Lefty Williams beat the charges in the Black Sox case must have an answer, jury nullification is the best one that examination of the record affords. ∎

Notes

1. See *Black's Law Dictionary*, Bryan A. Garner, ed. (St. Paul: West Publishing Co., 9th ed., 2009), 936.
2. See e.g., *State v. Ragland*, 519 A.2d 1361, 105 N.J. 189, 208–9 (NJ Sup. Ct. 1986): "Jury nullification is the power to act against the law. ... In its immediate application, it transforms the jury, the body thought to provide the ultimate assurance of fairness, into the only element of the [criminal justice] system that is permissibly arbitrary. ... [Jury nullification] is a power that is absolutely inconsistent with the most important value of Western democracy, that we should live under a government of laws and not of men."
3. Although Weaver was in attendance at each of the three pre-Series fix meetings, he denied accepting any payoff money and resolutely maintained his innocence of fix complicity. But in civil litigation later instituted by various White Sox players, fix gamblers Bill Burns and Billy Maharg placed Weaver inside Room 702 of the Sinton Hotel when a fix installment was paid after the Sox lost Game 2. For more detail, see William F. Lamb, *Black Sox in the Courtroom: The Grand Jury, Criminal Trial and Civil Litigation* (Jefferson, North Carolina: McFarland, 2013), 156–57.
4. The anticipated indictment of the eight players was first revealed in the *Chicago Tribune*, September 25, 1920.
5. See the *Philadelphia North American*, September 26, 1920.
6. The transcript of Cicotte's grand jury testimony has not survived, but portions of it are preserved in a June 1923 Cicotte deposition, read into the record of Joe Jackson's subsequent civil suit against the White Sox. The Jackson civil suit transcript is preserved at the Chicago Baseball Museum. Compare *Jackson Trial Transcript*, 1274–75, 1294–95, to the Associated Press dispatch published in the *Los Angeles Times*, September 29, 1920, and elsewhere.
7. The transcript of Jackson's grand jury testimony is one of the few surviving artifacts of the Black Sox criminal case. The transcript can be accessed online at http:www.1919blacksox.com/transcripts1.htm.
8. Compare *Jackson Grand Jury Testimony*, 14, to the bogus account published in the *Los Angeles Times*, September 29, 1920: "Jackson said that throughout the Series he either struck out or hit easy balls when hits would have meant runs." In fact, Jackson posted a Series-high .375 BA and paced the Sox attack with six RBIs.
9. Williams *Grand Jury Testimony*, 30.
10. *Chicago Evening American*, September 30, 1920.
11. Ibid.
12. See the *Boston Globe*, *Chicago Evening Post*, and *The New York Times*, September 29, 1920.
13. See *Black's Law Dictionary*, 351.
14. As subsequently affirmed by Illinois highest court in *People v. Lloyd*, 304 Ill. 23, 136 N.E. 505 (Ill. Sup Ct. 1922).
15. Chick Gandil as told to Mel Durslag, "This Is My Story of the Black Sox Series," *Sports Illustrated*, September 17, 1956.
16. The Illinois sports corruption statute would not take effect until July 1, 1922.
17. For a comprehensive account of PCL scandal, see Larry Gerlach, "The Bad News Bees: Salt Lake City and the 1919 Pacific Coast League Scandal," *Base Ball, A Journal of the Early Game*, Vol. 6, No. 1, (Spring 2012).
18. See *Black's Law Dictionary*, 7th ed., 585.
19. Typical was the review of the *Los Angeles Times*, July 22, 1921: "The State's chief witness ... hurled excellent ball, permitting the defense few hits in the grilling cross-examination." For other press raves about the Burns witness stand performance, see the *Chicago Tribune*, July 22, 1921, and *The New York Times*, July 23, 1921.
20. Some years after the trial, jury foreman William Barry would tell Judge Friend that the Grabiner testimony had more effect on the jury than that of any other witness. See the Eliot Asinof papers, circa 1963 Friend-Asinof interview, in the white penny notebook, Chicago History Museum.
21. Decades after the fact, ill-informed Black Sox commentators would assert that the Cicotte, Jackson, and Williams grand jury confessions

had been lost and were thus unavailable when the case came to trial. But the only things lost (stolen from the SAO evidence vault) were the original transcriptions of the testimony. The theft was discovered well in advance of trial and immediately remedied by having grand jury reporters Walter Smith and Elbert Allen create new transcripts from their shorthand notes of the Cicotte, Jackson, and Williams testimony. The authenticity and accuracy of the second generation transcripts were not disputed by Black Sox defense counsel at trial.

22. Important from an historical perspective, neither Cicotte nor Jackson nor Williams maintained that what they had told the grand jury was untrue. Rather, the defense wanted the confessions thrown out on legal grounds, asserting that reneged prosecution promises of leniency rendered the confessions involuntary in the Fifth Amendment-sense, and thus inadmissible as evidence. Joe Jackson's later claim of complete non-involvement in the Series fix was not unveiled until his April 1923 deposition for the back pay law suit that he instituted against the White Sox.

23. The Levi brothers had been targeted for prosecution by American League President Ban Johnson, the silent underwriter of much of the State's case. But little incriminating evidence was presented at trial against Lou, and none at all against Ben. Indeed, prosecutors interposed no objection to dismissal of the charges against the Levis once the State's case rested.

24. Later in the case, things got so hot between Frumberg and lead prosecutor George E. Gorman that the two almost came to blows. Gorman subsequently apologized and asked that his remarks about Fromberg be stricken from the record, as reported in the *Chicago Herald Examiner*, July 29, 1921.

25. As reported in the *Boston Globe* and *Washington Post*, July 30, 1921, and elsewhere.

26. As reported in newspapers nationwide. Selected excerpts of the summations of defense counsel have been posted at http://www.law.umkc.edu/faculty/projects/ftrials/blacksox.trial.summations.html.

27. *Chicago Tribune*, August 3, 1921.

28. Published in the *Chicago Tribune*, August 3, 1921.

29. As reported in the *Los Angeles Times*, August 3, 1921.

30. Ibid.

31. As quoted in the *Los Angeles Herald Examiner*, August 3, 1921.

32. Per the *Des Moines Evening Tribune*, August 3, 1921.

33. As reported in the *Des Moines Evening Tribune* and *Los Angeles Herald Examiner*, August 3, 1921.

34. Originally, Zork and Franklin were alleged to have instigated a fix revival attempt after the corrupted Sox players went rogue and unexpectedly won Game 3 of the Series. Discarded prosecution witnesses like Joe Gedeon and Joe Pesch would have filled in the details had prosecutors not decided to short-circuit their case during trial. Apart from the likely malice of AL President Ban Johnson, the impetus for the indictment of the Levi brothers is unknown. At trial, the prosecution proofs were embarrassingly meager, consisting of the fact that Lou Levi had been seen in the company of fix villain Abe Attell while the Series was ongoing, and that the brothers had won heavily betting on the Reds.

35. Except in organized crime cases tried in federal court [where jurors seem to give a dispensation to government use of the low-life witnesses], prosecutors will avoid using testimony by codefendants, if at all possible. The writer, a retired state/county prosecutor in New Jersey, went 24 years [from 1982 to 2006] between putting a cooperating codefendant in front of a jury.

36. In most jurisdictions, conspiracy law recognizes a principle called renunciation. Renunciation is the complete and voluntary abandonment of criminal purpose *before* the crime is committed, coupled with requirements that need not be specified here. Suffice it to say that renunciation has no application to the Black Sox case, as the object of the conspiracy was achieved before the 1919 Series started, and the moment that a co-conspirator like Abe Attell or Sport Sullivan placed a bet with some unsuspecting White Sox backer.

37. While on the witness stand testifying in support of the back pay lawsuit that he had initiated against the White Sox, Jackson denied—more than 100 times—that he had made the statements reposed in black-and-white in the transcript of his grand jury testimony. First astonished, then outraged, Wisconsin Circuit Court Judge John J. Gregory cited Jackson for perjury and had him incarcerated over night. Thereafter, Judge Gregory vacated the judgment awarded Jackson by the civil jury and dismissed the case. For more detail, see Lamb, 170–88.

38. See James Kirby, "The Year They Fixed the World Series," *American Bar Association Journal*, February 1, 1988.

39. The longstanding notion that the Black Sox were underpaid is demolished by Bob Hoie in "1919 Baseball Salaries and the Mythically Underpaid Chicago White Sox," *Base Ball, A Journal of the Early Game*, Vol. 6, No. 1 (Spring 2012); "Black Sox Salary Histories," *The Inside Game*, Vol. XIII, No. 1 (February 2013), and "Black Sox Salary Histories: Part II," *The Inside Game*, Vol. XIII, No. 2 (May 2013).

Pick Wisely

A Look at Whom Select Baseball Players Choose as Their Heroes and Why

Kevin Warneke, Ph.D., John Shorey, and David Ogden, Ph.D.

The 13-year-old third baseman from Colorado, who identified his race as Hispanic American, didn't look far from home when he named his favorite player, who also happened to be his favorite athlete and his hero: Colorado Rockies' Carlos Gonzalez. A 14-year-old Minnesotan, who proclaimed his primary position on his select baseball squad as third base, looked to an outfielder who plays for a California team as his hero, favorite athlete and favorite ballplayer: Mike Trout. This teen listed his race as Caucasian. And the 10-year-old left fielder from Missouri, who listed his race as African American, chose Wilber "Bullet" Rogan as his favorite baseballplayer and fellow Negro Leaguer Satchel Paige as his hero.

Although they played different positions, were different ages, and hailed from different states, the three select baseball players had one thing in common: Each boy chose a hero who shared his racial or ethnic identity. Children and the people they emulate have been the focus of previous research, predominantly in the early twentieth century with a renewed interest on children's attitudes toward those they admire. Viewers of the annual Little League World Series witness such interest anecdotally. Television broadcasts of that series typically include brief interviews with participants, where they state their names, the positions they play, and their favorite players. What these players never reveal is why they made their choices. This study delves into who select youth baseball players choose as their favorite player, favorite athlete, and hero in an attempt to discover patterns in the choices youngsters make.

Heroes provide children with role models, while giving them a way to understand their places in society.[1] To fully understand the influence that heroes—and subsequently role models—have over their subordinates, one must first understand that heroes and hero-worship are concepts that have endured throughout history.

Scottish philosopher, writer, essayist and historian Thomas Carlyle contended that it was impossible to stamp out reverence for great men. Hero-worship endures, according to Carlyle, while man endures.[2] Heroes have been defined as those who serve as models for personal conduct[3] and those who influence through aspirations and actions.[4] Heroes represent the ideal of what admirers would like to become, focusing especially on qualities they would like to develop.[5]

LITERATURE REVIEW

Michael Sullivan and Anre Venter sought to understand how and why people use the term "hero." While attempting to determine the parameters for the term's use, they first sought to define it. "For some, heroes are both a creation of and a service to society at large."[6] Based on the literature, they discovered that, on one level, heroes share the characteristic of being individuals placed in a public role because of some feat they performed or quality they possess. They reported a second theme among definitions of hero: the function the hero, or heroic figure, plays for those who view him or her as one. Focusing merely on the attributes and characteristics of those identified as heroic isn't enough. Attention must also be placed on the role that individuals have when determining whether to deem someone as a hero, or heroic. For their research, the authors defined heroes as people who "possess a skill, trait, or position that inspires an individual to imitate or strive to attain goals."[7]

Heroes shape a person's self-concept and the literature is ripe with the outcomes of possessing a hero: gaining persistence when facing adversity and promoting long-term career planning. "The focus is not merely on the attributes of the heroic figure but also takes into account the role that individuals have in whether they accept a figure's hero status."[8]

The impact that heroes have on their admirers can be significant, and Sullivan and Venter found that those identified as a hero have the same effect on their admirers' self-concept as their loved ones.[9]

Sullivan and Venter, while citing their investigation of the popular press, contend that although the concept of hero remains prevalent in society today, it is unclear what meaning the word conveys. "The term hero is commonly understood to be an individual who is viewed positively; but across context, the specific distinctions of who is a hero and what is heroic have differed."[10]

A study of 241 French 10- and 15-year-olds and 227 Spanish youths of the same age found that the younger participants preferred heroes with collectivist qualities while the older preferred them with individualized qualities.[11] The study noted that French female participants chose proximal—family and community-based—heroes more often than expected by chance, while French male participants chose this type of heroic figure less than expected. The male participants, however, chose distal heroic figures—art-science, political, film-television-video, religious, music, sport and modeling—more often than expected by chance.

Traits of exterior (outward appearance) of an athlete are worship facilitators for adolescents when choosing idols.[12] A study of 1,636 students attending 13 Taiwanese high schools found that those chosen as favorite idols were more often male (65 percent) than female. In addition, 67 percent chose actors, singers or athletes as their favorite idols, while 10 percent chose family, friends, or teachers. Finally, the study revealed that most participants—regardless of gender—chose a male media star as their favorites. The conclusion was that female participants saw male media stars as a safe and convenient romantic attachment, while identification attachment resulted in male participants choosing idols who were male.

The pretext that hero choices would be confined within the boundaries of gender and the natural selection of public figures, according to the literature, cannot be generalized. Of note were studies that explored a more personal approach to hero selection and compared gender differences in hero selection.[13,14]

A study of 111 boys, ages 11 to 21, suggests that because of a narrowing of time and space around boys, they see the life experiences of teachers and parents as too dated to be relevant for them. Likewise, according to the study, the gilded lifestyles of celebrities, including athletes, are thought to be alien. "This phenomenon forces boys to weigh up the positive and negative examples given by local, 'older brother' role models to the exclusion of more traditional figures." Participants had little desire to follow in their father's footsteps, thus opting away from the "historical" route to manhood.[15] They also saw those who found fame and fortune, as portrayed by the media, as "glossily distant to be useful role models."[16] This mindset results in the participants looking to "older brother" figures who lived where they lived and "whose positive and negative experiences in a world that boys can recognize provide trusted clues towards the next steps they themselves might, or might not, take."[17]

Shayla Holub, Marie Tisak, and David Mullins explored the gender differences in the choices children make as their heroes, the attributes of those chosen, and the characteristics shared by typical heroes. They discovered that while the majority of the girls in their study chose heroes personally known to them, boys chose personal and public figures equally often. Most boys chose male heroes, while the selections made by girls were mixed. Of note, however, the authors reported that both boys and girls collectively chose private heroes—family members, friends, teachers—more than they chose public figures.[18]

Gender is not the only factor that affects a youngster's choice of hero. Racial identity is also a factor. Sports have become so racialized in the United States that affinity for a sport also means an affinity for a race.[19] Thus, a youngster who favors basketball is also likely to favor and to focus on the African Americans who play it. That is, basketball belongs to African Americans.[20] Baseball, on the other hand, belongs to Caucasians, as do its heroes.[21] Coaches, school officials, and authority figures reinforce these stereotypes, as do parents.[22,23]

Mass media also serve a major role in stereotyping sports and its heroes. While the "whiteness" of baseball is celebrated in mass media such as movies (i.e. the films *Bull Durham*, *The Rookie*, and *Major League*, in which the only black character practices voodoo), mass media also reinforce and commercialize the "blackness" of basketball and its heroes. Reebok and other athletic apparel companies have built basketball players such as LeBron James, Allen Iverson, and Michael Jordan into icons and more. NBA player Vince Carter was made larger than life by a soft drink company that pitted Carter, a Toronto Raptor, against another kind of raptor—a computerized velociraptor.[24] Such commercial images make not only heroes of those NBA players,[25] but they also become cultural currency for African American youth, because "emulation of those players was important for membership in peer groups."[26] However, such hero worship makes African American youth feel as if they are part of a cultural "in-group."[27]

While much has been written generally about heroes and hero worship, children's hero conceptions are not commonly the focus of research studies. "Parents, teachers and researchers have had growing concern that an increase in superhero cartoons for young children has negatively influenced the play and behavior of this age group."[28] Public figures don't always serve as positive role models. "It is important to find out why children value these characters as heroes in order to better assess the influence these figures have on children."[29]

Based on findings in the literature and previous research on select baseball players, the authors addressed five research questions:

RQ #1: Are select ballplayers more likely to choose a favorite MLB player of their own race?

RQ #2: Are select ballplayers more likely to choose a hero of their own race?

RQ #3: Do more youth players choose proximal (private) heroes more than distal (public figures)?

RQ #4: Are select players of one race more likely to choose a ballplayer or parent as a hero?

RQ #5: Are younger players more likely than older players to cite a parent as a hero and less likely to cite a ballplayer as a hero?

METHOD

Youth select baseball players who competed in a national tournament held in June 2014 in Council Bluffs, Iowa, were the subjects of this study. Protocol stipulated by the University of Nebraska required that the researchers first approach a player's parent or guardian about the study to receive verbal consent to approach the players. With parental or guardian consent secured, the researchers then explained their survey and its focus to potential participants.

Players who agreed to participate were asked to complete a 10-question survey. The initial five questions were biographical in nature, focusing on their age, state of residence, position most frequently played, time in years playing select baseball, and race. The second five questions focused on their preferences: whether they had a hero and, if so, who that was; whether they had a favorite athlete (of any sport) and, if so, who that was; whether they had a favorite baseball player and, if so, who that was. Additionally, participants were asked the reason for their choice of favorite player, along with their favorite sport and the sport at which they thought they were best. Participants were asked to answer the questions without parental input, but the researchers provided explanations for the questions when asked. In some situations, the researchers read the questions to participants and recorded their responses for them. The researchers opted for a more basic definition of hero than used by Sullivan and Venter: "A hero is someone you look up to."[30]

RESULTS

Of the 396 players, ages 7 to 17, who completed the survey, 306 (78 percent) identified themselves as Caucasian, 25 (6.5 percent) African American, 42 (11 percent) Hispanic American, 9 (2.3 percent) Asian American, 5 (1.3 percent) Native American, and 6 (1.5 percent) Middle Eastern. The teams were from 23 states, with Colorado and Texas being the most represented states (103 players and 66 players respectively).

Of the 396 players, 277 participants indicated they had a hero. Almost half (134) chose a baseball player, while more than one third (96) chose a parent. Likewise, 347 of the respondents cited a favorite baseball player, and 140 of them named both a hero and a favorite baseball player, with 77 choosing the same baseball player as both.

In addressing the five research questions, the authors found the following:

RQ #1: Are select ballplayers more likely to choose a favorite MLB player of their race?

The 10-year-old center fielder from Colorado, who identified himself as Caucasian, chose Todd Helton as his favorite player, while the 11-year-old first baseman from New Mexico, who identified himself as Hispanic American, selected Boston designated hitter David Ortiz. Their choices replicated study results that players' choices of favorite players followed racial lines (see Table 1). Select players were significantly more likely to choose an MLB player of their own race than a player of a different race ($X2$ (8, N = 329) = 21.56, $p < .01$). Of the 271 white players, 148 named Caucasian MLB players as their favorites, while 10 of the 21 African American players selected MLB players of their race. Of the 37 Hispanic select players who chose a favorite MLB counterpart, 16 named an MLB Hispanic players. All results were significantly higher than expected by chance. The MLB players mentioned most often as favorite players were Mike Trout, Derek Jeter, Troy Tulowitzki, David Ortiz and Dustin Pedroia. (Jeter, who is biracial, was considered as African American for this study.)

Table 1. Race and Favorite Player

Favorite Player	N	Caucasian	African American	Hispanic	Other
Caucasian	271	148 (55%)	49 (18%)	69 (25%)	5 (2%)
African-American	21	3 (14%)	10 (48%)	8 (38%)	0
Hispanic American	37	14 (38%)	7 (19%)	16 (43%)	0

N = 329, X2 = 21.56, $p < .01$

RQ #2: Are select ballplayers more likely to choose a hero of their race?

When asked to name his hero, the 12-year-old Texan, who identified himself as African American, chose Jackie Robinson. As with RQ 1, select players' choices of heroes were race-based (see Table 2). Caucasian players were significantly more likely to choose a hero that was Caucasian, and the same racial pattern occurred for hero selections by African American youths and Hispanic youths ($X2$ (8, N = 159) = 17.70, p < .05).

RQ #3: Do more players choose proximal (private) heroes more than distal (public figures)?

While the 12-year-old third baseman from Texas chose Robinson as his hero, his teammate chose his father. For heroes, select ballplayers in this study chose most often, in the following order: Jackie Robinson, their parents, Andrew McCutchen, and Mike Trout. About 59 percent (164) selected distal heroes, who were primarily athletes and entertainers, with the majority (140) selecting a baseballplayer, while 41 percent (113) of the 277 respondents identified a family member or friend (proximal) as their hero. These results would seem to contradict the findings from the previously mentioned study by Walker in which participants leaned away from selecting public figures and their fathers as heroes, and opted toward a big brother figure.[31]

RQ #4: Are select players of one race more likely to choose a ballplayer or parent as a hero?

While ballplayers and parents were the most commonly cited heroes, there were no racial differences among those selections. According to a chi-square analysis, Caucasian players were just as likely as African Americans, Hispanics, and players of other races to choose a parent or ballplayer as heroes. These results reinforce those found by Gash and Rodriguez (2009) that indicated boys of similar age were more likely to choose distal heroic figures.[32]

RQ #5: Are younger players more likely than older players to cite a parent as a hero and less likely to cite a ballplayer as a hero?

For convenience in tabulation, respondents were broken into three age groups: 7 to 11, 12 to 14, and 15 to 17 years of age. Those three age brackets correspond to grade school, junior high school and high school, respectively (American School System, n.d.). A chi-square showed no significant difference in the selections by age groups (see Table 3). Despite that overall finding, most of those of junior high and high school age selected a ballplayer as their hero—as did the 13-year-old first baseman from Wisconsin who named Carlos Gomez as his hero.

The authors note that while their survey sought to determine whether participants chose their favorite players because of team allegiance, they did not gauge whether regional influences were prevalent in their participants' choices. This means the first baseman from Wisconsin could have chosen Gomez because he played for the Milwaukee Brewers at the time the survey was taken or the 13-year Colorado third baseman chose Gonzalez because he favors the Colorado Rockies.

DISCUSSION

Fifteen years ago, conservative Canadian journalist Ted Byfield lamented society's need for heroes as essential to one's psychology, as food and shelter are essential to one's physiology: "And if passing events do not produce heroes, we invent them, sometimes out of the most unpromising material."[33]

A study that involved in-depth interviews with 10 African American non-baseball players revealed that baseball does not provide the amount of role models—due partially to a lack of action in the sport—that basketball and football can.[34] Applying social role theory—which states that people, including youth, behave in ways that replicate the roles they are expected to play in society—youngsters tend to get involved with sports through the influence of their role models. "If baseball does not have enough marketable athletes to entice the young African American community, its popularity will take a backseat to sports that

Table 2. Race and Hero

Hero	N	Caucasian	African American	Hispanic	Other
Caucasian	135	73 (54%)	44 (33%)	16 (12%)	2 (1%)
African-American	12	4 (33%)	7 (59%)	1 (8%)	0
Hispanic American	12	2 (17%)	4 (33%)	6 (50%)	0

Note: Although 277 respondents named a hero, race of the hero could be verified in 159 cases. An example for when race could not be determined would be when the player named a relative. X^2 = 17.70, p < .05

Table 3. Age and Hero Selection

Age	Hero	
	Parent	Ballplayer
7–11	45	45
12–14	55	91
15–17	1	4

X^2 (2, N = 241) = 4.48, p = .106

provide such."[35] Of the 25 African American players in this current study, 21 had a favorite player; and 10 selected an African American MLB player. In addition, 10 African Americans in this current study chose a baseballplayer as their hero. Thus, African American youth players, like Caucasians and Hispanic Americans in the study, found no shortage of baseball players to call heroes. The young players in this study felt that baseball takes a backseat to no other sport.

Baseball players figured dominantly in the hero worship by those age 12 and older, reflecting previous findings. Although the previously cited research featured youths from France and Spain, and Taiwan respectively, their results mirrored the responses given by select baseball players—male participants were more likely to choose public heroes than private ones.[36] That is, 59 percent of the respondents in this study selected distal figures rather than family or friends as heroes, and the bulk of those heroes were baseball players. With that in mind, baseball organizations that are trying to interest youths in playing might enhance the allure of the game by focusing on baseball "heroes" who also might be potential heroes to those in a youth's peer group or family. This study provides evidence that certain heroes have wide popularity, like McCutchen and Trout. Role modeling is nothing new, but selecting the specific role models to resonate with specific groups has the potential to broaden the base of youth interest in the game.

Yi-Hsiu Lin and Chien-Hsin Lin provide evidence for using heroes to broaden a sport's appeal when they noted that youths have a tendency to select exterior traits in their heroes and they say that is due, in part, to the youths' relatively low cognitive functioning.[37] This lower cognitive functioning causes youths to be more susceptible to commercial and materialistic messaging. As Hugh Gash and Pilar Rodriguez point out, digital media and television play an important role in the construction of young people's heroes.[38]

Exploring the role of media in hero worship is beyond the purview of this study. However, the findings here indicate that older players tend to favor heroes who are outside their immediate social circle—although there was no statistically significant difference between the age groups—while grade-school-aged players were as likely to name a parent as their hero as they were to name a public figure.

Youths' selection and emulation of heroes raises other concerns, as reflected in the literature. Hero worship can have negative connotations, as implied by a survey conducted by the Kaiser Family Foundation. That survey of youngsters and how they viewed their

Like the 10-year-old Caucasian center fielder from Colorado, who chose Todd Helton as his favorite player, and the 11-year-old Hispanic American first baseman from New Mexico who selected Boston designated hitter David Ortiz, the youths studied were significantly more likely to choose an MLB player of their own ethnicity as a "hero" than a player of an ethnic background different from their own.

favorite athletes found the following: 74 percent of survey participants said it was common for a professional athlete to yell at a referee; 62 percent agreed that "trash talking" opponents was the norm; and 46 percent said it was common for athletes to take cheap shots at their opponents.[39] "Too often, the dark side of athletes—the steroid use, hard partying lifestyle and poor sportsmanship—overshadows an athlete's ability to play the game," Kay Ireland wrote. Then Ireland, citing the survey results, encouraged parents to consider the benefits and impact of the influence that athletes can have on their children and their lives. Survey results also indicated that the youthful respondents considered the same behaviors—yelling at a referee, trash talking and taking cheap shots—as normal while playing sports with their friends. "A spoiled-athlete mentality," she wrote, "may teach children that it's OK to yell and fight to get what they want."[40]

The results of this current study, however, may provide some consolation to parents and coaches who fear that youngsters are ill-equipped to select appropriate roles modes. Four of the five most often mentioned favorite players (Trout, Jeter, Tulowitzki, and Pedroia) and those MLB players who received most mentions as heroes (Robinson, McCutchen, and Trout) have not been publicly accused of criminal activity, use of performance-enhancing drugs, or otherwise questionable behavior. The results of this study, the authors contend, indicate that young baseball players choose wisely when selecting their heroes and favorite players.

CONSIDERATIONS AND FUTURE RESEARCH

Whether athletes are suitable to serve as role models falls beyond the scope of this study. What remains pertinent is determining what criterion youngsters, in this case select baseball players, use when making their choices. The authors asked participants to state the reason behind their selections for their favorite players—most prevalent was that their selections played on their favorite team—but did not ask for rationales for their choices as heroes. Those rationales would provide parents and coaches with information about why young ballplayers chose certain individuals as heroes and the role those heroes play in the players' ambitions and plans in continuing to play baseball. Such information also has implications for marketing baseball and baseball-related consumption to young players.

A larger sample of players, particularly African Americans and Hispanic Americans, is needed to qualify the findings in this study. A larger sample of minority players could also help us understand how hero worship might shed light on the paucity of African Americans in the highest levels of competition in the game and on the growing number of Hispanics playing baseball. ∎

ABOUT THE AUTHORS: The Fall 2013 edition of the *Baseball Research Journal* featured previous work by these authors on whether fans attending minor league baseball games paid enough attention to the action on the field to know the scores of those games (they did).

Notes

1. Shayla Holub, Marie Tisak, and David Mullins, "Gender Differences in Children's Hero Attributions: Personal Hero Choices and Evaluations of Typical Male and Female Heroes." *Sex Roles* 58 (2008), 567–78.
2. Thomas Carlyle, *On Heroes, Hero-Worship, and the Heroic in History* (London, England: Chapman and Hall, 1869).
3. Dixon Wecter, *The Hero in America: A Chronicle of Hero Worship* (New York, New York: Schribners, 1941).
4. Katie Pretzinger, "The American Hero: Yesterday and Today." *Humboldt Journal of Social Relations,* 4 (1976), 36–40.
5. John Caughey, *Imaginary Social Worlds: A Cultural Approach* (Lincoln, NE: University of Nebraska Press, 1984).
6. Michael Sullivan and Anre Venter, "Defining Heroes Through Deductive and Inductive Investigations," *The Journal of Social Psychology,* 150 (2010), 472.
7. Ibid, 473.
8. Ibid, 472.
9. Michael Sullivan and Anre Venter, "The Hero Within: Inclusion of Heroes Into the Self," *Self and Identity,* 4 (2005), 101–11.
10. Sullivan and Venter, "Defining Heroes Through Deductive and Inductive Investigations," 471.
11. Hugh Gash and Pilar Rodriquez, "Young People's Heroes in France and Spain," *The Spanish Journal of Psychology,* 12 (2009), 246–57.
12. Yi-Hsiu Lin and Chien-Hsin Lin, "Impetus for Worship: An Exploratory Study of Adolescents' Idol Adoration Behaviors," *Adolesence,* 42 (2007), 575–88.
13. Barbara Walker, "No More Heroes Any More: The 'Older Brother' as Role Model," *Cambridge Journal of Education,* 37 (2007), 503–18.
14. Holub, Marie Tisak, and David Mullins, "Gender Differences in Children's Hero Attributions: Personal Hero Choices and Evaluations of Typical Male and Female Heroes," *Sex Roles,* 58 (2008), 567–78.
15. Walker, "No More Heroes Any More: The 'Older Brother' as Role Model," 503.
16. Ibid, 515.
17. Ibid, 515.
18. Shayla Holub, Marie Tisak, and David Mullins, "Gender Differences in Children's Hero Attributions: Personal Hero Choices and Evaluations of Typical Male and Female Heroes." *Sex Roles,* 58 (2008), 567–78.
19. Ronald Hall, "The Bell Curve: Implications for the Performance of Black/White Athletes," *Social Science Journal,* 39 (2002), 113–18.
20. Ibid.
21. David Ogden, "The Welcome Theory: An Approach to Studying African-American Youth Interest and Involvement in Baseball," *Nine: A Journal of Baseball History and Culture,* 12 (2004), 114–22.
22. Othello Harris,"Race, Sport, and Social Support," *Sociology of Sport Journal,* 11 (1994), 40–50.
23. Steven Philipp, "Are We Welcome? African American Racial Acceptance in Leisure Activities and the Importance Given to Children's Leisure," *Journal of Leisure Research,* 31(1999), 385–403.
24. J. Steenhuysen, "Breaking a new spot for 'Gatorade Fierce," *Business Times.* Retrieved September 21, 2004 from http://adtimes.nstp.com.my/archive.
25. Brian Wilson and Robert Sparks, "It's Gotta Be the Shoes:" Youth, Race and Sneaker Commercials," *Sociology of Sport Journal,* 13 (1996), 398–427.
26. Ogden, "The Welcome Theory: An Approach to Studying African-American Youth Interest and Involvement in Baseball," 118.
27. Ketra Armstrong, "African-American Students' Responses to Race as a Source Cue in Persuasive Sport Communications," *Journal of Sport Management,* 14 (2000), 223.
28. Holub, Tisak, and Mullins, "Gender Differences in Children's Hero Attributions: Personal Hero Choices and Evaluations of Typical Male and Female Heroes," 576.
29. Ibid, 576.
30. Michael Sullivan and Anre Venter, (2010).
31. Walker, "No More Heroes Any More: The 'Older Brother' as Role Model."
32. Gash and Rodriquez, "Young People's Heroes in France and Spain."
33. Ted Byfield, "Why the Heroes We Manufacture These Days are of Such a Very Low Grade," *Newsmagazine,* 27 (2000), 68.
34. Michael Mudrick, "The Decline in Baseball Participation Amongst African American Youth," Digital Commons, retrieved Feb. 10, 2015, http://digitalcommons.uconn.edu/gs_theses/82.
35. Ibid.
36. Gash and Rodriquez, "Young People's Heroes in France and Spain."
37. Lin and Lin, "Impetus for Worship: An Exploratory Study of Adolescents' Idol Adoration Behaviors."
38. Gash and Rodriquez, "Young People's Heroes in France and Spain."
39. Kay Ireland, (2014). The pros and cons of the influence of sports athletes on kids, Livestrong.com., retrieved January 5, 2015, www.livestrong.com/article/371876-the-pros-cons-of-the-influence-of-sports-athletes-on-kids.
40. Ibid.

Harry & Larry

A Century of Confusion

Matthew Clifford

Sometimes research leads us to answers we never intended to find. My quest began in 2010 when I set out to review the history of an unlucky baseball pitcher named Sylvester "Syl" Johnson. This man had the honor to work with one of the most notorious baseball men in history, Tyrus Raymond Cobb. He was also hit by nine line drives off his own pitches, all of which led to broken bones. Sylvester joined the Detroit Tigers in 1922 and stayed until 1925. During those four years, he worked with a catcher named Charles Lawrence "Larry" Woodall. Johnson also shared the field with Detroit's powerhitting right fielder, Harry Edwin "Slug" Heilmann. In 2011, I found a black and white photograph taken in 1923. The picture included six members of the Detroit Tigers standing in front of a dugout with their temperamental skipper, Mr. Cobb. This pesky photo led me into a journey that would permanently affect my cross-reference methods. I had reviewed hundreds of pictures of the 1922 Tigers, the year Johnson began his major league career.

In a 1923 photo, the first fellow I spotted on the left was Bob "Fatty" Fothergill. Bob, a relief outfielder, was also signed in 1922 and I had previously examined several images from his rookie year. Don't assume that his nickname "Fatty" assisted my identification. The hefty gentleman's figure was not visible—the edge of the photograph trimmed at his neck. Fothergill's tired-eyed stare was the first feature I recognized. But, just to be sure, I cross-referenced the photo with Bob's picture on his profile page at Baseball-Reference.com. His weary-eyed glance stared back at me, verifying my guess.

The man standing to Fothergill's right was catcher Johnny Bassler. The only man smarter than the weather in the picture, Bassler wore a wool cardigan sweater with a calligraphy "D" on his chest. Johnny had facial features that were simple to remember. Baseball-Reference confirmed my memory.

The third man in the row was another no-brainer. The angry gape of Bobby Veach had frightened me when I initially started my research of the Tigers from the 1920s. Bobby's face was occupied by a pair of sharp and icy eyebrows that would make any player second guess themselves before confronting him. On reviewing his career, I learned that his menacing eyebrows did not match his upbeat demeanor. I read one story that Cobb had purposely instructed a player to taunt Veach when he stepped into the batter's box. Veach, known to have a friendly conversation with the opposing team's catcher before the pitch crossed the plate, had infuriated Cobb (who was not one to extend any courtesy to his opponents).

Veach occupied Detroit's left field from 1912 until 1923. This photograph captured one of the last days of Veach dressed in Detroit duds. The man standing to the right of Bobby Veach was a gentlemen who stuck out in more ways than one. Larry Woodall was born with the physical feature of ears that I would classify as "cab doors," like a small fan on both sides of his face.

The fifth man in the lineup was another 1922 rookie named Fred Haney. I noted Haney as the only third baseman and the shortest man in the picture. Just shy of five-foot-six, Fred's identity was confirmed by Baseball-Reference.com. I ran into a problem when I came to the sixth man in the lineup. Towering over Haney by seven inches stood Harry Heilmann. I recalled other photos I had seen of this legendary hitter. He reminded me of today's popular actor Russell Crowe. Crowe, known for his roles as James J. Braddock in

1923 Detroit Tigers Dugout Lineup Photo: Standing left to right: Bob Fothergill, Johnny Bassler, Bobby Veach, Larry Woodall, Fred Haney, Harry Heilmann, Ty Cobb.

MLB

the 2005 motion picture, *Cinderella Man*, and Maximus Meridius in the 2000 film, *Gladiator*, could have been Harry Heilmann's relative.

Worried that my interest in modern films might cloud my research judgment, I went to Baseball-Reference.com to compare Harry's profile picture with the 1923 photo. I found Harry's page but Harry wasn't there. His full name and every accurate stat of his career were there. But rather than finding my expected look-a-like shot of Russell Crowe, I found a snapshot of Woodall and his cab door ears! Why was Larry on Harry's page? I went back to Woodall's profile page on Baseball-Reference.com. Larry was there, accurately where he belonged. After clicking back and forth between Heilmann and Woodall, I determined two differences. On Larry's page, his photo showed his eyes looking up. On Harry's page, Larry's photo showed his eyes looking right at the camera. Then I saw something else. Larry's picture on Harry's page was a face shot, just like the other one—but there was a distinctive white space in the upper left-hand corner of the picture. I surfed the web to collect additional pictures of both players. My opinion that Heilmann and Crowe shared similar facial features was verified. Woodall and his protruding cab doors were also verified. Then I stumbled across a baseball card printed in 1960 that made my jaw drop.

Harry Heilmann (1924)
MLB

Lawrence Woodall (1924)
MLB

Card #65 "Harry Heilmann" from Fleer's 1960 Baseball Greats card set.

THE FLEER CORP / THE UPPER DECK CO. LLC / MLB

Card #65 from the 1960 Fleer set titled "Baseball Greats" was marked "Harry Heilman." But Heilmann's face was not on the face of the card—it was Larry Woodall in the same pose as appeared on his Baseball-Reference page. I purchased Card #65 from an online auction. Both the front and back of the card read "Harry Heilman." Harry's stats were printed on the backside but Woodall's face was undoubtedly affixed to the front.

Fleer had colorized the original 1923 Woodall photo by adding ink blasts of pink skin tone and blots of navy blue to enhance his Detroit ball cap. Below the modernized reproduction in bold, white print, read two words: "Harry Heilmann." Wow.

My first step to correct the error was to notify the National Baseball Hall of Fame and Museum in Cooperstown, New York. I traded letters with a brilliant and helpful gentleman named Freddy Berowski. Freddy agreed with my findings and thanked me for my "keen eye for detail" along with his surprise that Card #65 had gone unnoticed for so many years. I then contacted the web team at Baseball-Reference.com, pointing out the error, and suggesting that Harry's Card #65 may have led the creators of Heilmann's profile page in the wrong direction. Baseball-Reference.com immediately responded, and replaced Harry's photo with an accurate one in July 2011. I continued to review more photos of Harry and Larry before I contacted the Fleer Corporation. The powerhouse sports card company, founded in 1885, had been sold in 1992 to the Marvel comic book company, then to a private company, then to Upper Deck after it was declared bankrupt. As I researched Upper Deck, I found another error!

In 2001, Upper Deck had released a new baseball card series titled "Legendary Cuts." These expensive, limited number sets featured hand cut signatures of legendary baseball players. Some sets included players' signatures with authentic pieces of the player's bats and uniform swatches. Others included photographs of the players set next to their genuine autographs. Upper Deck continues to issue these sets today. In 2005, Upper Deck added a dual signature card to their Legendary Cuts set. One card was titled "DC-HC," and featured two of Detroit's most renowned baseball legends, Ty Cobb and Harry Heilmann. Named "DC" for "Dual Cuts" and "HC" for "Heilmann/Cobb," the card was hand numbered "1/1," signifying that only one card (featuring the signatures of Cobb and Heilmann) existed in the set. But there was a problem.

I found no fault with the lower half of the card displaying an accurate photo of Tyrus Cobb and the original cursive of his authentic autograph. But the upper half of the card displayed Heilmann's valid signature set next to a small, sepia and black colorized photo of Charles Lawrence "Larry" Woodall! When I found the card on an online auction website priced for $5,995, I contacted the seller about the error and the card disappeared from the Internet. I had learned long ago that error cards are worth more than their "corrected" cards. I felt as if I had tiptoed past a cat that got spooked and ran away. (On March 14, 2012, the Upper Deck Card DC-HC sold for a final private bid of $1,558.)

Meanwhile, I traded emails with Lyman Hardeman, the editor of the popular baseball card website "Old Cardboard." He agreed with my observation of Fleer Card #65. More interest followed after I contacted Rich Mueller, editor of the "Sports Collector Daily" website. In late July 2011, both sites graced me with digital ink as they presented details of my detection, which was cleverly coined "The Mix-Up of Harry & Larry." My Internet news story earned more interest a few weeks later. During my photograph review, I noticed that another baseball card company had committed several new errors. Panini America Incorporated has been in the business of sports collectibles and cards for years. In 2012, not long after my confusion between Harry & Larry was beginning to calm, Panini released their "National Treasures" baseball card series. These cards included old and recent baseball players' autographs, personal uniform swatches, and authentic baseball bat chips. Card #9 from Panini's 2012 National Treasures "League Leaders" set of 99 cards was titled, "Harry Heilmann" and wouldn't you know it, Harry's mug was missing from the face of the card, replaced by Larry's.

When Panini manufactured other categories titled "Legends" and "All-Decade," Heilmann's name and bat chips continued to be accompanied by Woodall's image, although some Heilmann cards from the "Legends" and "All Decade" categories were printed with accurate photos of Harry and some of Larry. Altogether, of the 488 Harry Heilmann cards issued by Panini in their 2012 National Treasures set, 334 had accurate photos of Harry and 154 had pictures of Larry. I attempted to contact the Upper Deck Company and Panini America Inc. by email and snail mail in 2012, but I have not received a reply to date.

Many of the Heilmann error cards from Panini's "National Treasures" that I had discovered and noted have been graded, authenticated, and inspected by trusted sports card grading companies. It's amazing that two men (who look nothing alike) were confused and permanently printed, graded, and sealed in the history annals of error cards. Then I found another problem that deserved some attention.

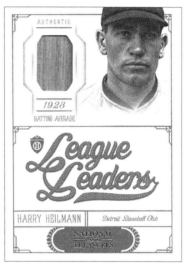

Card #9 "Harry Heilmann" from Panini's 2012 National Treasures "League Leaders"

Card #DC-HC "Cobb/Heilmann" from Upper Deck's 2005 Legendary Cuts "Dual Cuts."

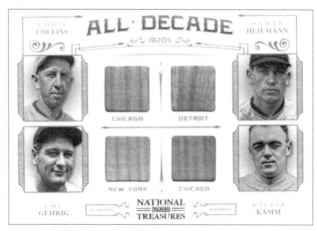

Card #5 "Collins/Gehrig/Heilmann/Kamm" from Panini's 2012 National Treasures "All Decade Quad."

Card #7 "Harry Heilmann" from Panini's 2012 National Treasures "Jumbo Bat .400 Club"

PANINI AMERICA INC. / MLB

Card #7 "Harry Heilmann" from Panini's 2012 National Treasures "Jumbo Bat Nickname"

PANINI AMERICA INC. / MLB

The Helmar Brewing Company, a prosperous beer franchise located in Detroit, released a set of "cabinet cards" in 2012. The owner of the company, Charles Mandel, created a successful brewing company and followed his personal passion to create old-time sports cards for today's modern collector. Helmar cards have a unique appearance and feel in comparison to the fresh, sharp-edged cards of new players. These new "old-time" cards are purposely discolored, scraped and weathered to create an aged look. The company releases cards of old-time players like Mel Ott, Ty Cobb, and—you guessed it—Harry Heilmann.

Mandel's company created cabinet cards, otherwise noted as "L3" cards. There are 207 cards measuring 9.5 inches tall and 4 inches wide in the 2012 set. Each features a separate player. Brilliant color and added details of branded leather and nine chips of Swarovski crystal cover the face of the card, above and below the player's photograph. The L3 card set is amazing… and so is Card #56. I examined this card and noticed Heilmann's name burned in the leather. Harry's name, along with the names of 204 star players from the Detroit Tigers are listed on the back side of the card. On the face of the card, surrounded by nine sparkling crystals, is the face of a catcher who never made any prominent records in the Detroit annals. It was a face I clearly recognized. Larry Woodall was staring back at me again.

I contacted the Helmar Brewing Company in 2013 and traded emails with Charles Mandel, who apologized for creating the Heilmann error card. I purchased the card happily and added it to the other Heilmann error cards I had been collecting for the past two years. Not long after I made contact with Mr. Mandel, I received an email from Bill Wagner. Known professionally as "Da Babe" or "Babe Waxpak," Wagner was a writer for the Scripps Howard News Service. Recognized for his writing talent and advice and enthusiasm as a sports card collector, Wagner inquired into the details behind "The Mix-Up of Harry & Larry."

After an interesting conversation, I was honored to work with the talented gentleman shortly before he announced his retirement. In late October 2013, the details of my discovery made press ink. Bill Wagner titled the story, "Error Corrected After 90 Years." By now I felt passionate about finding the origin of this error that had produced hundreds of cards confusing these two players since Fleer committed the initial error in 1960.

The first step of my investigation was to closely examine the details of the Woodall image used on Baseball-Reference.com and the cards issued by Fleer, Upper Deck, Panini, and Helmar. Every photo was an identical match. Each company changed the color of the image, but the shadows and physical image of Woodall remained the same, altered to conform to the setup and background of each company's design. Some companies took a "block shot" of the Woodall image, cut from the original photograph with four edges of the original background that surrounded Larry when the shot was taken.

Other companies cropped Woodall's image as they cut away the original background that surrounded Larry. These cut images were trimmed closely against

Helmar Brewing L3 Cabinet Card #56 "Harry Heilmann" (Full view and close-up)

HELMAR BASEBALL ART CARD CO. / MLB

Woodall's face, cap, uniform and shoulders. I wanted to know the details of the "white void" I noticed in the image on Heilmann's profile page on Baseball-Reference.com. I started a relentless search for the original image. I contacted libraries in Detroit and requested a search of images of Charles Woodall, Larry Woodall, and Harry Heilmann.

My digging paid off when one of my late night Internet image searches hit. ESPN.com had created a webpage on December 12, 2012, titled, "Hall of 100— Ranking All-Time Greatest MLB Players." I found the original photo of Larry Woodall incorrectly included on Harry Heilmann's ESPN.com webpage on which Harry was ranked as #110 in the "Honorable Mention" category. Similar to Baseball-Reference.com's stats and details, Heilmann's notations were correctly displayed with the wrong player's photograph.

I took a digital snapshot of the photo used by ESPN.com and enlarged it. I immediately spotted the reason for the "white void" I had seen. It was another player's elbow. In the background, facing the opposite direction from Woodall, a player stood on the left side of Larry with his arms and elbows resting on the top of the concrete dugout. Then I took a closer look at Fleer's Card #65. I could vaguely see the heavily colorized and shaded section occupying the upper left corner of the card, erasing the player's elbow from the original shot. The edge of the dugout extended from the player's elbow behind Woodall's head and reappeared over Larry's right ear. Fleer could not erase the dugout edge above Larry's ear.

The photo on ESPN, Baseball-Reference, and Fleer's card #65 were a match. ESPN's image added another detail that caught my eye. Their photo included a closer view of the top button of Woodall's uniform. A metal safety pin was clearly visible, used as a makeshift button. ESPN's photo was obviously the original

photograph, with no alterations. I compared that to Fleer's card #65, on which Woodall's top button is fastened and nicely detailed with a round button. Fleer had cleverly drawn a bright, white button over Woodall's safety pin. Fleer also colorized the black and white photo and attempted to blur the player's elbow in the upper left corner. A closer look at ESPN.com's picture revealed that the photograph was credited "AP Photo."

On September 11, 2013, I searched the Internet and found the website for the Associated Press. I searched through the images and found the "X" on my treasure map. APimages.com had a category titled "Harry Heilmann." I clicked on Heilmann's link and found three "Heilmann" photos. One was a 2010 photograph of Harry P. Heilmann, the assistant Chief Engineer of the Washington Metropolitan Area Transit Authority. Since my research didn't involve Washington trains, I skipped over the details of this "Heilmann." One, copyright number 2601010370, dated 1/1/1926 was an accurate image of the Tigers' Harry Heilmann, kneeling with one knee down while holding himself up with a bat. The third, dated 1/1/1923, was really Charles Lawrence "Larry" Woodall, a silver pin clasped under his Adam's apple and a clearly visible player facing away from him with relaxed elbows on top of a dugout.[1] It was a great sight to see: the original photograph. It was labeled copyright number 2601010266. My eyes focused to the lower right of the photo as I examined the original chalk used to number it. I noted the handwritten digits "16" in white grease pencil on the black and white photo. Considering that this original photo could be in reverse (as many pictures are), I concluded that this number could be "91" if the photo negative was upside down.

I had found what I had been looking for and I was thrilled.

I printed the picture and drew horizontal and vertical lines over it to create a grid. I did the same with

1923 Photograph of Lawrence Woodall, "The Original Picture That Started It All"

1960 Fleer's Baseball Greats Card #65 Photo / 1923 Original Photo of Larry Woodall (Comparison Circles: "Dugout/Ear," "Void/Collar," "Pin/Button," "Fold/Chest").

Fleer's card #65, Upper Deck's DC-HC, the Panini's cards, Helmar's card #56 and Baseball-Reference's erroneous photo. I was able to confirm that every photo included a dark shadow "void" on the left side of Larry's neck. This helped me to verify that all pictures were an identical match to the chalk-marked original AP photograph. Could there be a chance that AP had the original physical photograph in their archives? If they did, was it likely that the back of the photo was incorrectly labeled "Harry" instead of "Larry"? I considered the possibility that the artist responsible for taking the snapshot was the famous baseball shutterbug, Charles M. Conlon.

Conlon was known to take snapshots of players as they stood alone in a dugout. I quickly reviewed and eliminated Conlon's competitor, Chicago sports photographer George Brace, since Brace did not begin taking baseball photos until 1929. If this was an authentic Conlon shot, why was it owned by the Associated Press? I contacted the AP and requested a copy of the picture. My offer was rejected by the AP's contracted sales company, Replay Photos, who explained, "AP does not have the rights to sell this photo for personal use. Unfortunately Major League Baseball prevents us from having the rights to sell prints of Major League Baseball players, even for personal use." MLB owns the photos and allows AP the rights to license and distribute them to professional publishing companies. I asked Replay Photos to inspect the original photograph and check the blank reverse side for the names Larry and Woodall, explaining in tedious detail the errors I had found. Sadly, I never received a reply. In October 2013, Bill "Waxpak" Wagner contacted Associated Press and spoke with Paul Colford, AP's Director of Media Relations, to discuss the details of my error discovery. Colford advised Wagner, "We're unable, so many years later, to determine how the image came to be misidentified initially. However, it is properly identified now, so that any future licensor of the photo from AP images can be confident."[2]

Wagner's interview with AP and the specifics of the errors I discovered were added to Wagner's story: "Error Corrected After 90 Years." I believe it's possible that when Larry's original shot was taken, it was marked incorrectly with the name "Harry," and that started it all.

Both players were with the Tigers from 1920 through 1929. They were born eight days apart in 1894. Harry was elected to the National Baseball Hall of Fame in 1952. A year before he was given his baseball honor, Harry "Slug" Heilmann died in Southfield, Michigan, on July 9, 1951. Woodall passed away twelve years later on May 6, 1963, in Cambridge, Massachusetts.

Heilmann lived up to his handle, "Slug," collecting 2,660 hits during his 17-year career in the major leagues. In 1923 Harry earned an astounding .4027 batting average. Larry gathered 353 hits during his decade with Detroit. Although he never made the history books for anything outstanding during his time on the major league fields, Larry Woodall's face landed on popular baseball cards linking him with Harry Heilmann's statistics, Heilmann's name, and Heilmann's honors.

When I initially discovered the error, I couldn't help but imagine two photograph artists yelling back and forth to each other in a loud printing press office at the Fleer headquarters. Perhaps when the design of card #65 was in the process of production, one artist yelled "Harry" across the room to his co-worker—when he should have yelled "Larry." Maybe the back of the original Woodall photograph negative has the incorrect label. No matter what the truth is, the error carried on for almost 100 years and I was more than happy to be a part of its history. ∎

Notes

1. EDITOR'S NOTE: It is common practice for the AP and other historical photo collections to use "January 1" as a generic date indicating the year of the photo is known, but the exact day is not.
2. "Babe Waxpak/Sports Collectibles: Error Corrected After 90 Years," *Indiana Gazette*, October 19, 2013.

SABR BioProject Books

In 2002, the Society for American Baseball Research launched an effort to write and publish biographies of every player, manager, and individual who has made a contribution to baseball. Over the past decade, the BioProject Committee has produced over 3,400 biographical articles. Many have been part of efforts to create theme- or team-oriented books, spearheaded by chapters or other committees of SABR.

A PENNANT FOR THE TWIN CITIES:
THE 1965 MINNESOTA TWINS
This volume celebrates the 1965 Minnesota Twins, who captured the American League pennant in just their fifth season in the Twin Cities. Led by an All-Star cast, from Harmon Killebrew, Tony Oliva, Zoilo Versalles, and Mudcat Grant to Bob Allison, Jim Kaat, Earl Battey, and Jim Perry, the Twins won 102 games, but bowed to the Los Angeles Dodgers and Sandy Koufax in Game Seven
Edited by Gregory H. Wolf
$19.95 paperback (ISBN 978-1-943816-09-5)
$9.99 ebook (ISBN 978-1-943816-08-8)
8.5"X11", 405 pages, over 80 photos

MUSTACHES AND MAYHEM: CHARLIE O'S THREE TIME CHAMPIONS:
THE OAKLAND ATHLETICS: 1972-74
The Oakland Athletics captured major league baseball's crown each year from 1972 through 1974. Led by future Hall of Famers Reggie Jackson, Catfish Hunter and Rollie Fingers, the Athletics were a largely homegrown group who came of age together. Biographies of every player, coach, manager, and broadcaster (and mascot) from 1972 through 1974 are included, along with season recaps.
Edited by Chip Greene
$29.95 paperback (ISBN 978-1-943816-07-1)
$9.99 ebook (ISBN 978-1-943816-06-4)
8.5"X11", 600 pages, almost 100 photos

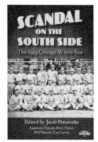

SCANDAL ON THE SOUTH SIDE:
THE 1919 CHICAGO WHITE SOX
The Black Sox Scandal isn't the only story worth telling about the 1919 Chicago White Sox. The team roster included three future Hall of Famers, a 20-year-old spitballer who would win 300 games in the minors, and even a batboy who later became a celebrity with the "Murderers' Row" New York Yankees. All of their stories are included in Scandal on the South Side with a timeline of the 1919 season.
Edited by Jacob Pomrenke
$19.95 paperback (ISBN 978-1-933599-95-3)
$9.99 ebook (ISBN 978-1-933599-94-6)
8.5"x11", 324 pages, 55 historic photos

WINNING ON THE NORTH SIDE
THE 1929 CHICAGO CUBS
Celebrate the 1929 Chicago Cubs, one of the most exciting teams in baseball history. Future Hall of Famers Hack Wilson, '29 NL MVP Rogers Hornsby, and Kiki Cuyler, along with Riggs Stephenson formed one of the most potent quartets in baseball history. The magical season came to an ignominious end in the World Series and helped craft the future "lovable loser" image of the team.
Edited by Gregory H. Wolf
$19.95 paperback (ISBN 978-1-933599-89-2)
$9.99 ebook (ISBN 978-1-933599-88-5)
8.5"x11", 314 pages, 59 photos

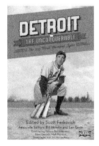

DETROIT THE UNCONQUERABLE:
THE 1935 WORLD CHAMPION TIGERS
Biographies of every player, coach, and broadcaster involved with the 1935 World Champion Detroit Tigers baseball team, written by members of the Society for American Baseball Research. Also includes a season in review and other articles about the 1935 team. Hank Greenberg, Mickey Cochrane, Charlie Gehringer, Schoolboy Rowe, and more.
Edited by Scott Ferkovich
$19.95 paperback (ISBN 9978-1-933599-78-6)
$9.99 ebook (ISBN 978-1-933599-79-3)
8.5"X11", 230 pages, 52 photos

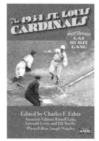

THE 1934 ST. LOUIS CARDINALS:
THE WORLD CHAMPION GAS HOUSE GANG
The 1934 St. Louis Cardinals were one of the most colorful crews ever to play the National Pastime. Some of were aging stars, past their prime, and others were youngsters, on their way up, but together they comprised a championship ball club. Pepper Martin, Dizzy and Paul Dean, Joe Medwick, Frankie Frisch and more are all included here.
Edited by Charles F. Faber
$19.95 paperback (ISBN 978-1-933599-73-1)
$9.99 ebook (ISBN 978-1-933599-74-8)
8.5"X11", 282 pages, 47 photos

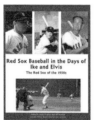

RED SOX BASEBALL IN THE DAYS OF IKE AND ELVIS: THE RED SOX OF THE 1950s
Although the Red Sox spent most of the 1950s far out of contention, the team was filled with fascinating players who captured the heart of their fans. In *Red Sox Baseball*, members of SABR present 46 biographies on players such as Ted Williams and Pumpsie Green as well as season-by-season recaps.
Edited by Mark Armour and Bill Nowlin
$19.95 paperback (ISBN 978-1-933599-24-3)
$9.99 ebook (ISBN 978-1-933599-34-2)
8.5"X11", 372 pages, over 100 photos

THE MIRACLE BRAVES OF 1914
BOSTON'S ORIGINAL WORST-TO-FIRST CHAMPIONS
Long before the Red Sox "Impossible Dream" season, Boston's now nearly forgotten "other" team, the 1914 Boston Braves, performed a baseball "miracle" that resounds to this very day. The "Miracle Braves" were Boston's first "worst-to-first" winners of the World Series. Includes biographies of every player, coach, and owner, a season recap, and other great stories from the 1914 season.
Edited by Bill Nowlin
$19.95 paperback (ISBN 978-1-933599-69-4)
$9.99 ebook (ISBN 978-1-933599-70-0)
8.5"X11", 392 pages, over 100 photos

SABR Members can purchase each book at a significant discount (often 50% off) and receive the ebook edtions free as a member benefit. Each book is available in a trade paperback edition as well as ebooks suitable for reading on a home computer or Nook, Kindle, or iPad/tablet.
To learn more about becoming a member of SABR, visit the website: sabr.org/join

Casey at the Stat

Ernest Thayer
(annotated by Russell Frank)

The outlook wasn't brilliant for the Mudville nine that day:[1]
The score stood four to two, with but one inning more to play,[2]
And then when Cooney[3] died at first, and Barrows[4] did the same,
A pall-like silence fell upon the patrons of the game.

A straggling few got up to go in deep despair.[5]
The rest Clung to the hope which springs eternal in the human breast;
They thought, "If only Casey[6] could but get a whack at that—
We'd put up even money now, with Casey at the bat."[7]

But Flynn[8] preceded Casey, as did also Jimmy Blake,[9]
And the former was a lulu,[10] while the latter was a fake;[11]
So upon that stricken multitude grim melancholy sat,
For there seemed but little chance of Casey getting to the bat.

But Flynn let drive a single,[12] to the wonderment of all,
And Blake, the much despisèd, tore the cover off the ball;[13]
And when the dust had lifted, and men saw what had occurred,
There was Jimmy safe at second and Flynn a-hugging third.[14]

Then from five thousand throats and more there rose a lusty yell;[15]
It rumbled through the valley, it rattled in the dell;
It pounded on the mountain and recoiled upon the flat,
For Casey, mighty Casey, was advancing to the bat.[16]

There was ease in Casey's manner as he stepped into his place;
There was pride in Casey's bearing and a smile lit Casey's face.[17]
And when, responding to the cheers, he lightly doffed his hat,
No stranger in the crowd could doubt 'twas Casey at the bat.

Ten thousand eyes were on him as he rubbed his hands with dirt;
Five thousand tongues applauded when he wiped them on his shirt;[18]
Then while the writhing pitcher ground the ball into his hip,
Defiance flashed in Casey's eye, a sneer curled Casey's lip.

And now the leather-covered sphere came hurtling through the air,[19]
And Casey stood a-watching it in haughty grandeur there.
Close by the sturdy batsman the ball unheeded sped—[20]
"That ain't my style," said Casey.[21] "Strike one!" the umpire said.

From the benches, black with people, there went up a muffled roar,
Like the beating of the storm-waves on a stern and distant shore;
"Kill him! Kill the umpire!" shouted someone on the stand;[22]
And it's likely they'd have killed him had not Casey raised his hand.

70

With a smile of Christian charity great Casey's visage shone;
He stilled the rising tumult; he bade the game go on;
He signaled to the pitcher, and once more the dun sphere flew;[23]
But Casey still ignored it and the umpire said, "Strike two!"[24]

"Fraud!" cried the maddened thousands, and echo answered "Fraud!"
But one scornful look from Casey and the audience was awed.
They saw his face grow stern and cold,[25] they saw his muscles strain,
And they knew that Casey wouldn't let that ball go by again.

The sneer is gone from Casey's lip, his teeth are clenched in hate,
He pounds with cruel violence his bat[26] upon the plate;
And now the pitcher holds the ball, and now he lets it go,
And now the air is shattered by the force of Casey's blow.[27]

Oh, somewhere in this favoured land the sun is shining bright,[28]
The band is playing somewhere, and somewhere hearts are light;[29]
And somewhere men are laughing, and somewhere children shout,
But there is no joy in Mudville—mighty Casey has struck out.[30]

Notes

1. Mudville's Win Probability (WP) was 36.7% at game time.
2. A home team coming up in the bottom of the 9th trailing by two runs has a Win Expectancy (WE) rate of 7.92%.
3. Cooney's slash line (batting average/on-base average/slugging average) was .272/.360/.361.
4. .192/.292./.212.
5. With two outs, Mudville's WE had fallen to 1.34%.
6. 302/.367/.447.
7. Casey's Win Probability Added (WPA) mark for the season stood at 1.31.
8. .313/.328/.363.
9. .252/.336/.324.
10. Flynn was also said to be a hoodoo, that is, a bringer of bad luck.
11. Blake was also thought to be a cake, that is, an easy out.
12. Flynn attained a maximum speed of 20.4 mph running from home to first.
13. Blake's drive had an exit velocity off the bat of 99.5 mph, a launch angle of 15.4 degrees and a maximum height of 30.9 feet.
14. Mudville's WE had now risen to 14.13%.
15. Peak stadium crowd noise is typically 130 decibels (dBA).
16. Casey has a career slash line of .290/415/.552 with runners in scoring position (RISP).
17. Studies show that smiling relieves stress.
18. A metric that would quantify the sound of applauding tongues is "in development," according to the Acoustical Society of America.
19. The pitcher achieved a 5.8-foot extension of his body toward home plate at the end of his delivery.
20. The Spin Rate of the pitch, a fastball, was 2,490 revolutions per minute (rpm). Its perceived velocity was 93.3 mph.
21. Casey swings at 65.1% of pitches inside the strike zone.
22. The only known case of umpicide occurred in 1899 in Lowndesboro, Alabama, when a player named Frank McCoy killed umpire Samuel Powell when Powell ruled his home run a foul ball. The call was not reviewable.
23. Extension, 6.5 feet; Spin Rate, 2345 rpm; Perceived Pitch Velocity, 94.5 mph.
24. The average player's batting average with a two-strike count is .160.
25. The average temperature of the human cheek is 32C.
26. Casey's bat was a 34-inch, 31-ounce Louisville Slugger.
27. Mudville resident Grace Satterley, rocking on her front porch 1.37 miles from the ballpark, reported feeling the breeze from Casey's swing.
28. The Mudville forecast called for gloomy skies with a 46% chance of depressing afternoon showers.
29. The lower end of the weight range for a human heart is about 8 ounces.
30. As a result of Casey's whiff, Mudville dropped below Youngstown, Ohio, as the unhappiest place in America in the latest Gallup-Healthways Well-Being Index.

Join SABR today!

If you're interested in baseball — writing about it, reading about it, talking about it — there's a place for you in the Society for American Baseball Research.

SABR was formed in 1971 in Cooperstown, New York, with the mission of fostering the research and dissemination of the history and record of the game. Our members include everyone from academics to professional sportswriters to amateur historians and statisticians to students and casual fans who merely enjoy reading about baseball history and occasionally gathering with other members to talk baseball.

SABR members have a variety of interests, and this is reflected in the diversity of its research committees. There are more than two dozen groups devoted to the study of a specific area related to the game — from Baseball and the Arts to Statistical Analysis to the Deadball Era to Women in Baseball. In addition, many SABR members meet formally and informally in regional chapters throughout the year and hundreds come together for the annual national convention, the organization's premier event. These meetings often include panel discussions with former major league players and research presentations by members. Most of all, SABR members love talking baseball with like-minded friends. What unites them all is an interest in the game and joy in learning more about it.

Why join SABR? Here are some benefits of membership:

- Two issues (spring and fall) of the *Baseball Research Journal*, which includes articles on history, biography, statistics, personalities, book reviews, and other aspects of the game.
- One expanded e-book edition of *The National Pastime*, which focuses on baseball in the region where that year's SABR national convention is held (in 2015, it's Chicago)
- 8-10 new and classic e-books published each year by the SABR Digital Library, which are all free for members to download
- *This Week in SABR* newsletter in your e-mail every Friday, which highlights SABR members' research and latest news
- Regional chapter meetings, which can include guest speakers, presentations and trips to ballgames
- Online access to back issues of *The Sporting News* and other periodicals through Paper of Record
- Access to SABR's lending library and other research resources
- Online member directory to connect you with an international network of SABR baseball experts and fans
- Discounts on registration for our annual events, including SABR Analytics Conference & Jerry Malloy Negro League Conference
- Access to SABR-L, an e-mail discussion list of baseball questions & answers that many feel is worth the cost of membership itself
- The opportunity to be part of a passionate international community of baseball fans

SABR membership is on a "rolling" calendar system; that means your membership lasts 365 days no matter when you sign up! Enjoy all the benefits of SABR membership by signing up today at SABR.org/join or by clipping out the form below and mailing it to SABR, Cronkite School at ASU, 555 N. Central Ave. #416, Phoenix, AZ 85004.

- - - ✂ -

SABR MEMBERSHIP FORM

	Annual	3-year	Senior	3-yr Sr.	Under 30
U.S.:	❏ $65	❏ $175	❏ $45	❏ $129	❏ $45
Canada/Mexico:	❏ $75	❏ $205	❏ $55	❏ $159	❏ $55
Overseas:	❏ $84	❏ $232	❏ $64	❏ $186	❏ $55

Add a Family Member: $15 for each family member at same address (list on back)
Senior: 65 or older before 12/31/2015

All dues amounts in U.S. dollars or equivalent

Participate in Our Donor Program!
I'd like to desginate my gift to be used toward:
❏General Fund   ❏Endowment Fund   ❏Research Resources   ❏_____
❏ I want to maximize the impact of my gift; do not send any donor premiums
❏ I would like this gift to remain anonymous.

Note: Any donation not designated will be placed in the General Fund.
SABR is a 501 (c) (3) not-for-profit organization & donations are tax-deductible to the extent allowed by law.

Name _____

Address _____

City _____ ST_____ ZIP_____

Phone _____ Birthday _____

E-mail: _____
(Your e-mail address on file ensures you will receive the most recent SABR news.)

Dues $_____

Donation $_____

Amount Enclosed $_____

Do you work for a matching grant corporation? Call (602) 496-1460 for details.

If you wish to pay by credit card, please contact the SABR office at (602) 496-1460 or visit the SABR Store online at SABR.org/join. We accept Visa, Mastercard & Discover.

Do you wish to receive the *Baseball Research Journal* electronically?: ❏ Yes   ❏ No
Our e-books are available in PDF, Kindle, or EPUB (iBooks, iPad, Nook) formats.

Mail to: SABR, Cronkite School at ASU, 555 N. Central Ave. #416, Phoenix, AZ 85004

The Enigma of Hilda Chester

Rob Edelman

The New York Yankees have their Bleacher Creatures. The crosstown Mets had Karl "Sign Man of Shea" Ehrhardt, while "Megaphone Lolly" Hopkins was the super-fan of the Boston Red Sox and Braves. Cleveland Indians, Chicago Cubs, Detroit Tigers, and Baltimore Orioles rooters have respectively included John "The Drummer" Adams, Ronnie "Woo Woo" Wickers, Patsy "The Human Earache" O'Toole, and "Wild Bill" Hagy. Then there are the Brooklyn Dodgers, whose off-the-field attractions included their Sym-Phony, Eddie Bottan and his police whistle—and Hilda Chester and her cowbell.

Hilda, otherwise known as "Howlin' Hilda," was a product of the outer-borough "woiking" classes: a dees-dem-dose, toidy-toid-'n'-toid Brooklynite. Granted, when interviewed, she was capable of using the King's English. More often, however, her responses were pure Brooklynese. She criticized one-and-all by pronouncing, "Eatcha heart out, ya bum," and identified herself by declaring, "You know me. Hilda wit da bell. Ain't it t'rillin'?" And she is as much a part of Dodgers lore as Uncle Robbie and Jackie Robinson, Pistol Pete, Pee Wee, and "Wait 'til next year." "I absolutely positively remember Hilda Chester because I often sat near her in the Ebbets Field bleachers," recalled Murray Polner, the author of *Branch Rickey: A Biography*. "Brooklyn Dodger fans all recognized her cowbell and booming voice." (Polner added: "There was another uber-fan who would scream, 'Cookeee'—for Lavagetto.")[1]

Hilda's reputation even transcends the Borough of Churches. Bums author Peter Golenbock labeled this "plump, pink-faced woman with a mop of stringy gray hair" the "most famous of the Dodger fans—perhaps the most famous fan in baseball history,"[2] while Bill Gallo of the *New York Daily News* called her "the most loyal and greatest fan to pass through the turnstiles of the Flatbush ballpark."[3] The *Los Angeles Times* cited her as "perhaps the greatest heckler of all time" who would "scream like a fishmonger at players and managers, or lead fans in snake dances through the aisles."[4] Seventy years earlier, *The Sporting News* had christened her "the undisputed Queen of the Bleachers, the Spirit of Brooklyn, the Bell of Ebbets Field, and we do mean Bell."[5]

Despite these accolades, little is known about Hilda Chester outside of baseball—and this was her preference. While piecing together the facts of her life, it becomes apparent that she was the product of a hard-scrabble youth and young adulthood, one that she steadfastly refused to acknowledge. Writer Thomas Oliphant, whose parents got to know Hilda in the Brooklyn ball yard, described her background as "truly the stuff of legend, much of it unverifiable.... My father...told me that behind her raucous behavior was a tough, often sad life, but that she was warm and decent under a very gruff exterior."[6] What is certain, however, is that whatever joy Hilda took from life came from her obsessive love of sports—and especially her devotion to the Brooklyn Dodgers.

So little is known about Hilda that the place of her birth cannot be confirmed. According to the United States Social Security Death Index, she was born on September 1, 1897.[7] No location is listed; most sources cite her birthplace as Brooklyn, but this may be conjecture given her identity as a Dodgers fanatic. More than likely, Hilda was born and raised on the East Side of Manhattan, but no one knows the identities of her parents or the circumstances under which she settled in Brooklyn.[8] In fact, in 1945 Hilda was queried as to what brought her to Brooklyn. "I liked da climate!" was her sarcastic response.[9]

What is certain is that Hilda was a product of urban poverty. "Home was never like this...," she noted in a 1943 interview in *The Sporting News*. "I haven't had a happy life. The Dodgers have been the one bright spot. I do not think I would want to go on without them." The article observed, "Nothing Hilda does startles [the Brooklyn players] any more. She is one of the family." Tellingly, the paper also reported, "Any further efforts to inquire into Hilda's early history meet a polite 'Skip it!' And when Hilda says 'Skip it,' she means it."[10]

Reportedly, Hilda played ball in her youth. "As a young girl she was willing to sock any boy who wouldn't let her play on the baseball teams...," noted journalist Margaret Case Harriman.[11] For a while, she was an outfielder for the New York Bloomer Girls and she hoped to one day either make the majors or establish a women's softball league. But this was not

NATIONAL BASEBALL HALL OF FAME LIBRARY, COOPERSTOWN, NY

Hilda Chester and her famous cowbell.

to be, and so she transformed herself into a rabid Brooklyn Dodgers booster. The story goes that, when Hilda was still in her teens, she would hang around the offices of the *Brooklyn Chronicle* in order to be the first to learn of the Dodgers' on-field fate.

Various sources note that Hilda was married at one time but that her husband had passed away. A daughter, Beatrice, was a product of their union, and the child also had baseball in her blood. As "Bea Chester," she played briefly in the All-American Girls Professional Baseball League. In 1943 she was with the South Bend Blue Sox, where she was the backup third baseman, appearing in 18 games and hitting .190. The following season she joined the Rockford Peaches, where she made it into 11 games. Her batting average in 42 at bats was .214.[12]

While playing for the Blue Sox, recalled Lucella MacLean Ross, "I had two different roommates. One was Betty McFadden, and the other was Bea Chester. She's a lady they have never traced as an All-American girl. Her mother was quite famous.... they used to call her 'Hilda the Bell-Ringer.' Her name was Hilda Chester."[13]

After the 1945 campaign, Bea "retired" as a professional ballplayer. In 1948 columnist Dan Parker reported that Hilda "is a grandma now and has decided to bring up young Stephen as a jockey instead of a Dodger shortstop."[14]

The AAGPBL website features a photo of Bea but also reports, "This player has not been located. We have no additional information." However, the young woman in the picture bears a marked resemblance to the photo of a Beatrice Chester that appears in the June 1939 yearbook of Thomas Jefferson High School, located in the East New York section of Brooklyn. Are the two one and the same? It certainly seems so. For one thing, this Beatrice Chester is cited as her school's "Class Athlete." She is dubbed "the 'he-man' of girls' sports" who "bowls, plays ping pong...She possesses letters in tennis, volley ball, basketball, baseball, hockey, shuffleboard, deck tennis, badminton...she has won a trophy at Manhattan Beach for the hundred yard dash, the running broad jump, and in baseball and basketball throw."[15] (In 1945, Hilda admitted to Margaret Case Harriman that Beatrice was a "very good soft-ball player." Harriman asked her where her daughter played. Hilda did not cite the AAGPBL. Instead, she "hastily" responded, "Oh, up at that school she don't go to no more."[16])

Most telling of all, the Jefferson yearbook notes, "To relieve the monotony of winning awards, Beatrice plays the mandolin and banjo." On two occasions, a younger musically-inclined Beatrice Chester was cited in the *Brooklyn Daily Eagle* reportage of events sponsored by the Brooklyn Hebrew Orphan Asylum. In February 1932, the paper covered "an afternoon entertainment staged by the boys and girls who live in the institution." One was Beatrice Chester, who performed a mandolin solo.[17] Then in December 1933, at an event sponsored by the asylum's women's auxiliary, Beatrice "played several selections on a mandolin..."[18]

What emerges here is that Hilda and Beatrice were Jewish, and Beatrice was a "half-orphan:" a child with one parent, but that parent was incapable of looking after her. Observed Montrose Morris, a historian of Brooklyn neighborhoods, "By 1933, during the Great Depression, the [asylum] estimated that 65% of their children had parents, but the parents were too poor to take care of them."[19]

Given her lack of finances, one cannot begin to calculate how many Dodgers games Hilda saw during this period, nor can it be determined exactly when she became an Ebbets Field habitué. *The Sporting News* reported that she began regularly attending games "when a doctor told her to get out in the sunshine and exercise an arm affected by rheumatism."[20] It was not until the late 1930s, however, that Hilda was a conspicuous Ebbets Field presence. That was when Larry MacPhail, the Dodgers' new president and general manager, inaugurated Ladies' Day in the ballyard; one afternoon each week, for the price of a dime, women could file into the bleachers. "The price was right," Hilda recalled years later. "I used to come to the park every Ladies' Day. I was like any other ordinary fan. Then I started to get bored…," and this resulted in her transformation from one of the anonymous masses into a uniquely colorful Dodgers devotee.[21]

Additionally, Hilda had long been unable to secure steady employment. But then the Harry M. Stevens concessionaire hired her to bag peanuts before sporting events; her job was to remove the peanuts from their 50-pound sacks and place them into the smaller bags that would be sold to fans. When she wasn't redistributing peanuts, she could be found selling hot dogs for Stevens at New York-area racetracks, a job she kept for decades. And she relished her employment. "They're all so good to Hilda," she observed. "When you got no mother, no father, it's nice to have a boss that treats you nice."[22]

On game days in Brooklyn, Hilda would grab a spot at the Dodgers players' entrance and greet them upon their arrival. She then would make her way to her seat in the center field bleachers where she loudly yelled at the players, her booming voice echoing throughout the stadium. After the game, she would situate herself along the runway beneath the stands that led to the team's locker room and either applaud or console her boys, depending upon the final score.

Her employment with Stevens aside, sportswriters began providing Hilda with passes, which further enabled her to mark her Ebbets Field turf. Initially, she preferred the cheap seats to the grandstand. "What, go down there and sit with the shareholders?" she once quipped, "And leave these fine friends up here…. All my friends (are) here. They all know me! They save my seat for me while I am checking the boys in every day. Leave them? Never."[23] She added, "There are the real fans. Y'can bang the bell all y'darn please. The 55-centers don't fuss so much about a little noise."[24]

Hilda was not exclusively a baseball devotee. During the offseason, she made her way to Madison Square Garden to root for the New York Rangers, and she exhibited the same hardnosed devotion to the hockey team as she displayed in Brooklyn. On February 27, 1943, the *Brooklyn Daily Eagle* printed the following Hilda query: "Just a few lines to let you know I couldn't wait for today's *Eagle* to see what kind of writeup you gave the Rangers last night after that game with Detroit. I think it's a rotten shame the way those referees treat our Rangers. I thought it was only in baseball they play dirty. Now I think it's worse in hockey. How come?"[25] Nonetheless, Ebbets Field and

its environs were her preferred home-away-from-home. Hilda and her daughter were occasionally observed knocking down pins at Freddie Fitzsimmons's bowling alley, located on Empire Boulevard across the street from the field.[26]

Various stories chart the manner in which Hilda expanded her repertoire from voice to cowbell. The most commonly reported is directly related to a heart attack she suffered in the 1930s. Her doctor eventually ordered her to cease bellowing at ballplayers, which led to her banging a frying pan with an iron ladle. They were replaced by a brass cowbell, which reportedly was a gift from the Dodgers' players in the late 1930s. She also was noted for waving a homemade placard for one and all to see. On it was an inscription: "Hilda Is Here."

After suffering a second heart attack in August 1941, Hilda found herself confined to Brooklyn's Jewish Hospital. "The bleacher fans have taken on a subdued atmosphere since the absence of the bell-ringing Hilda," reported the *Brooklyn Daily Eagle*, "but she sends them all her best regards and urges them 'to keep their thumbs up and chins out and we'll clean up the league'." While being prepared for a medical procedure, Hilda pinned a Dodgers emblem to her hospital gown and asked if she could hold onto a *Brooklyn Daily Eagle* clipping of Dixie Walker and Pete Reiser.[27] Her health status was covered in the media, with the paper running a photo of a smiling Hilda, holding what presumably was the Walker-Reiser clipping, above the following caption: "Howlin' Hilda Misses Dodgers: From a bed in Jewish Hospital Hilda Chester, popular bell-ringing bleacherite, roots for her faithful Dodgers to bring home the bacon."[28]

After being bedridden for two weeks, Hilda announced that she was planning to leave the hospital and make her way to Ebbets Field for a game against the rival New York Giants. "I will be calm," she told the *Brooklyn Daily Eagle*. "Oh, yes. I have to be calm. But—sure, I'll take my bell along, just for luck. And will I ring it when our boys show them Giants how to play ball? Sure, I will, just for luck. And, oh yes, I guess I'll cheer a little, too, for Leo [Durocher] and Dixie [Walker] and the rest of the boys."[29] So against doctors' orders, Hilda returned to Ebbets Field because, as she explained, her boys "needed me."[30]

While hospitalized, Hilda had been visited by no less a personage than Durocher, who then was the Bums' skipper. It was for good reason, then, that Durocher was a Hilda favorite. After the 1942 season, scuttlebutt had it that the Dodgers were about to fire Leo the Lip. "[W]hat's all this noise going on about not re-signing Leo Durocher N.L. best Mgr., again in 1943," Hilda wrote the *Brooklyn Daily Eagle*. "You know, I know that we all know whom we have but who knows what we will get. For the past two seasons Leo did a wonderful job and for that reason must the Dodgers get a new Mgr." The missive was signed "HILDA CHESTER, 100% real loyal Dodger bleacher rooter." Her mailing address was 20 DeKalb Avenue in downtown Brooklyn.[31]

During the 1945 campaign, The Lip faced a felonious assault charge for allegedly donning brass knuckles and helping to beat up John Christian, a medically-discharged veteran. Hilda immediately came to Leo's defense. "The pernt is this: Christian had been pickin' on nearly all the Dodger players for more'n a month—with a verce like a foghorn," she declared. "He shouldn't been usin' langwidge that shocked the ladies."[32] In court, Hilda was called to the witness stand and promptly perjured herself, claiming that Christian had called her a "cocksucker"—and the manager merely was defending her honor.

By this time, Hilda occasionally accompanied the team on short road trips; "I'm travelin' right along in da train wit da boys," she declared in 1945. "Ain't it t'rillin'?"[33] During the war years, she also appeared at the team's temporary spring training site at Bear Mountain in upstate New York. "Close to 500 watched the Dodgers in action on the Sabbath," reported the *Brooklyn Daily Eagle* during spring training in 1943. "A sizeable delegation of Brooklyn fans were headed by Milton Berle, the comic, and Hilda Chester, the cowbell girl."[34]

Hilda was by then a semi-celebrity who was synonymous with the Dodgers brand, and who was cited in the same sentence as big-name entertainers. *New York Post* columnist Jerry Mitchell dubbed her "the Scarlett O'Hara of Ebbets Field," and her name even occasionally appeared in game coverage.[35] "Whether it was Durocher, Charley Dressen, Johnny Corriden or Hilda Chester, someone was responsible for a lot of wild masterminding in a wild and at times fantastic game," wrote *The New York Times* Louis Effrat, reporting on the Dodgers' tenth-inning victory over the Boston Braves in August 1944.[36]

And certainly, Hilda reveled in her fame. "I notice in [your] Sunday magazine section you gave me a little plug," she wrote *Times* columnist Arthur Daley. After thanking him, she added, "For heaven's sake, don't call me a character." She signed the missive "Hilda Chester, The Famous One."[37]

It was around this time that Hilda went Hollywood. *Whistling in Brooklyn* (1943), an MGM comedy, stars

Red Skelton as "The Fox," a popular radio sleuth who is a prime suspect in a series of murders. He is chased into Brooklyn and winds up at Ebbets Field, where the Dodgers are playing an exhibition with the Battling Beavers, a House of David-style nine. "The Fox" dons a fake beard and impersonates "Gumbatz," the Beavers' starting pitcher, in a sequence that features such real-life Dodgers as Leo Durocher, Billy Herman, Arky Vaughan, Ducky Medwick, and Dolph Camilli.

As Herman comes up to bat, a female fan is shown on-camera and yells out what is best translated as: "Will ya get it wound up son of a seven, you Gumbatz." Could it be? Yes, it's none other than Hilda Chester. ("Beware, Hollywood!" observed columnist Alice Hughes in the *Reading Daily Eagle*. "Hilda Chester, most famous rooter of our beloved Brooklyn Dodgers, has been playing a bit in [the] Red Skelton movie, 'Whistling in Brooklyn,' some of it filmed in the Dodgers' ball park—so look out Hedy Lamarr and Greer Garson!")[38]

Additionally, *Brooklyn, I Love You* (1946), a Paramount Pictures short highlighting the Dodgers' 1946 season, features such Brooklyn stalwarts as Durocher, Pee Wee Reese, Pete Reiser, Eddie Stanky, Red Barber—and Hilda. A Hilda-ish fan, played by character actress Phyllis Kennedy, appears in several scenes in *The Jackie Robinson Story* (1950), the first "42" biopic; the Hilda-inspired Sadie Sutton, a gong-beating fan, is one of the minor characters in *The Natural*, Bernard Malamud's 1952 novel. Around this time, Hilda began popping up on radio and TV shows. For example, on April 19, 1950, she guested on a *This Is Your Life* radio tribute to umpire Beans Reardon. Among those appearing on the July 23, 1956, edition of *Tonight!*, with Morey Amsterdam substituting for host Steve Allen, were "Diahann Carroll, vocalist," "Oscar Peterson, jazz pianist," and "Hilda Chester, Dodger fan." Then on March 7, 1957, Hilda guested on *Mike Wallace's Night Beat* interview program. Her fellow interviewee was Gerald M. Loeb, a founding partner of E.F. Hutton & Co.

Across the years, Hilda formed warm personal relationships with players. In 1943, *The Sporting News* reported that "Brooklyn's No. 1 rooter...always remembers the Dodgers' birthday with cards, visits them in hospitals when they're ill or injured and consoles them in their defeats."[39] Noted Dixie Walker: "She never forgets a birthday. She sends us the nicest cards you ever saw, on all important occasions. I think she's wonderful."[40] Hilda the super-fan even had kind words for Dodgers' management. Of Branch Rickey, she observed: "Anything the boss does, he knows what he's doin'." But clearly, Leo the Lip was her favorite. "They don't come any better in my book," she declared.[41]

On one occasion, in a well-reported anecdote, Hilda actually affected the outcome of a game. Whitlow Wyatt was the Dodgers' starting pitcher. It was the top of the seventh inning; the year was either 1941 or 1942. The story goes that, as center fielder Pete Reiser took his place in the field, Hilda handed him a note and instructed him to deliver it to Leo Durocher. Upon returning to the bench, Reiser gave it to his manager— and Durocher assumed that the missive was from Larry MacPhail. It read: "Get [Dodgers reliever Hugh] Casey hot. Wyatt's losing it." Upon taking the hill, Wyatt surrendered a hit and Durocher promptly replaced him with Casey, who almost lost the game. An irate Durocher berated Reiser for handing him the note without explaining that it was from Hilda rather than MacPhail.

(As the years passed, different versions of the story were cited. For example, as early as 1943, *The Sporting News* reported that Hilda had written: "Better get somebody warmed up, Casey is losing his stuff out there."[42] In a 1953 *Brooklyn Daily Eagle* column, Tommy Holmes—after observing that "in 1941, [Hilda] was the unchallenged dream boat of the cheap seats"—recalled that she had written: "[Luke] Hamlin seems to be losing his stuff—better get Casey warmed up."[43] Then in 1956, Reiser claimed that the Dodgers' starting pitcher that day was Curt Davis, rather than Wyatt.[44] But the essence of the tale remains unchanged.)

During the 1943 campaign, after the Dodgers dropped their ninth game in a row, Tommy Holmes observed, "When nobody else loves the Dodgers, Hilda Chester will…"[45] Perhaps Holmes was a bit optimistic. Just before the 1947 season, Hilda abruptly switched her allegiance to the New York Yankees. It was noted in *The Sporting News* that her "feelings have been hurt by certain persons in the [Dodgers] business office. It seems Hilda wrote in for her customary seat, but got a bill for $24.50, instead. She angrily denied the presence of Laraine Day [the Hollywood actress who was Durocher's wife at the time] had anything to do with it. 'Laraine?' she said. 'That's Leo's headache'."[46] Queried *Brooklyn Daily Eagle* columnist George Currie, "[W]hat is Ebbets Field ever going to be again, without her cowbell?"[47]

But Hilda never could become a true-blue American League devotee. Later that season, she and her "Hilda Is Here" banner began inhabiting the Polo Grounds; by the following year, the New York Giants had become her team of choice, in part because she claimed to have had difficulty obtaining 1947 World

A statue of Hilda Chester now stands in the National Baseball Hall of Fame in Cooperstown.

Series tickets, but also because, midway through the campaign, her favorite baseball personality left his Ebbets Field managerial post for the vacated one in Coogan's Bluff. *The Sporting News* published a photo of Hilda and an unidentified female fan holding a large sign with "Leo Durocher" on it. In responding to a question about her health, Hilda explained, "I hardly ever get pains now, except for what they done to my Leo."[48]

All was soon forgiven, however, and Hilda returned to her outfield perch at Ebbets Field. In fact, she was presented with a lifetime pass to the Flatbush grandstand; eventually, in a departure from her loyalty to the center-field denizens, she was given a reserved seat near the visitors' dugout. In 1950 she was asked if she ever received free Ebbets tickets. "Free tickets!" she bellowed. "I never accepted free tickets. They always give me complementaries."[49]

The cowbell was not the only gift to Hilda from her Brooklyn "boys." In August 1943 she was presented with a silver bracelet that featured her first name across the band and a small baseball dangling from the chain. "Was Hilda the happiest woman in Brooklyn last night?" queried *The New York Times*. "Silly question!"[50] In August 1949, the Dodgers awarded her a charm bracelet for her "loyalty" as the team's number one fan. On Mother's Day 1953, after she dyed her hair "a flaming red," team owner Walter O'Malley—in a pleasant mood because the Dodgers were completing a winning home stand and had just bested the

Philadelphia Phillies—had a florist deliver to her a large bouquet with a note inscribed, "To Brooklyn's newest redheaded mother." *The Sporting News* reported: "Long after the game Hilda was still outside Ebbets Field, displaying her flowers to all and sundry."[51] In 1955, the Dodgers announced their all-time all-star team, as determined by fan vote. A ceremony was held at Ebbets Field on August 14. Various Dodgers who were present and in the stands or dugouts were acknowledged. They included Billy Herman, Leon Cadore, Otto Miller, Arthur Dede, Gus Getz, and one non-ballplayer: Hilda Chester.

By the 1950s, Hilda's mere presence at Ebbets Field was enough to spur on the Dodgers. But she still sporadically employed her lungpower. On one occasion, she yelled to a young Dodgers broadcaster, "I love you Vin Scully!" Apparently, a mortified Scully did not respond, and her follow-up line to him was, "Look at me when I speak to you!"[52] Meanwhile, her iconic status was acknowledged by Dodgers ballplayers. Recalled Ralph Branca: "She was better known than most of us, and if you stunk she'd let you know it." Added Duke Snider, "She'd be in her box by the third-base dugout and keep hollering at you until you acknowledged her." But the Duke of Flatbush admitted, "She had a great knowledge of the game and of game situations. It was her life."[53]

Near the end of the 1955 season, *The Sporting News* reported that "Dodgers players, headed by Pee Wee Reese (who else?), gave Hilda a portable radio… Now Hilda can tune in on the Bums, wherever they may be."[54] However, "wherever they may be" would soon be a long way from Brooklyn, as it was announced that the team would be abandoning the Borough of Churches and heading west, to relocate in Los Angeles.

Hilda, like all Brooklyn diehards, was furious. At first, she was in denial about the situation. "The Dodgers ain't gonna move to Los Angeles," she declared in March 1957. "I saw some games in Los Angeles a few years back. Why, the place was like a morgue…no rootin'…no cheerin'…how are the Bums gonna feel at home there?"[55] As the days turned to months, though, it became clear that the Dodgers' new anthem would be "California, Here I Come." Writing in the *Los Angeles Times* in July, Jeane Hoffman declared, "If you want one reporter's opinion, our guess is that if L.A. comes up with what O'Malley wants, the city has got him—even if Brooklyn threw in the Gowanus River and Hilda Chester to try and keep him there."[56]

Of course, the Dodgers did leave after the 1957 season. During their inaugural campaign in Los Angeles, the closest they got to Brooklyn was Philadelphia, when they played the Phillies—and Hilda pronounced that she "wouldn't be caught dead" there.[57] In June 1958, Dick Young quoted her from her perch selling hot dogs at one of the New York racetracks: "You oughta hear how the horseplayers talk. They hate O'Malley."[58]

In 1960, upon the razing of Ebbets Field, Hilda and five members of the Dodger Sym-Phony appeared on *Be Our Guest*, a short-lived CBS-TV program. (The other guests included Ralph Branca, Carl Erskine, and *Phil Silvers Show* regulars Maurice "Doberman" Gosfield and Harvey Lembeck.) Hilda joined the Sym-Phony in performing a number, to the tune of "Give My Regards to Broadway," which included a revised lyric: "Give our regards to all Dem Bums and tell O'Malley, 'Nuts to you!'" Hilda asked host George DeWitt if the show was being broadcast in color. The answer was "black-and-white," which displeased her because she had dyed her hair for the occasion. She and the musicians were described as being "still Dodger rooters, but only for the departed Brooklyn club." All were given original Ebbets Field seats.[59]

A year later, it was announced that Hilda "will be honored as America's No. 1 baseball fan" during ceremonies at the opening of the National Baseball Congress tournament in Wichita, Kansas.[60] But then she quietly faded from view. Occasionally, her name would pop up in the media. In 1963, Dan Daniel noted that "the last I heard of Hilda was that she was employed by the Stevens brothers in their commissary department at the New York race tracks."[61] Still, she steadfastly maintained her Dodger ties. In 1969, Dixie Walker noted that he hadn't been back to Brooklyn "for years" but was quick to add, "Ah, but last September I got a birthday card from Hilda Chester. She never misses a one."[62] Rumor had it that she no longer resided in the New York metropolitan area. "I understand she's in retirement in Florida," declared Dodgers super-fan Danny Perasa.[63] However, Dick Young reported that "the cowbell-ringing zany of the old Dodger days" is "ill at age 71. Drop her a note at: 144–02 89th Avenue, Queens, N.Y. 14480."[64]

In the early 1970s, Hilda's address became the Park Nursing Home in Rockaway Park, Queens. Writer Neil Offen showed up at the home with the intention of interviewing her. "I'm sure she won't want to talk, not about baseball, not about those days," explained a nursing home employee. "She doesn't like to talk about them anymore. She doesn't even like to talk about them to us." However, Offen got to speak with Hilda on the telephone. "The old days with the Brooklyn Dodgers, no, that's out," she insisted. She noted that there was "no particular reason" for her reluctance to reminisce, but she quickly added, "It's all over, that's it. That's the only reason. I'm sorry. That's all I can say. I'm sorry. But it's all over. That's it. I'm sorry. I'm sorry."[65]

Hilda Chester was 81 years old when she passed away in December 1978. Matt Rothenberg, Manager of the Giamatti Research Center at the National Baseball Hall of Fame and Museum, reported that she died at St. John's Episcopal Hospital in Queens and was buried in Mount Richmond Cemetery on Staten Island, which is operated by the Hebrew Free Burial Association.

What emerges here is that, for whatever reason, Hilda's indigent state was not addressed by any surviving family member. According to the Association's mission statement, "When a Jewish person dies and has no family or friends to arrange for the funeral, or if the family cannot afford a funeral, we assure that the deceased is treated with respect demanded by our traditions. The deceased is buried in Mount Richmond Cemetery in Staten Island where our rabbi recites memorial prayers over the grave. Whether they die in a hospital, nursing home, or a lonely apartment, the New York area's poorest Jews are not forgotten."[66]

Various sources list Hilda's death date as December 1. However genealogical researcher Scott Wilson reported that her fate was altogether different—albeit no less tragic. According to Wilson, she "died alone at 81 at her home at Ocean Promenade, Far Rockaway, Queens. Found December 9, with no survivors or informant, she was taken first to Queens Mortuary, then to Harry Moskowitz at 1970 Broadway, through the public administrator. Buried December 15, 1978, and a stone placed by the Hebrew Free Burial Association in the 1990s, sec. 15, row 19, grave 7, Mt. Richmond Cemetery…"[67] Andrew Parver, the Association's Director of Operations, confirmed Wilson's reportage and noted: "It doesn't appear that she had any relatives when she died." He added that Hilda's "stone was sponsored by an anonymous donor" and that "our cemetery chaplain has a vague recollection of someone visiting the gravesite more than 15 years ago."[68]

At her passing, Hilda was the definition of a has-been luminary—and her demise went unreported in the New York media. But in subsequent years, her memory has come alive in the hearts of savvy baseball aficionados. Events sponsored by The Baseball Reliquary, which was founded in 1996 and describes itself as "a nonprofit, educational organization dedicated to fostering an appreciation of American art and culture through the context of baseball history," begin with a ceremonial bell-ringing which pays homage to Hilda. All attendees are urged to bring their own bells and participate in the ceremony.

"It's a great way to engage the audience and a perfect way to remember Hilda," explained Terry Cannon, the organization's Executive Director.

Additionally, The Reliquary hands out the Hilda Award, which recognizes distinguished service to the game by a baseball fan. According to Cannon, the prize itself is "a beat-up old cowbell…encased and mounted in a Plexiglas box with an engraved inscription." But he was quick to note that, while Hilda is the Reliquary's "unofficial symbol" and "perhaps baseball's most famous fan," she remains "somewhat of a mystery woman. I'm not aware of any existing family members.… Had she died today, of course, that news would have been on the front page of every paper in New York."[69]

Hilda also has a presence at the National Baseball Hall of Fame and Museum, where an almost life-size fabric-maché statue of her and her cowbell, sculpted by Kay Ritter, is displayed with several other ballyard types. Hilda is all smiles as she rings her bell; affixed to her dress is a button that says: "I'LL TELL THE WORLD I'M FROM BROOKLYN N.Y." Three years after her death, she was a character in *The First*, the Joel Siegel-Bob Brush-Martin Charnin Broadway musical about Jackie Robinson. And thirty-plus years after her passing, *Howling Hilda* (also known as *Howling Hilda and the Brooklyn Dodgers*), a one-person biographical musical set at the start of the Dodgers' 1957 season, was penned by Anne Berlin and Andrew Bleckner and presented at various venues.

"I happened upon her and her story quite by accident and fell in love with her instantly," explained Berlin. "She was one of the most colorful people I had ever read about.… She had a very musical sounding voice to me. With musicals you have to have a voice before you can tell a story. Hilda Chester was all voice—I could hear her voice clearly and thought she would make a wonderful subject for a musical."

"I think she was ahead of her time. Today her cowbells would be tweeted—pictures of her would be on Instagram. She would have a Facebook page called The Brooklyn Dodgers' Greatest Fan. She knew how to market herself. She took an interest and love and made herself indispensable to it.… She's coarse, abrupt, gruff, but at the same time she's someone who can't get enough of these guys. This was her family. She's a product of her class, her environment, and Brooklyn. I feel the Dodgers were her family—her real family did not matter to her."[70]

Hilda Chester may be long-gone, but she is not forgotten—and, if she could speak today, her response to all the hubbub surely would be: "Ain't it t'rillin'!" ∎

Acknowledgments

Audrey Kupferberg; Lois Farber; Murray Polner; Jean Hastings Ardell; Anne Berlin; Jim Gates, Matt Rothenberg, Sue MacKay, and Cassidy Lent of the National Baseball Hall of Fame and Museum; Terry Cannon of The Baseball Reliquary; Andrew Parver, Director of Operations, Hebrew Free Burial Association; Mark Langill, Team Historian and Publications Editor, Los Angeles Dodgers.

Additional Sources

Jean Hastings Ardell. *Breaking into Baseball: Women and the National Pastime.* Carbondale: Southern Illinois University Press, 2005.

Notes

1. Interview with Murray Polner, March 21, 2015.
2. Peter Golenbock. *Bums: An Oral History of the Brooklyn Dodgers.* New York: G.P. Putnam's Sons, 1984, 60.
3. http://www.nydailynews.com/sports/more-sports/duke-snider-brooklyn-dodgers-boys-summer-baseball-treasure-ebbets-field-article-1.117552.
4. http://articles.latimes.com/2013/may/01/sports/la-sp-erskine-20130502.
5. J.G.T. Spink. "Looping the Loops." *The Sporting News*, April 22, 1943, 1.
6. Thomas Oliphant. *Praying for Gil Hodges: A Memoir of the 1955 World Series and One Family's Love of the Brooklyn Dodgers.* New York: St. Martin's Press, 2005, 158.
7. https://familysearch.org/search/collection/1202535.
8. Rich Podolsky. "The Belle of the Brooklyn Dodgers." *Saratoga Summer 2003*, Summer, 2003.
9. Margaret Case Harriman. "The Belle of the Brooklyn Dodgers." *Good Housekeeping*, October 1945, 257.
10. Spink, 1.
11. Harriman, 256.
12. http://www.aagpbl.org/index.cfm/profiles/chester-bea/213.
13. Jim Sargent. *We Were the All-American Girls: Interviews with Players of the AAGPBL, 1943–1954.* Jefferson, North Carolina, MacFarland & Company, 2013, 105.
14. Dan Parker. "The Broadway Bugle." *Montreal Gazette*, May 24, 1948, 15.
15. Mildred Danenhirsch. "The Miss of Tomorrow." *Thomas Jefferson High School Yearbook*, June, 1939, 75–76.
16. Harriman, 19.
17. "Child Box Fund Brings $2,000 to Hebrew Orphans." *Brooklyn Daily Eagle*, February 23, 1932, 6.
18. "Asylum Given Substantial Aid By Auxiliary. *Brooklyn Daily Eagle*, December 14, 1933, 22.
19. http://www.brownstoner.com/blog/2012/09/walkabout-saving-abrahams-children.
20. "Hilda Clings to Lip, Clangs for Giants." *The Sporting News*, August 18, 1948, 14.
21. Louis Effrat. "Whatever Hilda Wants, Hilda Gets in Brooklyn." *The New York Times*, September 3, 1955, 10.
22. Carl E. Prince. *Brooklyn's Dodgers: The Bums, the Borough, and the Best of Baseball: 1947–1957.* New York, Oxford: Oxford University Press, 1996, 89.
23. Spink, 11.
24. Sam Davis. "No Fair Weather Fans in Flatbush, and When You Hear the Gong, It's Hilda Chester Time at Ebbets Field." *Sarasota Herald-Tribune*, September 28, 1943, 6.
25. "Sincerely Yours: Ralph Trost Answers the Mail." *Brooklyn Daily Eagle*, February 27, 1943, 9.
26. Hugh Fullerton, Jr. "Sports Roundup." *The Gettysburg Times*, February 3, 1944, 3.
27. "Brooks' No. 1 Fem Fan 'Benched' By Illness." *Brooklyn Daily Eagle*, August 21, 1941, 1.
28. http://www.brooklynvisualheritage.org/howlin-hilda-misses-dodgers.
29. "It's All Over, Terry, Our Ace Feminine Fan Is On the Mend." *Brooklyn Daily Eagle*, September 3, 1941, 3.
30. "Defies Doctors' Orders to See Dodger Games." *Brooklyn Daily Eagle*, September 8, 1941, 1.
31. "Sincerely Yours: Ralph Trost Answers the Mail." *Brooklyn Daily Eagle*, November 21, 1942, 9.
32. Jack Cuddy. "Leo's Alleged Lawsuit Divides Brooklyn Fans." *Los Angeles Times*, June 12, 1945, 10.
33. Harriman, 258.
34. "Flock Is Getting Into Shape Fast." *Brooklyn Daily Eagle*, March 22, 1943, 9.
35. Jerry Mitchell. Sports on Parade. *New York Post*, January 29, 1943, 41.
36. Louis Effrat. "Dodgers Set Back Braves in 10th, 8–7." *The New York Times*, August 6, 1944, S1.
37. Arthur Daley, "Sports of the Times: Short Shots in Sundry Directions." *The New York Times*, June 12, 1947, 34.
38. Alice Hughes. "A Woman's New York." *Reading Daily Eagle*, April 29, 1943, 14.
39. Oscar Ruhl, "Purely Personal." *The Sporting News*, August 12, 1943, 9.
40. Spink, 11.
41. Davis, 6.
42. Spink, 11.
43. Tommy Holmes. "Daze and Knights." *Brooklyn Daily Eagle*, August 22, 1953, 9.
44. "'McPhail's Order' for Leo Proved to Be Work of Hilda." *The Sporting News*, April 4, 1956, 16.
45. Tommy Holmes. "Dodgers Drop 9th Straight, 7 to 4." *Brooklyn Daily Eagle*, August 8, 1943, 24.
46. Paul Gould. "Even Hilda Quits Dodgers, shifts to Yankee Stadium." *The Sporting News*, April 9, 1947, 20.
47. "George Currie's Brooklyn. *Brooklyn Daily Eagle*. April 9, 1947, 3.
48. "Hilda Clings to Lip, Clangs for Giants," 14.
49. Oscar Ruhl. "From the Ruhl Book." *The Sporting News*, May 3, 1950, 21.
50. Roscoe McGowen. "Dodgers Overcome By Braves, 7 to 4; Defeat 9th in Row." *The New York Times*, August 8, 1943, S1.
51. (Roscoe) McGowen, "Hilda, Now Redhead, Gets Big Bouquet From O'Malley." *The Sporting News*, May 20, 1953, 11.
52. http://lasordaslair.com/2012/01/21/dodgers-in-timehowlin-hilda-chester.
53. Podolsky.
54. Roscoe McGowen. "It Was 25-Man Job,' says Smokey, Dodging Orchids." *The Sporting News*, September 14, 1955, 5.
55. "Hilda Claims Bums to Stay." *Toledo Blade*, March 8, 1957, 31.
56. Jeane Hoffman. "Soul of Irish Charm: O'Malley Adopts 'Wait and See' Policy in Face of N.Y. Headlines." *Los Angeles Times*, July 18, 1957, C-6.
57. Gay Talese. "Brooklyn Is Trying Hard to Forget Dodgers and Baseball." *The New York Times*, May 18, 1958, S3.
58. Dick Young. "Clubhouse Confidential." *The Sporting News*, June 18, 1958, 19.
59. "Hilda and Sym-Phoney [sic] Band Bid Adieu to Ebbets Field." *The Sporting News*, February 17, 1960, 27.
60. "Hilda Chester to Be Cited as Top Fan at NBC Tournament." *The Sporting News*, February 15, 1961, 21.
61. Dan Daniel. Mary, Lollie, Hilda—Loudest Fans in Stands." *The Sporting News*, February 2, 1963, 34.
62. John Wiebusch. "Dixie…Hilda…Leo…Shades of Daffy Dodgers." *Los Angeles Times*, February 27, 1969, F1.
63. Michael T. Kaufman. "For the Faithful, There Will Never Be a Coda to the Sym-Phony of the Brooklyn Dodgers." *The New York Times*, April 11, 1971, 77.
64. Dick Young. "Young Ideas." *The Sporting News*, February 15, 1969, 14.
65. Neil Offen. *God Save the Players.* Chicago: Playboy Press, 1974, 96–97.
66. http://www.hebrewfreeburial.org/what-we-do.
67. Scott Wilson. *Resting Places: The Burial Sites of Over 10,000 Famous Persons.* Jefferson, North Carolina: McFarland & Co., 2007, 134.
68. Interview with Andrew Parver, April 22, 2015.
69. Interview with Terry Cannon, March 24, 2015.
70. Interview with Anne Berlin, March 12, 2015.

Larry Twitchell's Big Day

With Notes About Individual Total Bases

Brian Marshall

I was researching information related to an afternoon game held on May 30, 1894. Bobby Lowe had four home runs in that game. I came across this line in *The Washington Post*: "Lowe's work with the stick was unparalleled, his four home runs making a League record and his total bases equaling Larry Twitchell's famous record."

I had been under the impression that Lowe's 17 total bases was the record for an individual in a single nine-inning game, later equaled by Ed Delahanty, and wasn't aware that someone had established the mark prior to Lowe. This led me to research the matter and upon further review, it became clear that Twitchell only had 16 bases and not 17. This explains why the major-league record for total bases in a single nine-inning game was listed for many years as being shared by Bobby Lowe and Ed Delahanty, and not by Larry Twitchell.

Larry Twitchell's big day came on August 15, 1889, in a game between the Cleveland Spiders and the Boston Beaneaters, played at League Park in Cleveland, Ohio.[1] The *Cleveland Leader* described Cleveland native Twitchell as a "good natured and affable young man who rakes flies out of left field" and also "the same Larry who played in every vacant lot in Cleveland in his boyhood days."

The boxscore in Figure 1 indicates that Larry Twitchell was perfect on the day with a batting average of 1.000 based on his six hits in six at bats with one base on balls for a total of seven plate appearances:

1. **First Inning** – single to left field scoring Stricker, left on base
2. **Third Inning** (led off) – triple up against the left field fence, Twitchell scored on Tebeau's single
3. **Fourth Inning** – triple to center field scoring Stricker, Twitchell scored on Tebeau's double
4. **Sixth Inning** (led off) – double to right-center field, Twitchell scored on Tebeau's single
5. **Seventh Inning** (led off) – home run to left-center field
6. **Eighth Inning** – base on balls, Twitchell scored on Tebeau's home run
7. **Ninth Inning** – triple to center field, left on base

Larry Twitchell debuted for the Detroit Wolverines in 1886 and would go on to play for seven teams in the National League, Players League, and American Association.

When it was all said and done, Twitchell's six hits were comprised of one single, one double, three triples and a home run for a total of 16 total bases and included hitting for the cycle.

From a team perspective, Cleveland scored in every inning, amassed 27 hits, including 11 extra base hits, and 48 total bases, none of which was an NL record at the time.[2] Regarding the Cleveland team effort, *The Cleveland Leader* said, "Cleveland broke the League batting record for the season and made one of the best records ever made in the history of the organization. Twenty-seven hits for a total of forty-eight bases doesn't grow on every tree and never grew in Cleveland before, that's sure."

The Leader further commented as follows:

"Kid" Madden, the energetic young gum-chewing pitcher of the Bean Eaters, was in the box and was kindly kept there for nine long and enthusiastic

Figure 1. BOX SCORE: Cleveland at Boston, August 15, 1889

CLEVELAND SPIDERS
Manager – Tom Loftus

Batting, Fielding and Stolen Bases

Player	AB	R	H	BA	1B	2B	3B	HR	BB	SO	SH	SB	PO	A	E
Paul Radford, rf/lf	7	2	4	0.571	2	1	1	0	0	1	0	0	1	0	1
Cub Stricker, 2b	4	3	2	0.500	1	0	0	1	3	0	1	2	3	4	0
Ed McKean, ss	7	1	2	0.286	2	0	0	0	0	2	1	0	1	7	0
Larry Twitchell, lf/p	6	5	6	1.000	1	1	3	1	1	0	0	0	2	1	0
Patsy Tebeau, 1b	7	2	5	0.714	3	1	0	1	0	0	0	0	1	1	0
Jimmy McAleer, cf	6	1	2	0.333	1	1	0	0	0	0	1	0	1	0	0
Bob Gilks, 1b	3	2	1	0.333	1	0	0	0	3	0	0	0	12	1	0
Chief Zimmer, c	6	1	4	0.667	4	0	0	0	0	1	0	0	6	4	1
Jersey Bakely, p/rf	1	1	1	1.000	1	0	0	0	0	0	0	0	0	0	0
Henry Gruber, p	3	1	0	0.000	0	0	0	0	1	1	1	0	0	2	0
Totals	50	19	27	0.540	16	4	4	3	8	5	4	2	27	20	2

Pitching

Player	IP	H	SO	BB	HBP	WP	B	W	L	R		LOB	DP	BE
Jersey Bakely, p	1.0	0	0	4	1	0	0	0	0	4		13	3	2
Larry Twitchell, p	1.0	0	0	1	0	0	0	0	0	0				
Henry Gruber, p	7.0	10	3	5	0	1	0	1	0	4				
Totals	9.0	10	3	10	1	1	0	1	0	8				

BOSTON BEANEATERS
Manager – Jim Hart

Batting, Fielding and Stolen Bases

Player	AB	R	H	BA	1B	2B	3B	HR	BB	SO	SH	SB	PO	A	E
Hardy Richardson, lf	5	0	1	0.200	1	0	0	0	0	0	0	0	1	0	1
King Kelly, c	3	1	1	0.333	1	0	0	0	2	0	0	1	7	4	1
Billy Nash, 3b	5	0	0	0.000	0	0	0	0	0	0	0	0	2	5	0
Dan Brouthers, 1b	3	2	2	0.667	2	0	0	0	2	0	1	0	8	0	0
Dick Johnston, cf	3	1	1	0.333	1	0	0	0	2	0	0	0	1	2	0
Joe Quinn, 2b	4	2	1	0.250	1	0	0	0	1	1	1	0	5	2	2
Pop Smith, ss	3	2	1	0.333	1	0	0	0	2	1	0	2	2	5	0
Charlie Ganzel, rf	4	0	1	0.250	1	0	0	0	0	1	0	0	1	0	0
Kid Madden, p	4	0	2	0.500	2	0	0	0	1	0	0	0	0	2	0
Totals	34	8	10	0.294	10	0	0	0	10	3	2	3	27	20	4

Pitching

Player	IP	H	SO	BB	HBP	WP	B	W	L	R		LOB	DP	BE
Kid Madden, p	9.0	27	5	8	1	0	0	0	1	19		10	0	1
Totals	9.0	27	5	8	1	0	0	0	1	19				

Umpire in Chief: Tom Lynch at HP

Runs by Inning

	Inning									
	1	2	3	4	5	6	7	8	9	Totals
Cleveland Spiders	1	1	3	2	1	6	1	3	1	**19**
Boston Beaneaters	0	4	0	1	1	1	0	0	1	**8**

innings while the infants fattened up their batting averages, the base hit column was swollen until its own mother wouldn't recognize it, and the total base column looks like the fat man of the dime museum.

The Twitchell performance on August 15 wasn't simply limited to his batting and fielding exploits, he also pitched in the game. Twitchell started the game in left field but was called in to pitch in the second inning. Jersey Bakely was the starting pitcher for Cleveland but he walked the first four Boston batters in the bottom of the second and hit the next batter.[3] Bakely went to right field, Radford went from right to left, and Twitchell went from left field to pitcher. The first batter that Twitchell faced was Kid Madden, the Boston pitcher, and Twitchell walked him, forcing in another run. Then a hit was muffed by Radford in left field which scored another run, Boston's fourth in the inning. Ganzel was thrown out at the plate on Kelly's hit to McKean and Madden was thrown out at the plate on Nash's hit to Twitchell, who threw to Zimmer, who was also able to throw out Nash at first for a double play. Gruber started the third inning in the box for Cleveland which presumably sent Twitchell back to left field and Radford to right field.

An interesting sideline regarding Twitchell's big day has to do with the topic of individual total bases. There was misleading information in the published accounts at the time and those after the fact. The 16 total bases registered by Twitchell surpassed the previous NL mark of 15, which was held by Dan Brouthers. In a game played on Friday September 10, 1886, Brouthers, playing for the Detroit Wolverines, had five hits against the Chicago White Stockings: three home runs, one double, and one single. The Twitchell total bases mark also surpassed the record in the American Association (AA), which was also 15, and was also established in 1886. The AA mark was set by Guy Hecker, a pitcher for the Louisville Colonels, in the second game of a doubleheader played on Sunday August 15, 1886, against the Baltimore Orioles. The *Louisville Courier-Journal* reported, "Hecker broke all previous batting records for a single game, making three home runs and three singles, a total of six hits which yielded altogether fifteen bases. He was at the bat seven times and made seven scores."

The *Baltimore Sun* stated, "The feature of the game was Hecker's tremendous and unparalleled batting. He made three home runs and three singles, with a total of fifteen bases, which has never been equaled in the history of the national game. Hecker also made seven scores out of seven times at bat." The *Baltimore American* agreed: "Hecker made a remarkable record out of seven times at bat. He secured seven runs and five hits, three of them being home runs, and yielding him a total of fourteen bases."

The *American* coverage was very misleading because the boxscore listed Hecker with six hits, not five, as they had mentioned in their writeup, and to make matters worse they listed Hecker as having a double in the breakdown below the boxscore. Some simple math based on Hecker having had five hits, as the *American* stated, comprised of three home runs, a double and a single, would yield a minimum of 15 bases, not 14 as the article had stated. The *Baltimore American* statistical portion of their coverage is so contradictory, as it related to some of the metrics for Hecker, that it becomes hard to identify what really happened and causes one to wonder what they were basing their information on.

The game write-up in *Sporting Life* ran as follows: "The afternoon game was remarkable for the wonderful and unprecedented batting of Hecker, who broke the individual batting record for a single game. He was seven times at bat and made three home runs, two doubles and a single. An error gave him a base once, and he scored seven runs, thus beating the record in three different ways—home runs, total bases and number of runs."

In the breakdown below the boxscore, *Sporting Life* contradicted themselves by not listing Hecker as having a single double, let alone two doubles.

Regarding Brouthers's performance of September 10, 1886, the *Sporting Life* write-up read, "Both clubs hit very hard and Brouthers made a remarkable display, in five times at bat getting five hits for a total of fifteen bases, three of the hits being home runs. This leads the League record and almost equals Hecker's record of sixteen bases."

The mention of Hecker's record being 16 bases is not correct as, apparently, he only had 15 bases in the August 15, 1886, game. It should be pointed out that the Hecker marks for runs scored and home runs in a game by a pitcher are also long-standing major-league records, whereas the total bases mark, while an AA record, was short lived from a major-league perspective.

The story of the total bases doesn't end with the Hecker AA game in 1886. It actually revealed the omission of a performance by George Strief, in addition to an error in the number of total bases. The *Louisville Courier-Journal* stated the following:

No Association player ever before made three home runs in a championship game, or reached a total of fifteen bases. The best records were made by Orr, the big batter of the Metropolitans, and Larkin, the heavy slugger of the Athletics. These players tied for the honor, each having made a total of eleven bases last year, Orr against Caruthers, of the St. Louis Browns, and Larkin against Morris, of the Pittsburghs. Hecker's performance is thus four points better than that of either Orr or Larkin. In the National League, Anson, of Chicago, once made three home runs in a single game, but his total number of bases did not equal Hecker's record yesterday.

The issue with the preceding, as reported in the *Louisville Courier-Journal*, is threefold.

1. The total bases mark that Hecker surpassed was stated incorrectly as 11 when it was 13.

2. The 11 total bases was incorrectly implied as the previous mark. George Strief had established a mark of 14 bases in a single game after both of the Orr and Larkin performances.

3. It was incorrectly implied that Anson had the only previous three-home-run performance in a single game. There were at least two others, being Williamson and Manning, both in 1884 along with Anson.

The Orr performance was on June 12, 1885, against the St. Louis Browns at the Polo Grounds. *The New York Times* reported the game as follows:

The 1,500 persons who attended the Metropolitan-St. Louis game on the Polo Grounds yesterday witnessed a most remarkable feat in batting. It was performed by David Orr, the first baseman of the Mets. He went to the bat six times, and hit the ball safely on each occasion. One of his hits, a line ball to the left field, yielded him a home run; another to the centre field gave him three bases. Besides these he made two doubles and two singles—in all a total of thirteen bases.

The Larkin performance was on June 16, 1885, against the Pittsburgh Alleghenys in Philadelphia. The *Philadelphia Record* reported it this way:

The Pittsburgh club was beaten to the tune of 14 to 1 by the Athletic nine at the Jefferson Street ground yesterday. Morris, the visiting club's crack left-handed pitcher was batted for a total of thirty-four bases, and Larkin, the Athletic Club's centre fielder, equaled Orr's great batting record. He was six times at bat and made six safe hits, with a total of thirteen. The first hit was a home run, the second a three-bagger, the third a double, and the fourth a single. Then came another double, and he completed the great record by a clean single in the ninth inning.

Both David Orr of the Metropolitans and Henry Larkin of the Athletics hit for the cycle, and had the exact same batting statistics which consequently yielded the exact same total bases.

The performance that was completely omitted from the the *Louisville Courier-Journal* newspaper article covering the Hecker game, and at least one subsequent publication, was that of George Strief of the Athletics on June 25, 1885, in a game against the Brooklyn club in Brooklyn. The importance of the Strief game was that it superseded, from a total bases and date perspective, both the Orr and Larkin performances since Strief registered 14 bases on four triples and a double in five hits

Figure 2. Progression of Total Bases for Both the NL and AA

TBs	NL Player	Date	Hit Composition	AB	H	BA
17	Bobby Lowe	May 30, 1894	4 x HR + 1 x 1b	6	5	0.833
	Ed Delahanty	July 13, 1896	4 x HR + 1 x 1b	5	5	1.000
16	Larry Twitchell	August 15, 1889	1 x HR + 3 x 3b + 1 x 2b + 1 x 1b	6	6	1.000
15	Dan Brouthers	September 10, 1886	3 x HR + 1 x 2b + 1 x 1b	5	5	1.000

TBs	AA Player	Date	Hit Composition	AB	H	BA
15	Guy Hecker	August 15, 1886	3 x HR + 3 x 1b	7	6	0.857
14	George Strief	June 25, 1885	4 x 3b + 1 x 2b	5	5	1.000
13	David Orr	June 12, 1885	1 x HR + 1 x 3b + 2 x 2b + 2 x 1b	6	6	1.000
	Henry Larkin	June 16, 1885	1 x HR + 1 x 3b + 2 x 2b + 2 x 1b	6	6	1.000

and five at bats. Not to mention the fact that the four triples was not only an AA record for the most triples in a single game by an individual, it was also a major-league record at the time. The game write-up in *Sporting Life* read, "Strief and Pinckney [sic] hit safely every time they went to the bat. The former made four three baggers and a two bagger, a total of 14 hits [sic], which beats Orr's and Larkin's record."

The New York Times reported as follows: "The contest at Washington Park, in Brooklyn, yesterday, between the Brooklyn and Athletic Clubs, was marked by very heavy batting. Strief, of the Athletics, led in the heavy work. He made four three-base hits and a double."

In conclusion, the most appropriate way to emphasize the impact of the Twitchell performance on August 15, 1889, is to let the records that he set and/or equaled speak for themselves.

1. Set the NL record for most total bases by an individual in a single game with 16. (Previous NL record was 15 total bases by Dan Brouthers on September 10, 1886, with three home runs, one double, and one single in five hits.)

2. Equaled the NL record for most extra base hits by an individual in a single game with five. (George Gore, of the NL Chicago White Stockings, had five extra base hits with three doubles and two triples in five hits on July 9, 1885.)

3. Equaled the NL record for the most hits by an individual in a single game with six. (NL record was broken by Wilbert Robinson with 7 hits on June 10, 1892 {1}.)

4. At the very least equaled, if not set, the NL record for the most triples by an individual in a single game with three. (NL record was broken by Bill Joyce with four triples on May 18, 1897.)[4]

Honorable mention: Twitchell scored five runs which was one shy of the NL record. ∎

Author's Notes

A progression of total bases leaders for both the NL and AA is listed in Figure 2.

Team names and the spelling of player names was based on that as listed on Baseball-Reference.com.

References

"BOSTON VS CINCINNATI: Home Run Record Broken," *Washington Post*, Thursday, May 31, 1894, 6.

"THEY HIT THE BALL: The Giant Killers Give a Wonderful Exhibition of Heavy Batting," *Cleveland Leader*, Friday, August 16, 1889, page unknown.

"THEY HIT THE BALL: The Spiders Play Havoc With Kid Madden's Curves," *Cleveland Plain Dealer*, Friday, August 16, 1889, 4.

"ENOUGH FOR ONE DAY: The Louisvilles Win a Game From Kilroy and Another Off Conway: Hecker Breaks the Batting Record With Three Home Runs and Three Singles: Doubling the Dose," *Louisville Courier-Journal*, Monday Morning, August 16, 1886, page unknown.

"BASEBALL: The Baltimores Lose Two Games at Louisville on Sunday," *Baltimore Sun*, Monday, August 16, 1886, page unknown.

"NOW WITHOUT A CATCHER: The Baltimores Lose on Sunday as Well as Any Other Day: Afternoon Game," *Baltimore American*, Monday, August 16, 1886, 4.

"BASE BALL: American Association: Games Played Sunday, Aug. 18," *Sporting Life*, Volume 7, Number 20, August 25, 1886, 2.

"BASE BALL: The National League: Games Played Friday, Sept. 10," *Sporting Life*, Volume 7, Number 23, September 15, 1886, 4.

"A GREAT FEAT IN BATTING: Orr Hits Caruthers for Thirteen Bases," *The New York Times*, Saturday, Jun 13, 1885, 2.

"PITTSBURGH OVERWHELMED: A One-Sided Slugging Game—Larkin Equals Orr's Great Batting Record," *Philadelphia Record*, Wednesday Morning, June 17, 1885, 4.

"THE AMERICAN ASSOCIATION: Games Played June 25," *Sporting Life*, Volume 5, Number 12, July 1, 1885, 6.

"ON THE DIAMOND FIELD," *The New York Times*, Friday, Jun 26, 1885, page 2.

"BASE-BALL: Chicago 31, Buffalo 7," *Chicago Tribune*, Wednesday, July 4, 1883, 7.

Bill Felber, Editor. *Inventing Baseball: The 100 Greatest Games of the 19th Century*. Phoenix, AZ: Society for American Baseball Research, Inc., 2013.

John B. Foster, Editor (Compiled by Charles D. White). *Spalding's Official Base Ball Record*, part of the Spalding "Red Cover" Series of Athletic Handbooks, No. 59R. New York, NY: American Sports Publishing Company, 1924.

John B. Foster, Editor (Compiled by Charles D. White). *The Little Red Book: Spalding's Official Base Ball Record*, part of the Spalding's Athletic Library, No. 59B. New York, NY: American Sports Publishing Company, 1928.

Notes

1. The day was a little cool, given the time of year, with a temperature of about 64°F, the skies were partly cloudy and there was a light breeze from the southwest.

2. There was a game played on July 3, 1883, between the Chicago White Stockings and the Buffalo Bisons in which Chicago registered 32 hits, including 16 extra base hits, 14 of which were doubles, and 50 total bases.

3. The four consecutive batters that were walked by Bakely were Brouthers, Johnston, Quinn, and Smith which forced in a run and the batter that was hit by Bakely was Ganzel which forced in another run.

4. Regarding the three triples, it may have been the NL record at the time. I was unable to find a reference that categorically stated when the single game record for triples by an individual was established prior to the Joyce performance.

The Colonel and Hug

The Odd Couple...Not Really

Steve Steinberg and Lyle Spatz

Jacob Ruppert believed that hiring Miller Huggins as his manager after the 1917 season was the first and most important step in turning the Yankees from also-rans into champions. Under Ruppert's ownership and Huggins's leadership, the Yankees would dominate the decade of the 1920s, winning six pennants and three World Series.

At first glance, the two could not have been more different. Ruppert, an urbane New Yorker, was a man of great wealth, which he used freely to indulge himself. He had a mansion on Fifth Avenue, a country estate, and a 113-foot yacht. He raced and bred horses and dogs, and he collected rare books, art, and jade pieces. He also was a meticulous dresser. "He commonly carries a serious expression," wrote Damon Runyon. "He wears clothes of the latest cut, is very particular about his apparel, but never deviates from snowy white linen shirts and collars."[1]

Pitcher Waite Hoyt said of Ruppert, "His Rolls Royce always looked brand new when it was 10 years old. He was that way about everything."[2] Author Jack Moore wrote, "In many ways he belonged to the world of New York society that Edith Wharton described so beautifully and devastatingly in her novels. ... He relished the title [Colonel] and conducted his affairs with the Yankees as though he were their general."[3]

Huggins, a no-nonsense Midwesterner, had little interest in what others thought of him, and certainly

not what they thought of his appearance. He had no extravagances. His greatest joy came from fishing, smoking his pipe, and golf, which he started playing late in life.

These differences came close to dooming the Ruppert-Huggins collaboration at the start, according to *Sporting News* publisher J. G. Taylor Spink's description of their first meeting. "Coupled with his gnome-like appearance, the cap accentuated his midget stature, and made Huggins look like an unemployed jockey. And Colonel Ruppert, an immaculate dresser, instinctively shied away from a cap-wearing job applicant."[4]

Ruppert, especially as a younger man, was a partygoer and a member of many social clubs. As a congressman, he was a regular at White House receptions, held by his fellow New Yorker Teddy Roosevelt. Home in New York, he would often dine in one of the city's better restaurants, like Delmonico's, and then spend the evening socializing at the Lambs Club, the New York Athletic Club, or one of the several German societies to which he belonged.

He was also a risk-taker, especially when it came to fast cars. In 1902, he and fellow congressman Oliver Belmont were arrested in Washington for driving almost 20 miles per hour, well above the posted speed limit.[5] Ten years later, Ruppert was racing his motorcycle against a garage owner driving a car. When the car slammed into a tree, the driver was killed.[6]

Huggins's typical evening was spent at home with his sister, Myrtle, with whom he lived. And the only time he may have been seen in a car that was going too fast, it would have been as a passenger. He would sometimes ride along with Babe Ruth, another fast and risky driver.

Yet, in the more important matter of building winning baseball teams, Ruppert and Huggins were surprisingly alike.

1. Both had been reared by strict fathers, who had attempted to dictate their careers. Ruppert's father had been more successful at it, dismissing his son's early dreams of being a baseball player and later, his plan to enter West Point. "My dad, who was a brewer,

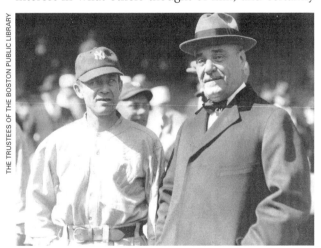

The architects of the Yankees' dominance in the 1920s, Miller Huggins and Jacob Ruppert.

said, 'This West Point stuff, this ball playing business, is all nonsense. You go into the brewery.'"[7]

Huggins was less the obedient son. "The head of our family," recalled his sister Myrtle, "was a strict Methodist who abhorred frivolity and listed baseball as such, especially baseball played on Sunday."[8] Huggins became a ball player in spite of his father's wishes, usually under an assumed name when he began playing as a semiprofessional. And on those evenings spent at home with Myrtle, he would sometimes have a glass of wine, something which his father would have frowned on.

2. By nature, both Ruppert and Huggins were intensely private men—aloof, blunt, and not interested in their personal popularity. "Despite the fact that he is one of the smartest men that ever trod on a ball field, and is a lawyer in the bargain," wrote a *New York Sun* columnist about Huggins, "he does not seem to realize what assets popularity and publicity can be to a successful manager."[9]

It was much the same with Ruppert: He was a "regal mystery" said one reporter. "There was about him a reserve that made such a [close] relationship difficult."[10] The Colonel "was not one to pal around with the boys," Rud Rennie wrote in the *New York Herald-Tribune*. "For the most part, he was aloof and brusque."[11] Even his fellow owners found him distant.

3. Neither man was "colorful," someone reporters could rely on to do or say something provocative. Huggins had no more personality, wrote one New York reporter, "than a stark old oak tree against a gray winter sky."[12] Ruppert also had a bland personality. A 1934 editorial in *Baseball Magazine* noted, "The genial Colonel has never cared overmuch for the spotlight. … He is, first and foremost, a businessman, and showmanship is not his forte."[13]

4. Both were lonely men. Damon Runyon wrote, "Huggins always struck me as rather a pathetic figure in many ways early in his managerial career. He was inconspicuous in size and personality. He seemed to be a solitary chap, with few intimates. He wasn't much of a mixer. … But the little man 'had something,' no doubt of that."[14]

Ruppert, too, was lonely. "He was a simple man, and direct, but he had moments of loneliness," explained George W. Sutton Jr., who handled public relations for him. "Sometimes when he was busy he would stop and ask me about my farm, and talk like that until something turned him back into the business machine."[15]

5. Being bachelors only added to their loneliness, though they had different views on marriage. Huggins told Dan Daniel, "That's my one big regret. Married life gives a man varied interests."[16]

When he was younger, Ruppert said he did not want to marry because "it was too much fun being single."[17] He later said, "There are too many attractive girls in New York to ever allow a man to be lonesome."[18]

As an older man, he became close to Helen Weyant, a woman who became the informal hostess at his upstate mansion. She was much younger than Ruppert, and there is no evidence of a romantic relationship between them, or between Ruppert and any woman. He was more like a kindly old uncle; so kindly, he left Weyant a third of his estate.

6. While Ruppert was a fan the Yankees, he still treated them as a business. "If a machine in my business wears out I replace it," he said. "I am always looking at improved machines; improved property. I study efficiency in business. Baseball is a sport; it is a hobby, but it is a business. I want the most out of baseball."[19]

Yet a similar quotation from Huggins could easily be mistaken for something Ruppert said. Operating a ball club, he believed, was "the quality of being able to look ahead and size up the future by the signs of the present. … In a way this business instinct is nothing but a keen gambling sense. It is knowing when to throw a lot of new capital into the organization."[20]

7. Having control of their "business" was key to both men. To the extent possible, they wanted to control their own destinies. Ruppert couldn't coexist with his partner, Til Huston. Ed Barrow described them as "two self-willed personalities, who by background, manner, and outlook were worlds apart."[21] Likewise,

Huggins couldn't coexist with Branch Rickey. When Rickey became his boss in St. Louis, after the 1917 season, he knew all personnel decisions would be made by Rickey and left the Cardinals for the Yankees.

8. The Colonel and "Hug" were excellent judges of personnel, who looked for the same personality traits in potential hires, which were a man's disposition and his belief in putting the team first. Ruppert's key hires were brilliant. In addition to Huggins, he brought in Ed Barrow as his business manager, Joe McCarthy as a successor to Huggins, and George Weiss to develop and run the farm system.[22]

Few men Huggins traded away went on to star elsewhere. No less an authority than John McGraw had said back in 1915, "Miller Huggins is my ideal of a real leader.... He can take a player who has shown only a mediocre supply of ability on some team and transform him into a star with his club."[23]

9. Dealing with Babe Ruth's often childish and outrageous behavior caused trials and tribulations for both, particularly Huggins. Eventually, they each would have to confront the Babe, and each would come out on top.

Ruth had repeatedly ignored his manager and violated club rules for years. In 1925, with the Yankees and the Babe in deep slumps (they were 27 games out of first place, and he was batting .266), Huggins decided it was a good time for him to crack down. With Ruppert's backing, he suspended Ruth for two weeks and fined him $5,000. The following season, Ruth and the Yankees made stunning comebacks. The Babe led the New Yorkers to the first of three consecutive pennants, leading the league in runs, runs batted in, and the first of six consecutive home run crowns.

The ultimate Ruppert-Ruth confrontation came ten years later, in 1935. Ruppert had repeatedly refused Ruth's request to manage the club. With the 39-year-old Babe's aging body and on-field performance breaking down, Ruppert declared it was time for the Yankees to move on. "The success of the Yankees is no longer intertwined with, and dependent upon, the success of Ruth," he said.[24]

Despite the headaches he gave them, Ruppert and Huggins benefited greatly from having Ruth on their team. He not only led them to success on the field, his popularity had helped them take away a good portion of New York's fans from John McGraw's Giants.

"Up to a couple of years ago, the Yanks were just the 'other New York team.' But the immense personal popularity of Babe Ruth and the dynamite in the rest of that Yankee batting order have made the Yanks popular with the element that loves the spectacular," wrote Sid Mercer.[25]

10. Both Ruppert and Huggins understood the demands of owning and managing a team in New York. The New York fans and press were no different than they are today. Keeping them happy was a constant battle, something both men understood. "The psychology of New York is entirely different.... You've got to make good!" Huggins said.[26] "The whole trouble is that we [the Yankees and the Giants] are New York clubs," he said. "If we were located in Kankakee things would be different.... 'Beat New York' is the slogan of the land, and when it can't be done, the boys start slinging mud."[27]

"This is one city where the public demands a winner, but you can't palm off inferior goods on them," Ruppert had said as early as 1918.[28] "Yankee fans want a winning ball club," he explained a decade later. "They won't support a loser."[29]

Ruppert and Huggins with Yankees' front office fixture (1921–45) Ed Barrow.

11. Both men had a fierce will to win. When Huggins was a young player on the Reds, Ned Hanlon, who had managed the legendary, win-at-all-costs Baltimore Orioles of the 1890s, said of his attitude (and that of one of his teammates), "The game is everything to them. Victories make them feel as though they owned the earth; defeat makes them angry."[30]

As the manager of the Yankees, Huggins said, "It is our desire to have a pennant winner each year indefinitely. New York fans want championship ball, and the Yankees can be counted on to provide it."[31]

Ruppert's approach was no different. "I want to win the pennant five more years in a row if we can. We are going ahead to get any good ball player we can. Winning pennants is the business of the New York Yankees."[32] Ruppert said, "Huggins was never content. He always felt that no matter how strong the Yankees were, they could be just a little stronger."[33]

Just before he died, Ruppert revealed the winning formula. "Money alone does not bring success. You must also have brains, organization, and enterprise. Then you've got something."[34]

12. Because of their intense desire to win, the difficulties of staying on top haunted Ruppert and Huggins, as they agonized over the Yankees' success. W. O. McGeehan said of Ruppert, "The Colonel has an infinite capacity for mental anguish and likes to do his worrying early."[35] Ruppert said in early 1928, "A slide, a broken leg, and the finest ball player may jump into baseball oblivion. That has happened before; it may happen again. We must have replacements."[36]

The 1927 Yankees had swept the World Series in four games and were already being talked about as the greatest team ever. Yet sportswriter Walter Trumbull observed at the baseball meetings that winter, "The case of Miller Huggins is almost pathetic. He is trying desperately to build up the Yankees. That is a tough job, a little perhaps, like trying to add a bit of height to Mount Everest."[37]

Despite cries from around the league to break up the Yankees, both men recognized the difficulties of staying on top. Ruppert's response to the other owners was to build up

Ruppert and Huggins with a familiar face of the Yankees: Babe Ruth.

their teams, not tear down his. He compared running the team to keeping his brewery on top, where if a part or a machine broke down, he replaced it.

Huggins's response to the "Break up the Yankees" crowd was more philosophical. In 1928, after the Yankees had again swept the Series, Huggins sounded an alarm. "Time will take care of the Yankees, as it takes care of everything else. This team, powerful as it is, will crack and break, no matter what any of us does to keep it up. The history of all great teams and all great personal fortunes is the same. They dominate the scene for a while but they don't last. Great teams fall apart and have to be put together again."[38]

13. Each had faced substantial obstacles along the way, Huggins on the field and Ruppert with his brewery and with challenges to his ownership of the Yankees. Huggins had to deal with repeated challenges to his authority, beginning in 1913, when he took over as manager of the Cardinals. A 1922 *Sporting News* editorial noted, "Perhaps never in the history of the game has a manager been so flouted, reviled, and ridiculed."[39]

Prohibition robbed Ruppert of his primary source of income with the brewery. And he had to take on (and take down) the president of his league, Ban Johnson, and then his co-owner, Til Huston.

14. Baseball meant the world to the two lonely bachelors and brought meaning to their lives. Ruppert told Taylor Spink in 1937, "It seems to me I never have got around to doing the

things I wanted to do most. For example, when I was a youngster, I wanted to be a ball player." He also said, "I was never able to be a major league catcher. That was my boyhood ambition."[40]

In 1918, three years after purchasing the Yankees, Ruppert wrote, "I have got a lot of excitement out of this magnate business and no doubt there is much more coming to me before I am through."[41] After acquiring Ruth, Ruppert told the press that it was his "life purpose" to give New York a championship team.[42] And in 1923, "Here I am deeper than ever in baseball and more in love with the game than ever."[43]

Damon Runyon wrote after the 1923 championship season, "The possession of great wealth is an old story to him. There was no novelty for him, no thrill, in the buying excesses of great wealth. It was the thing that money couldn't buy that brought him his big, bright hour."[44]

Huggins once said, "I fell in love.... The object of my love, though, was no lady. It was

Although on the surface, Huggins and Ruppert seemed worlds apart, the two men had striking similarities.

baseball."[45] He had little outside of baseball in his life. On off days during the season, he would often go to the Yankees' offices downtown. "Baseball is my life. I'd be lost without it. Maybe, as you say, it will get me some day—but as long as I die in harness, I'll be happy."[46] And of course it did get him, and he did die in harness.

Unlike Ruppert, Huggins did not want recognition. Christy Walsh said, "He played his part on the ball field without giving a thought to the grandstand or the critics. As for publicity, he loathed it almost as much as he belittled so-called personal popularity."[47] Even Walsh, Huggins's agent, said: "You know him intimately, and you don't know him at all."[48]

Ruppert told sportswriter Sid Mercer: "Take it from me, Sid, money is only a burden after you have enough for a comfortable living. It becomes a responsibility.... Here I am trying to snatch a few days with my ball team and I'll bet you I'll have to cut my vacation short."[49]

15. Sometimes, when the pressure of managing in New York became overwhelming, Huggins would reflect on his earliest days in baseball. "I probably had the most fun in my baseball career when I captained the Fleischmann Mountaineers.... That was a joy ride that year—1900—we won about 60 out of 66 games."[50] Bob Connery, a lifelong friend who scouted for Huggins in St. Louis, said said, "Those five years with the Cardinals were happier than any five years in New York, even when Huggins was winning pennants."[51]

Ruppert also longed for some of the simpler pleasures of the game, denied him by his position. He lamented to Taylor Spink in 1937, "I could not buy the liberty and the freedom of the youngster who could barely spare 50 cents that got him into the bleachers. That's money, and that's responsibility for you."[52]

16. These were men of impeccable integrity. During the Black Sox scandal, Ruppert promised that, "for my life and yours, baseball will be kept clean."[53] Damon Runyon once wrote, "I believe Colonel Ruppert would sacrifice his entire baseball investment rather than knowingly be a party to an unsportsmanlike action."[54]

His reaction to the Yankees' sweep of the 1927 World Series sweep is instructive. "I am happier in what I believe is a great thing for baseball," he said. "It will cost us something like $200,000, but there can be no talk now of stringing a series out. We wanted to win in four straight games and we did, because we have a wonderful team."[55]

Huggins established his reputation for decency at the outset of his professional career. When St. Paul Saints owner George Lennon sold Huggins to the Cincinnati Reds, he told reporters, "He is a finer man than he is a ballplayer."[56]

Along with integrity, both had a sense of duty to take care of people. Ruppert's aide, George Perry wrote, "He was a hard-boiled man to some, but they judged him entirely from externals. The charity he gave never will be known. He never sought publicity that way."[57]

During the days of the Federal League war, when St. Louis had three Major League teams and the Cardinals' finances were shaky, Huggins covered the team's payroll out of his own pocket. *The Sporting News* wrote in an editorial, "He [Huggins] was all there was to the club, practically under petticoat management even to the extent of being its financial savior."[58]

17. Moreover, Ruppert and Huggins were fiercely loyal to and trusting of one another. After the 1922 World Series, the Yankees' second consecutive Series loss to the Giants, the press again was calling for Ruppert to replace Huggins. But the colonel remained steadfast; he re-signed Huggins and said, "Maybe these people who are firing him and hiring others know more about it than I do.... This talk is ridiculous. We are for Huggins, first, last and all the time."[59] A year later, Huggins rewarded him with the Yankees' first world championship.

Then in the disastrous summer of 1925, with Yankees on their way to a seventh-place finish, Ruppert said, "It would be shabby treatment to remove him now or at any other time.... Huggins can remain in control of my team as long as he feels like it."[60]

After the 1924 season, Huggins declared, "Ruppert is a wonderful man to work with.

After seven years of close association I guess two men get to understand each other pretty well. If I really want a man, he will go the limit to get him. And he never tires of winners."[61]

18. Additionally, both men were visionaries. Ruppert saw the potential of Sunday baseball, building Yankee Stadium, and building up the farm system, but he was by no means perfect: he lagged in the areas of integration, night baseball, and the radio broadcasts of games.

Huggins, who had been a quintessential deadball-type player, foresaw the coming of the longball era and urged Ruppert to acquire Ruth.

Though seemingly very different, together the shared legacy of Jacob Ruppert and Miller Huggins was the establishment of an enduring winning franchise, a dynasty that lived long after they were gone. "Getting him was the first and most important step we took toward making the Yankees champions," Ruppert said. "Him" was not Babe Ruth, but rather Miller Huggins.[62]

Sportswriter Warren Brown wrote: "We never have run across anyone else who stressed winning as much as Col. Jake Ruppert."[63] "Winning was a mania with him," wrote Sid Mercer after Ruppert's death.[64]

"The combination of brains and money," wrote F. C. Lane of the two New York clubs (also John McGraw's Giants), "is a hard pair to beat.... The attempt to divorce wealth and intelligence from all advantage has never succeeded anywhere."[65]

Rupert and Huggins would have one more thing in common: perhaps fittingly, both would be long overlooked for formal recognition, which in baseball means election to the Hall of Fame. Huggins did not reach Cooperstown until 1964 and Ruppert not until 2013. ◼

Notes

1. Damon Runyon, *New York American*, December 27, 1924.
2. Eugene Murdock, *Baseball Players and their Times: Oral Histories of the Game* (Westport, CT: Meckler Publishing, 1991), 41.
3. Jack B. Moore, *Joe DiMaggio: A Bio-Bibliography* (Westport, CT: Greenwood Press, 1986), 37.
4. Spink's account appeared years later in "Looping the Loops," *Sporting News*, October 21, 1943. Spink was not present at the meeting but probably received firsthand accounts from both Ruppert and Huggins.
5. "O. H. P. Belmont, Too Speedy, Arrested," *New York Herald*, March 26, 1902.
6. "John Gernon Killed Racing Mr. Ruppert," *New York Herald*, June 29, 1912.
7. J. G. Taylor Spink, "Three and One," *The Sporting News*, August 19, 1937.

8. Myrtle Huggins, as told to John B. Kennedy, "Mighty Midget." *Collier's*, May 24, 1930, 18. Years later, James Huggins became reconciled to his son's playing baseball and even bragged that the skill he showed was hereditary. Henry F. Pringle, "A Small Package," *New Yorker*, October 8, 1927, 25.

9. Shortstop, "Huggins Fails to Snare Popularity," *New York Sun*, June 15,1919.

10. Frank Graham, *The New York Yankees* (New York: G. P. Putnam's Sons, 1948), 248.

11. Richard Tofel, *A Legend in the Making: The New York Yankees in 1939* (Chicago: Ivan R, Dee, 2003), 8.

12. Hyatt Daab, "Timely News and Views in the World of Sport," *New York Evening Telegram*, October 26, 1920.

13. Editorial, *Baseball Magazine*, March 1934, 434.

14. Damon Runyon, "Between You and Me," *New York American*, September 27, 1929.

15. "New Owners of Yanks Recover Enough to Talk," *Chicago Daily Tribune*, January 22, 1939.

16. Dan Daniel, "Late Chief's Policies to Govern New Yank Pilot," *New York Evening Telegram*, September 27, 1929. Daniel revealed these comments only after Huggins's death.

17. Fred Lieb, *Baseball as I Have Known It* (Lincoln: Bison Books, 1996), 228.

18. Betty Kirk, "Jacob Ruppert, 'Born Bachelor,' Sees Day Coming with Marriage Extinct," *New York Evening Telegram*, June 13, 1928.

19. Frank F. O'Neill, "Loud Wails in Wake of Yank Deal," *New York Evening Journal*, January 6, 1928.

20. Will Wedge, "Business Instinct in Baseball," *New York Sun*, April 17, 1926.

21. Edward G. Barrow, with James M. Kahn, *My Fifty Years in Baseball* (New York: Cowan-McCann, 1951), 123.

22. Former Yankees pitcher Bob Shawkey was Huggins's immediate successor, but Ruppert replaced him after one season.

23. "Hug May Capture Pennant, but not in 1915—Says McGraw," *St. Louis Post-Dispatch*, June 23, 1915.

24. Dan Daniel, "Ruppert Sees Boom Year and Pennant for Yanks," *New York Evening Telegram*, undated article in Jacob Ruppert file, National Baseball Hall of Fame Library and Archives.

25. Sid Mercer, "Whole City Busy with 'Dope,'" *New York Evening Journal*, October 3, 1921.

26. Miller Huggins, "Serial Story of his Baseball Career: Getting New York Angle Huggins' Biggest Problem at Start of Managership," *Chapter 50, San Francisco Chronicle*, March 11, 1924.

27. Joseph Gordon, "Yankee Pilot Waxes Furious at Accusation," *New York American*, December 16, 1927.

28. Jacob Ruppert, "Building a Winning Club in New York: An Interview with Col. Jacob Ruppert," *Baseball Magazine*, June 1918, 253.

29. Rud Rennie, "Stop Squawking!" *Collier's*, March 4, 1939, 11.

30. Ned Hanlon, "Jake [Weimer] and Little Hug are Shining Examples," *Cincinnati Times-Star*, April 30, 1906.

31. Miller Huggins, *The Sporting News*, August 4, 1927.

32. Frank F. O'Neill, "Loud Wails in Wake of Yank Deal," *New York Evening Journal*, January 6, 1928.

33. Frederick G. Lieb, "Ruppert Praises Word of Huggins," *New York Evening Telegram*, September 21, 1923.

34. Rud Rennie, "Stop Squawking!" 61.

35. W. O. McGeehan, "Down the Line," *New York Herald Tribune*, March 11, 1925.

36. Frank F. O'Neill, "Loud Wails in Wake of Yank Deal," *New York Evening Journal*, January 6, 1928.

37. Walter Trumbull, "The Listening Post," *New York Evening Post*, December 13, 1927.

38. Joe Vila, "Setting the Pace," *New York Sun*, December 26, 1928.

39. Editorial, *The Sporting News*, October 26, 1922.

40. J. G. Taylor Spink, "Three and One," *The Sporting News*, August 19, 1937.

41. Jacob Ruppert, "Building a Winning Club in New York," 254.

42. "Ruth Bought by New York Americans for $125,000, Highest Price in Baseball's Annals," *The New York Times*, January 6, 1920.

43. W. O. McGeehan, "Ruppert Lives to Learn Baseball Men Have Class," *The Sporting News*, December 27, 1923.

44. Damon Runyon, "Deserved Tribute to Colonel Ruppert," *The 1924 Reach Official American League Guide*, 243.

45. Miller Huggins, "How I Got that Way," *New York Evening Post*, October 2, 1926.

46. Ford Frick, "Huggins Born 49 Years Ago, Starred with Cardinals," *New York Evening Journal*, September 25, 1929.

47. Christy Walsh, *South Bend* [Indiana] *News-Times*, September 1929, exact date not known.

48. Warren Brown, "So They Tell Me," *Chicago Herald and Examiner*, September 27, 1929.

49. Sid Mercer, "The Colonel," *New York Journal-American*, January 17, 1939.

50. Miller Huggins, "Huggins Wins his Sixth Flag," *New York Sun*, September 29, 1928. Future Major League stars on the Fleischmann Mountaineers team included Doc White and Red Dooin.

51. Fred Lieb, *The St. Louis Cardinals* (New York: G. P. Putnam's Sons, 1948), 69.

52. J. G. Taylor Spink, "Three and One," *The Sporting News*, August 19, 1937.

53. William L. Chenery, "Foul Ball!" *The New York Times*, October 3, 1920.

54. Damon Runyon, "Runyon Says," *New York American*, December 27, 1924.

55. "Ruppert Happy, Though Smile Cost $200,000 in Receipts," *The New York Times*, October 9, 1927.

56. *Cincinnati Commercial Tribune*, "Huggins Got $1,000 of Purchase Money," March 8, 1904.

57. George Perry, "Three and One: Looking Them Over with J. G. Taylor Spink," *The Sporting News*, March 2, 1939.

58. "The Change Huggins Makes," *The Sporting News*, November 1, 1917.

59. John Kieran, "Huggins Will Manage Yanks Next Season, Says Club Owner," *New York Herald Tribune*, October 10, 1922.

60. Joe Vila, "Ruth May Pay Heavy Penalty for Getting Back too Quickly," *The Sporting News*, July 2, 1925.

61. Frederick G. Lieb, "Huggins Will Stay with Yanks Indefinitely; No Longer has Any Thought of Retiring," *New York Telegram and Evening Mail*," December 26, 1924.

62. Jacob Ruppert, "The Ten Million Dollar Toy." *Saturday Evening Post*, March 28, 1931, 18.

63. Warren Brown, "All in a Week," *Chicago Herald and Examiner*, January 15, 1939.

64. Sid Mercer, "The Colonel: Victory Always his Aim," *New York Journal-American*, January 20, 1939.

65. F. C. Lane, "The Shadow of New York on the Baseball Diamond," *Baseball Magazine*, August 1923, 398.

Babe Ruth, Brooklyn Dodgers Coach

John McMurray

Of all the facets of Babe Ruth's long and distinguished career, his time as a coach with the Brooklyn Dodgers in 1938 has received the least consideration. Perhaps that is justified: Ruth coached for less than a full season with the Dodgers, and first base coaches seldom make an obvious imprint. Yet Ruth's time with Brooklyn is consequential, both because, even as a non-player, Ruth was the team's biggest attraction, and because his time with the Dodgers effectively put an end to any remaining prospects the former New York Yankees star still had to become a major league manager.

NO OPPORTUNITY TO MANAGE WITH THE YANKEES

Ruth, as is well known, had longed to become manager of the New York Yankees, only to be passed over as player-manager when Joe McCarthy was hired prior to the 1931 season. According to Leigh Montville, Ruth considered the position of player-manager with the Yankees to be a "natural progression," and Ruth was cognizant that other prominent contemporary stars such as Ty Cobb, Rogers Hornsby, and Tris Speaker had each taken on such a role. Still, team owner Jacob Ruppert, mindful of Ruth's extensively documented immaturity, got to the crux of the matter when he asked his star player, "How can you manage a team when you can't manage yourself?"[1]

Mark Armour and Dan Levitt have noted that Ruppert made a habit of hiring "highly skilled men who offered very little drama or personality," such as Ed Barrow, who served essentially as the team's general manager. Ruth was the opposite: jovial, mercurial, and not focused enough to fulfill the job's responsibilities at a high level. "[T]he idea of [Ruth] being the Yankee manager seems completely incongruous from what we know about Ruppert, and, particularly, Barrow. The two might have wanted the likeable Ruth to manage in the Major Leagues—but certainly not for the Yankees."[2]

Ruth had hurt his own cause in attempting to become a major league manager by adopting a surly tone with McCarthy, by refusing to consider minor league managerial positions, and even by reportedly choosing to ignore an invitation following the 1933 season to meet with Detroit Tigers owner Frank Navin about the team's managerial job, electing instead to go on vacation in Hawaii. It was against this backdrop of squandered chances and self-inflicted setbacks that Ruth found himself still desiring a position as a major league manager but without any plausible chance of ever taking over the Yankees.

AFTER THE YANKEES, RUTH JOINS THE BRAVES— AN UNHAPPY EXPERIENCE

As recounted by Montville, Judge Emil Fuchs, his team in severe financial straits, wanted to acquire Ruth from the Yankees to play for his Boston Braves in 1935, primarily to draw fans to the ballpark. "That is all [Fuchs] wanted, an attraction. He wanted the Babe to ride the elephant."[3] But Fuchs's promises, including his strong implication that Ruth was in line to manage the team, were misleading and unsupported.

In enticing Ruth to join the Braves as a free agent, "the judge would offer a bunch of fine-sounding but hollow inducements that contained phrases like 'vice-president' and 'stock options' and 'opportunity to manage' while gaming with Jacob Ruppert to get the aging Ruth out of New York.[4] "The deal had a stench to it from the beginning," said Montville. "[Ruth] said he wanted to be a manager, period. The other parties took that desire and bent it to fit their needs. The Babe never knew what hit him."[5]

So, when Ruth's on-field performance in Boston was subpar (a .181 batting average in 28 games) and his physical ability to play waned, it was perhaps a surprise only to Ruth that Fuchs would want no more of him. The Associated Press summarized the situation between Ruth and Fuchs concisely: "Finally, their differences took so acute a turn that Ruth, in sheer disgust, quit the game."[6]

Montville said Claire Ruth called the day that she and Babe left Boston "one of the blackest days of their lives," while Ruth reportedly labeled Fuchs a "dirty double-crosser" who "would double cross a hot bun."[7] In joining the Dodgers three years later, Ruth, surely, had to be expecting better treatment and at least a reasonable chance that he would one day become the team's manager.

THE DODGERS COME CALLING

A) The state of affairs with the Brooklyn Dodgers in 1938

Burleigh Grimes—short-tempered and terse, and therefore the opposite of Ruth in personal temperament—was then Brooklyn's manager, though Grimes would never come close in that position to the high level of success he had enjoyed during nine seasons as a star pitcher for the team. In 1937, Grimes's first season as manager, Brooklyn finished sixth in an eight-team league, and, as of June 18, 1938, was sitting at an undistinguished 22–31. Five three-game losing streaks, two four four-game losing streaks, and one five-game losing streak during the first ten weeks of the season took away from whatever temporary pep was generated by the team's occasional offensive outbursts.

Dolph Camilli, who joined Brooklyn in 1938, was recalled in his *New York Times* obituary as "the first building block in the Dodgers' recovery from a string of dreary seasons."[8] The pall, though, clearly still hung over the team in 1938, when Camilli was the team's unquestioned top performer. Camilli led Brooklyn with 24 home runs, more than doubling any teammate's total. Pitching was a sore spot, as all but two regular Brooklyn hurlers had losing records for the season, the performances of Vito Tamulis and Freddie Fitzsimmons standing out from the rest.

Catcher Babe Phelps, an All-Star in 1938, played in fewer than half of the team's games due to injury.[9] The lineup was otherwise a collection of players who never made a notable mark (Johnny Hudson, Ernie Koy, and Goody Rosen) or older stars with little left (like eventual Hall of Famers Kiki Cuyler and Waite Hoyt). At a time when personal attachments to uniform numbers admittedly meant less than they do today, the incongruity of the Dodgers' 1938 season was neatly encapsulated by the fact that slick-fielding second baseman Pete Coscarart, who hit no home runs that season, continued to wear Ruth's famous number three uniform number—even after Ruth joined the team.[10]

Beyond manager Grimes, the real influence on the shape of the 1938 Dodgers was held by executive Larry MacPhail and team captain Leo Durocher. Durocher, then 32, had a mere .219 batting average that season as the club's shortstop, but he held an outsized influence on the team, as Brooklyn's unofficial manager-in-waiting and a constant check on Grimes's already shaky managerial influence. With MacPhail, Durocher, and Grimes—probably in that order—as the team's day-to-day center of influence, the 1938 Brooklyn Dodgers had a contentious trio pulling the strings.

B) Receiving a contract to coach in Brooklyn

Then, on June 15, 1938, against the Dodgers at Ebbets Field, Cincinnati's Johnny Vander Meer threw the second of his consecutive no-hitters, with Durocher making the last out.[11] In a season made up largely of lows, being no-hit at home during the first major league night game ever played in New York was surely the nadir of the season to date.[12] After that game, the *New York Times* bitingly described the Dodgers as "being reduced to the irreducible minimum of baseball accomplishment."[13] At the same time, Ruth was in attendance, apparently only as a spectator, and his appearance at that game, according to biographer Robert Creamer, left an impression on MacPhail and provided motivation to hire Ruth:

"Vander Meer's feat was front-page news, but earlier in the evening the biggest excitement in the ballpark was the arrival of Babe," said Creamer. "A stir ran through the crowd and fans swarmed around him. Larry MacPhail, who had become executive vice-president of the Dodgers that year, was doing everything he could to pump life into the then-moribund franchise. He remembered the Babe Ruth Day he had put on in Cincinnati three years earlier, and the crowd the Babe attracted."[14]

Given the unenthusiastic attendance at Dodgers games and the challenge the team faced in drawing fans against two other strong teams in New York, it made sense to try to recruit the former Yankee star, who had been out of baseball—and largely out of public view—since leaving baseball as an active player in 1935.

"To have [Ruth] in a Dodger uniform would be a coup," said Creamer. "MacPhail discussed the idea with his manager, Burleigh Grimes, and with Leo Durocher, the Dodger shortstop who had been made team captain in late May. MacPhail was grooming

Burleigh Grimes was manager of the Dodgers in 1938, but Larry MacPhail was already grooming Leo Durocher to take over the helm.

Durocher to succeed Grimes, who was well aware that this was his last year as manager. Larry talked to Ruth and offered him $15,000 to put on a uniform and be a coach for the rest of the year. The Vander Meer game was on June 15; Ruth met with MacPhail, Grimes and Durocher the next day and signed a contract."[15]

According to the Associated Press, "Ruth was playing golf in Tuckahoe, N.Y., when Larry S. MacPhail, energetic general manager of the Dodgers, announced he had been signed for the duration of the 1938 season. 'It's great to be back,' the Babe said. 'I would have been back long before if I had the chance to hook on with some major league club. But what could I do? I didn't get any offers. You can't make a guy give you a job. When I was offered one I grabbed it quick.'"[16]

There was one personal drawback to the timing of Ruth's signing: "The only lament the Babe had was that he would have to default in the Leawood club tournament—just when he appeared on his way toward winning another silver cup. 'Not only that,' the Babe groaned, 'but I'll have to blow another tournament at St. Albans. I'm in that, and winning that, too.'"[17]

Accounts of Ruth's signing differ. Whereas Creamer wrote that Ruth was signed to a contract the day after the Vander Meer game for what he implies was Brooklyn's first and only offer, a contemporary Associated Press story said that the Dodgers had been negotiating with Ruth "for a week or more" and that there was at least one prior contract offer.[18] That said, there seems little doubt that Ruth's appearance at the Vander Meer no-hitter was the serendipitous tipping point which led to his arrival in Brooklyn.

Interestingly, the *Chicago Daily Tribune*, too noting weeklong rumors that Ruth was to join the Dodgers as a coach, also cited the influence of Ford Frick in facilitating the deal:

To some familiar with behind [sic] scenes working of baseball the hand of Ford Frick, the National league [sic] president, is seen. Frick, as a former baseball writer, was once Babe Ruth's ghostwriter and still is his friend. Frick sponsored MacPhail in Brooklyn. Thus, Frick is seen as bringing the two together on the Brooklyn club.[19]

Perhaps less plausibly, the same account cites an anonymous team official who claimed that it was Grimes who prodded the team to hire Ruth in the first place.[20]

Labeling Ruth as baseball's "forgotten man," the Associated Press account noted on the day after Ruth's hiring that "Brooklyn officials insisted that Burleigh Grimes would remain as manager, but baseball writers believed Ruth would take over the job no later than the start of the 1939 season."[21] The interplay between Ruth and Durocher would influence the latter portion of the 1938 Brooklyn Dodgers season more than any of the team's on-field accomplishments.

Ruth, too, quashed early rumblings that he was in line to take over as Brooklyn's manager:

"You'd like a club of your own, wouldn't you, Babe?" he was asked.

"Sure, I would," he replied, and then side-stepped the managerial comment by turning to the idea that he might own a club. It has been rumored in that past that the Babe would head a syndicate to buy the Brooklyns.

"But that would cost plenty of dough," he added. "And there's a chance I would lose all I made in baseball that way."

Officials of the Brooklyn club insist, however, that Grimes will remain as manager and that Ruth was hired as a coach and nothing more. No promise was given Ruth that eventually he would be given a shot at the manager's job, they declared.[22]

The team's record aside, Grimes's hold on the manager's job was shaky even before Ruth arrived. Grimes, who was described as having had "a stormy career in organized baseball" at the time he took over the Dodgers for Casey Stengel in 1936, found himself dealing with internal dissension on the club early in the 1938 season.[23] In May, pitcher Luke Hamlin, perturbed about being removed from a game, complained about it loudly to the press, leading MacPhail to comment that "this is the rankest piece of insubordination on the part of a major league baseball player since I have been in baseball. Some players think they are managing the club instead of Grimes."[24] MacPhail's assurance that Grimes was "the boss, and I mean boss" for the rest of the 1938 season was undoubtedly taken with a grain of salt by followers of the Dodgers.[25]

INITIAL SUCCESS

Ruth's presence on the field for the first time as a coach for the Brooklyn Dodgers quickly grabbed fans' attention and probably served as the highlight of Ruth's brief time in Brooklyn. Creamer recounted Ruth's first day of coaching:

His debut with the Dodgers was on June 19, a Sunday doubleheader with the Cubs, and it was a box office success. Artistically, it was not so good, because Babe did nothing in batting practice. But when he toddled out to the coaching lines in his familiar pitty-pat trot there was a great welcoming cheer. Except for Durocher, the players liked him and enjoyed his presence. His penchant for nicknames led him to call Dolf [sic] Camilli Cameo and Vito Tamulis Tomatoes. He told stories on the bench and made noise in the clubhouse. It was stimulating. Kiki Cuyler, a thirty-eight-year-old outfielder who starred with the Pirates and with the Cubs and was now in his last season, sat in a corner of the dugout watching him and said, "That guy is amazing. He even does something to me." Grimes said years later, "When he spoke everyone listened, all but Durocher."[26]

In noting Ruth's return, the Associated Press account made it clear that the day itself, which included Tot Pressnell returning from injury in the first game of a doubleheader and a no-hit attempt by Clay Bryant in the second game, was of secondary concern to the arrival of the former Yankees star: "What mattered was—the Babe was back."[27] The spectacle of Ruth's presence indeed was the story, as John Kieran declared, "Sound the loud trumpet! Or as John Keats put it: 'What pipes and timbrels? What wild ecstasy?' It's *Prometheus Unbound*, if a title from Shelley may be borrowed for the great occasion."[28]

The Associated Press noted, "The fans were on hand early to watch [Ruth's] every move, to nudge each other and whisper, 'I bet the old guy can still hit 'em. I'll bet he'll ruin that scoreboard in a week.' They cheered him when he went up to the plate in batting practice, went wild with delight when he smacked a long ball foul and gave him a hand no coach has ever received before when by quick thinking he held Pressnell at third in the midst of a crucial three-run rally for the Dodgers in the fifth inning of the opener.[29]

"Pressnell was rounding third when a wild throw shot past the Cubs' Rip Collins at first. The ball hit the grandstand and snapped back to the waiting Collins. As it did, Ruth wheeled and held Pressnell at third. He saved a run, for Collins' throw to Gabby Hartnett was fast and true."[30]

Even though Ruth was credited with saving a run during the team's 6–2 victory during the first game of that doubleheader, the team's run of consistently average play continued. Another three-game losing streak followed on the heels of Ruth's first game. From the time Ruth joined the Dodgers until he departed on October 13, the team accumulated a record of 47–49,

a modest improvement from its tepid start but not enough to make an impression with Brooklyn's fans, who had witnessed only six winning seasons since the Brooklyn Robins played in the 1920 World Series.

From a performance standpoint, the 1938 season for the Brooklyn Dodgers proceeded uneventfully. With the Dodgers frequently mired in seventh place, the team could not compare either with the first-place Yankees or with the pennant-contending Giants. Following Ruth's arrival, the Dodgers finished the month of June with a 4–5 record. The month of July was a bit better, with a month-long record of 16–13. It would be one of only two winning full months the Dodgers would enjoy all year long. The most distinctive moment from the second half of the season may well have been Brooklyn's victory over the St. Louis Cardinals in the first game of a doubleheader on August 2, the only major league game in which yellow baseballs have been used.

But, in terms of attendance—the primary reason why Ruth was signed as a coach, after all—Brooklyn was much improved. By the end of the 1938 season, the Dodgers would draw 663,087 fans at home, nearly 200,000 more fans than they did the year prior and close to 100,000 more than the National League average that season.[31] Ruth, without question, made his mark at the gate.

The early part of August proved to be quite eventful for Ruth. Following a loss to Cincinnati at home on August 5, Ruth raced to the hospital, where his daughter Julia had taken ill. According to *The New York Times*:

> George Herman (Babe) Ruth, rushed by motor cycle escort from Ebbets Field, where he had been coaching the Brooklyn Dodgers, gave his 22-year-old adopted daughter, Julia, 500 cubic centimeters of his blood in a transfusion at 6 o'clock last night at the Manhattan Eye, Ear and Throat Hospital, 210 East Sixty-fourth [sic] Street. After the transfusion, Ruth rested for an hour and then drove his wife, Mrs. Claire Ruth, home. Fifty youngsters from the neighborhood of the hospital met him at its doors as he left, asking for his autograph. He told them he was forced to refuse because his right arm felt weakened.[32]

Then, on August 7, Ruth was ejected from a game for the first time as a coach: "Umpire Beans Reardon gave Babe the 'heave-o' in the fourth inning of the first game of the double header with Cincinnati, when Ruth protested too vigorously a decision on Buddy Hassett. Trapped between bases, Hassett was ruled out when

Reardon held he ran off the base path. For several minutes, fans chanted, 'we want Ruth.'"[33]

A tempest in a teapot surrounding Ruth occurred one day later, when William Harridge, president of the American League, appeared to be dismissive of Ruth's value to the Dodgers, suggesting in an interview with George Kirksey of the United Press that the American League would eschew the "hoopla" that seemed to be present in the National League. Retorted MacPhail:

> I resent, however, the thinly veiled cracks about Babe Ruth, our coach. Mr. Harridge may consider Ruth a 'Ballyhoo Man.' In any event, Mr. Harridge could not find a place for him in the American League. Ruth has made a valuable contribution to the spirit and morale of our club. He has worked in harmony with Burleigh Grimes (manager), Tom Sheehan (a coach), and Leo Durocher (team captain), and he has been an inspiration to the younger players. There will be a place for Babe in our organization just as long as he desires to be with us.
>
> Harridge's slur at Ruth—coming from a head of an organization that has ballyhooed clowns like Nick Altrock and Al Schacht for years and directed at a man who did as much for the American League and baseball as did George Herman Ruth—is the essence of bad taste and punk sportsmanship.[34]

THE FEUD WITH LEO DUROCHER

Outside slights notwithstanding, it was the internal turmoil building up with Durocher that would prove decisive for Ruth. Bad blood had existed between Ruth and Durocher for nearly for a decade, when Durocher and Ruth were teammates with the Yankees for parts of three seasons. Famously, Ruth branded young Durocher as "The All-American Out" and accused Durocher of stealing Ruth's wristwatch, a charge fervently denied by Durocher.[35] Temperamentally, of course, it is difficult to conceive of two more different personalities than the good-natured, fun-loving Ruth and the combustible Durocher.

One issue related to their respective roles and performances: Durocher, according to Creamer, was "functioning more like the assistant manager Ruth had been in name only with the Braves."[36] At the same time, Ruth offered an ostensibly lackadaisical approach to relaying signals at first base, effectively leaving the duties to others, which in no way enhanced his appeal as a potential manager or raised his stature in the eyes of an already dismissive Durocher. "Ruth's attitude

The Dodgers wanted Ruth for his box office drawing power, not his coaching expertise.

towards signals was that of the Grand Seigneur, not the dim-witted peasant," said Creamer. "He tended to ignore them. As a Dodger coach, he was not involved with them—Grimes was often on the coaching lines himself, at third base—and Babe spent most of the time waving his arms, clapping his hands and shouting encouragement.[37]

More simply, Gerald Eskenazi writes: "In fact, Ruth could barely get the signals straight as the first base coach."[38]

It was a signal for a hit-and-run play, apparently during a game on August 19, which Ruth called for and relayed to Durocher at bat, that made things boil over.[39] Even though Durocher got the game-winning hit, Durocher, according to Eskenazi, was angry that Ruth had called for such a risky play with the game on the line in extra innings.[40]

"Durocher was furious and yelled that Babe didn't have the brains to give such a sign. Babe heard it. 'Durocher, I've been wanting to smack you down for a long time,' roared the Babe," writes Eskenazi.[41]

Creamer described it as a "flaming argument" between Durocher and Ruth in the clubhouse, which may also have involved Cookie Lavagetto.[42]

"[Ruth and Durocher] tangled and the scuffle left a mark under Ruth's eye," writes Creamer. "But Grimes said, 'Durocher got mad, not Ruth. I grabbed Leo and pushed him back. It's not true about a punch hitting Babe. Not a hand was laid on him, though I guess Leo would have belted him if I hadn't stopped him.' Whatever good will Ruth's presence in uniform might have generated among owners looking for a manager was destroyed by the mocking talk about his inability to give signals, and the dispute with Durocher served as the coup de grâce to his dying hope of ever being one."[43]

Whether Ruth threw a punch or not, he apparently took blame for the scuffle. The Washington Post noted after the season that "our old hero, Mr. George Herman Ruth, stubbed his toe again. Babe parked his golf clubs to become a Flatbush coach with a promise of landing the job if he could prove his talent. There was a fight in the clubhouse with Durocher. Boss Larry Macphail [sic] sided with 'Lippy' and the Babe lost again."[44]

PARTING FROM THE DODGERS

With a 69–80 season complete and the Dodgers being branded "the problem children of the major leagues," to the surprise of few, Grimes was dismissed as Brooklyn's manager on October 10 and replaced by Durocher.[45] Grieving from his own father's recent death, Durocher confirmed that Ruth would not continue coaching for Brooklyn. According to one account, "In naming his two coaches, Charlie Dressen and Bill Killifer (sic), Durocher said the Bambino had not 'been available' for a coaching job."[46] Euphemisms aside, Ruth obviously would not be afforded an opportunity to remain with the Brooklyn Dodgers with Durocher as manager.

As Ruth left the team, the suggestion endured that the tiff with Durocher was indeed the tipping point: "The Babe, after coming out of retirement this past midseason to coach at first base for the seventh place Dodgers, attracted bumper crowds. He and Durocher had a spat one day in the clubhouse, probably costing Ruth whatever chance he may have had to manage the team next year."[47]

Though not discussed in widespread terms until it actually occurred, Ruth's leaving the Dodgers seemed to have been expected for some time. "It was definite weeks ago that the Babe wouldn't be back with Brooklyn next year," according to the Boston Globe, more than a week after Ruth was let go. "He and Lippy Leo Durocher, the Dodgers' new manager, weren't exactly Damon and Pythias in one or two clubhouse sessions. So when Lippy Leo was apprised of his appointing to succeed 'Boiling Boily' Grimes (and most baseball people will tell you this was long before Larry MacPhail was willing to admit it to the general public) the Babe knew he and the daffiness boys were parting company."[48]

THE END OF RUTH'S MANAGERIAL PROSPECTS

A week later, the Boston Globe suggested that Ruth might soon have a managerial position in the American Association, which, of course, never materialized.[49] "I've had some offers—sure," he explained. "But they were nothing I wanted. You know, I don't have to worry about where my next meal is coming from, so I can take what I want."[50] Ruth's parting from the Dodgers had an air of finality to it, as he was not mentioned, at least publicly, for other managing opportunities at the time.

A major league managing opportunity, of course, never came, even though Ruth's desire to manage was well-advertised over many years. It is assumed that Ruth never wanted to go to the minor leagues to prove his managerial mettle, and Ruth's incandescent personality combined with the extraordinary fanfare his mere presence drew may have been more of a distraction than any owner hiring a manager wanted to assume.

Ruth's brief time as a Brooklyn coach almost certainly cost him what few supporters he may have had left in his longstanding quest to become a major league manager. Fair or not, Ruth's apparent reputation for not focusing on the details of coaching may well have been more determinative of his future prospects than was the row with Durocher, which was seemingly out of character for Ruth. While Ruth was an obvious drawing card as a coach for the Dodgers, there is little evidence that he did much in Brooklyn to hone his managerial skills or to establish a reputation as an instructor, motivator, or tactician.

Ruth's arrival as a Brooklyn Dodger coach in 1938 seemed, at first glance, to offer him a plausible path to a managerial position and a way to overcome the unfair treatment that Ruth received with the Braves in 1935. But with MacPhail being firmly in Durocher's corner and Durocher being staunchly opposed to Ruth, there is no realistic way to expect that Ruth could ever have been named manager of the Dodgers under that arrangement. Paralleling his time with the Boston Braves, the opportunity to coach the Brooklyn Dodgers was, for Ruth, a case of being in the wrong place at the wrong time. Ruth, it seems, deserved better fortunes. ■

Acknowledgments

With thanks to the Baseball Hall of Fame for providing clippings of vintage articles cited in this piece.

Notes

1. Leigh Montville, *The Big Bam: The Life and Times of Babe Ruth.* New York: Broadway Books 2006, 333.

2. Mark L. Armour and Daniel R. Levitt, *In Pursuit of Pennants: Baseball Operations from Deadball to Moneyball.* Lincoln: University of Nebraska Press 2015, 84–85. As Armour and Levitt note, Ruth eschewed the Detroit opportunity thinking it would remain open. Instead, Navin, unwilling to wait, hired Mickey Cochrane, who managed the Tigers to American League pennants in both 1934 and 1935.

3. Montville, 337.

4. Ibid., 338.

5. Ibid., 337.

6. Associated Press, "Ruth to Get $15,000 As Coach For Brooklyn: Baseball Writers Believe the Babe Is Likely to Be Manager Not Later Than 1939," *Daily Boston Globe*, June 19, 1938, C25.

7. Montville, 343–44.

8. Richard Goldstein, "Dolph Camilli, Who Led Dodgers to '41 Pennant, Dies at 90," *The New York Times*, October 22, 1997. Camilli was acquired in a trade with the Philadelphia Phillies shortly before the season began, on March 6, 1938.

9. Dave Camerer, "Phelps May See Action in West: Ailing Dodger Catcher Now Ready." Clipping from Phelps' Hall of Fame file. Though no publication is given, the date of the story is August 23, 1938. It notes that Phelps had "split his thumb" from a foul tip off of the bat of Harry Danning on July 1.

10. See http://www.baseball-almanac.com/teams/baseball_uniform_numbers.php?t=BRO and http://www.baseball-reference.com/teams/BRO/1938-uniform-numbers.shtml. It is interesting to note that Topps issued a baseball card of Ruth in 1962 (#142), subtitled 'Coaching With the Dodgers,' clearly showing him wearing uniform number 35 with the Dodgers. His Brooklyn uniform with number 35 was also auctioned in 2008: http://sports.espn.go.com/ mlb/news/story?id=3705111.

11. James W. Johnson, "Johnny Vander Meer." SABR BioProject biography. Available at http://sabr.org/bioproj/person/14ff1abe.

12. Roscoe McGowen, "40,000 See Vander Meer of Reds Hurl Second No-Hit, No-Run Game in Row: Dodgers Bow, 6–0, in Night Inaugural," *The New York Times*, June 16, 1938, 27.

13. John Kieran, "All in Fun, or the Babe Comes Back," *The New York Times*, June 19, 1938, 64.

14. Robert W. Creamer, *Babe: The Legend Comes to Life,* New York: Fireside, 1974, 410–11.

15. Ibid., 411.

16. Associated Press, "Ruth to Get $15,000 As Coach For Brooklyn: Baseball Writers Believe the Babe Is Likely to Be Manager Not Later Than 1939," *Daily Boston Globe*, June 19, 1938, C25.

17. "Ruth Returns to Baseball as Dodger Coach," *Chicago Daily Tribune*, June 19, 1938, A1

18. Ibid.

19. "Ruth Returns to Baseball as Dodger Coach," A1

20. Ibid.

21. Associated Press, "Ruth to Get $15,000 As Coach For Brooklyn: Baseball Writers Believe the Babe Is Likely to Be Manager Not Later Than 1939," *Daily Boston Globe*, June 19, 1938, C25.

22. Associated Press, "Babe Ruth, the Man Whom Baseball Forgot, Comes Back to the Majors as Coach of the Dodgers," *Washington Post*, June 19, 1938, X1.

23. "Dodgers Name Grimes Pilot for One Year: Succeeds Stengel for Reported $9,000," *Chicago Tribune*, November 6, 1936, 31.

24. Associated Press, "Grimes Is Boss of Dodgers: MacPhail Will Tell the Players Plenty," *Boston Globe*, May 6, 1938, 26.

25. Ibid.

26. Creamer, 411. In fact, Cuyler would have been age 39 at the time of the quotation.

27. Associated Press, "28,013 Fans Cheer Babe at Brooklyn: Ruth Helps Flock Win Opener, 6–2; Cubs Take Second," *Washington Post*, June 20, 1938, 14.

28. John Kieran, "All in Fun, or the Babe Comes Back," *The New York Times*, June 19, 1938, 64.

29. Ruth occasionally coached at third base as well.

30. Associated Press, "28,013 Fans Cheer Babe at Brooklyn: Ruth Helps Flock Win Opener, 6–2; Cubs Take Second," *Washington Post*, June 20, 1938, 14. It is worthwhile to note that a mere nine days into his time with Brooklyn, Ruth was the center of attention once again, as his car he was driving was "in a collision with another car, glanced off both a stone wall and a tree and then turned over on its side." Ruth, uninjured, proceeded to coach the Dodgers the same day. See "Babe Ruth in a Crash: Baseball Coach Escapes Injury in Collision in Jersey," *The New York Times*, June 29, 1938, 17.

31. Baseball Almanac attendance data, available at www.baseball-almanac.com/teams/laatte.shtml. In 1937, 482,481 fans attended games at Ebbets Field. Average home attendance there in 1938 was 570,103.

32. "Blood of Babe Ruth is Given to Daughter: He Speeds on Motor Cycle from Ball Field to Hospital," *The New York Times*, August 6, 1938, 15.

33. Associated Press, "Ruthless: Ump Ejects Protesting Babe; Grimes Out for Bandit Act," *Daily Boston Globe*, August 8, 1938, 7.

34. "McPhail (sic) Resents Harridge's Blast Against Babe Ruth," *Washington Post*, August 10, 1938, 21.

35. Leo Durocher, SABR BioProject Biography, available at http://sabr.org/bioproj/person/35d925c7.

36. Creamer, 413.

37. Ibid., 413–14.

38. Gerald Eskenazi, *The Lip: A Biography of Leo Durocher.* New York: William Morrow and Co. 1993, 99.

39. Creamer, 414.

40. Eskenazi, 99.

41. Ibid.

42. Creamer, 414.

43. Ibid.

44. Paul Mickelson (AP Sports Writer), "Fight in Clubhouse Cost Ruth Job with Dodger Club," *Washington Post*, October 14, 1938, X25.

45. United Press, "Dodgers Cut Grimes Off: Change Held Needed, May Pick Durocher, Frisch Has Chance," *Washington Post*, October 11, 1938, X18.

46. No publication given, "Babe Ruth is Dropped as Coach," October 13, 1938.

47. Ibid.

48. "Babe Ruth Appears to Be Definitely Out of Baseball," *Daily Boston Globe*, October 21, 1938, 30.

49. Ibid.

50. Ibid.

The Sultan of Swag

Babe Ruth as a Financial Investment[1]

Michael Haupert

On the morning of January 6, 1920, New Yorkers awoke to a headline in *The New York Times* that screamed "Ruth bought by New York Americans for $125,000, highest price in baseball annals."[2] It was dramatic, albeit incorrect (the actual price was $100,000). Secondary headlines correctly predicted that Ruth would be getting a new contract, and reported that Yankees skipper Miller Huggins was already en route to California to ink the slugger to a "large salary." The *Times* correctly reported that Ruth had two years remaining on a three-year contract calling for $10,000 per annum, but Ruth, reacting to the sale, had promised that he would not play for that amount, hence the urgent trip by Huggins.[3] The *Times* gushed that "Ruth was such a sensation last season that he supplanted the great Ty Cobb as baseball's greatest attraction," and in obtaining the services of Ruth for next season "the New York club made a ten strike which will be received with the greatest enthusiasm by Manhattan baseball fans."[4] They went on to report that the Yankees were prepared to offer Ruth a contract of $20,000 per year, twice what he was being paid by Boston. He would prove to be worth every penny of that contract...and far more.

Curiously, the Boston and New York papers did not necessarily react in the way one might expect. The day after the purchase was announced, the *Times* decried the Ruth sale, complaining that "it marks another long step toward the concentration of baseball playing talent in the largest cities, which can afford to pay the highest prices for it. That is a bad thing for the game; and it is still worse to give a valuable player stranded with a weak club the idea that if he holds out for an imposing salary he can get somebody in New York or Chicago to buy his services."[5]

The *Boston Herald*, on the other hand, urged fans to be patient and wait to see how the trade worked out. Boston had a history of selling stars, having previously parted with Cy Young and Tris Speaker, and still had five World Series titles to show for it, including three of the previous four.

The *Boston Post* was less optimistic, arguing that Ruth was special. "He is of a class of ball players that flashes across the firmament once in a great while and who alone bring crowds to the park, whether the team is winning or losing."[6]

No less a sage than the venerable Connie Mack thought it was a good thing for baseball. "Ruth will be a more valuable man to the Yankees than he would have been to the Red Sox. As a matter of fact, New York needed him more than Boston."[7] While this is now widely recognized by economists as being true from a financial perspective, at the time Mack was focused more on the impact on the field. He felt Ruth was more valuable to the Yankees than the Red Sox because the latter was well fortified with outfielders and was a well-balanced club despite the loss of Ruth.

History would prove Mack wrong. While the Red Sox actually improved the first two years after selling Ruth, rising from a 66-win sixth-place finish in 1919 to fifth place with 72 wins in 1920 and 75 wins (good for another fifth-place finish) in 1921, that would be their high water mark for the next 13 years. After the sale of Ruth, the Red Sox would suffer through 14 consecutive losing seasons, never rising above the second division, and finishing dead last six consecutive seasons (1925–30) and eight times in a nine-year span. The Yankees, on the other hand, won seven pennants and four World Series with the Babe, and suffered through only one losing season in the 15 he was on their roster, finishing lower than third place only once. Not only did Ruth lead the Yankees to success in the standings, but he would prove to be a box office draw in his own right.

The press recognized this potential. The day after the sale was announced the Times predicted that "with Babe Ruth on the club the Yankees will become a strong attraction in Florida."[8] As if to prove the prognostication correct, a headline the next day announced that the city of Jacksonville, Florida planned to advertise the Yankees' spring trip there "like a circus" in order to reap the benefits of the expected interest Ruth would generate. The Jacksonville Tourist and Convention bureau announced they were implementing an extensive advertising campaign to bring visitors to the city during the time the Yankees were there playing the Dodgers. The city announced they would upgrade West Side Park, where the Yankees practiced, and Sally League Park, spring home of the Dodgers. The Rotary

Club of Jacksonville announced they would also help with the campaign to boost the visit of the ball clubs, and the city of Jacksonville would enjoy several holidays during the training session.[9]

The New York Times recognized the value of Ruth "as the super attraction in all baseball." They correctly predicted that his popularity and impact on the team would make him "the game's greatest drawing card, his power in this respect enhanced through that record deal, performing in the largest city of the major leagues. It will not be surprising if the Yankees of 1920 set new records for home attendance in a season, likewise for attendance on the road." Ruth not only "brings in dollars at the gate but he helps to make the team a pennant contender, which further adds to the worth of his presence on the club…[he] would have been a "good buy" at a figure higher than the sum disbursed. He should pay for himself in a few years at best."[10] Indeed, despite commanding the highest salary in MLB for 13 of his 15 years in pinstripes, Ruth turned out to be arguably the most profitable investment the Yankees ever made.

A BRIEF HISTORY OF THE YANKEES

The New York Yankees, the most storied franchise in Major League Baseball history, had an inauspicious beginning. The team was moved from Baltimore in 1903 as the American League sought to establish a foothold in New York. The franchise was sold to two local owners, William Devery and Frank Farrell, who were able to accomplish something that American League President Ban Johnson had been attempting to do for two years: secure enough land in Manhattan to construct a ballpark. The rival leagues went beyond mere refusal to cooperate: they resorted to out and out war. Andrew Freedman, owner of the National League New York franchise, was a Tammany Hall insider, and he used his political connections to keep the American League at bay by preventing them from securing the necessary land to construct a stadium in which to house a team.

However, when Tammany power lapsed, Farrell and Devery were aligned with the new powers. Johnson took advantage of this connection when he sought out the pair to purchase the Baltimore team and transfer it to Manhattan.[11] Their first order of business was to build a ballpark on acreage on Washington Heights overlooking the New Jersey palisades. The press dubbed the franchise with several nicknames referencing the location of their stadium, including "Hilltoppers" and "Highlanders."

Devery and Farrell sold the franchise after the 1914 season for $460,000.[12] The new owners of the Yankees were a pair of well-heeled local businessmen—Colonel Tillinghast L'Hommedieu Huston and Colonel Jacob Ruppert. Equally as important as their wealth was their business acumen. Ruppert had been raised in the brewery business, and Huston was a successful engineer. Both men had an interest in baseball, and more importantly, knew how to make money, recognizing that investing in a quality product might mean short term losses in order to procure long term gains.

The Yankees had been playing in the shadow of the Giants since their arrival in town. Now that men with sufficient funds owned the team, the Yankees made the necessary moves toward profitability. They began by improving the playing talent, resulting in a more competitive team, which in turn generated greater fan interest and gate revenue. After the colonels bought the team, they improved in the standings from sixth place in 1914 to consecutive third place finishes in 1919 and 1920, followed by three straight trips to the World Series.

THE RUTH PURCHASE

The Yankees were not an instant success either on or off the field. It wasn't until the 1920s that the team consistently began to win and generate profits. Not coincidentally, it was 1920 when Babe Ruth first appeared in their lineup.

The most famous and financially successful move the Yankees made was the purchase of Babe Ruth. He contributed to a Yankee powerhouse that appeared in six World Series in the decade following his arrival in town and attracted so many patrons that the Yankees constructed a monument called Yankee Stadium to house them.[13]

Ruth cost the Yankees $100,000 in January of 1920. Baseball lore claims that the Boston Red Sox, owned by Broadway magnate Harry Frazee, sold Ruth because Frazee was strapped for cash after the dismal failure of one of his shows. The legend further adds that the sale price of Ruth was only part of the purchase agreement. In addition, the Yankees allegedly loaned Frazee in excess of $300,000 to shore up his theaters or pay the former owners of the Red Sox. No evidence exists in the Yankees' account books that such a loan took place. The $100,000 purchase price (erroneously reported as $125,000 in newspapers at the time) is well documented. It took the form of $25,000 in cash plus three $25,000 promissory notes due on November 1 of 1920, 1921, and 1922. The interest rate was 6 percent, for a total cost, including interest, of $108,750.[14]

The matter of the loan is hard to analyze without any evidence. While it is possible the loan took place,

LIBRARY OF CONGRESS: BAINES COLLECTION

Ed Barrow moved from the front office of the Red Sox to the Yankees and acquired Ruth and many other players from the Sox during his tenure.

depending on its terms it may have had no relation to the Ruth purchase. The decision to loan money to Harry Frazee appears to be a separate financial decision. The only way in which it would have an impact on the value of the Ruth purchase was if the terms of the loan were better than the market rate. For example, if a condition of the sale of Ruth to the Yankees was that Jacob Ruppert loan Harry Frazee $300,000 at zero interest over a period of ten years, then the true cost of Ruth increases by the amount of interest that Ruppert would have collected on the $300,000.

There are a couple of problems with this scenario, however. First, it is apparent from examining the Yankees' account books that the loan, if it was ever made, was not made by the Yankees. It could only have been made by Ruppert or Huston privately. Since Ruppert was the primary negotiator in the Ruth deal, it stands to reason that if any loan was made, it would have been from Ruppert.

If the loan was made by Ruppert, then it seems unlikely that he would have made it at below market rates. The deal to secure Ruth provided revenues to the Yankees, of which Ruppert was only a fifty-percent owner. In addition, it seems even less likely that he would make such a financial arrangement given the strained relationship that existed at the time between Ruppert and Huston. The rift between the two men would eventually grow to the point where Ruppert bought out Huston in 1923, becoming sole owner of the franchise for the remainder of his life.

If a loan was made from Ruppert to Frazee as a condition of the Ruth sale, but the loan was at the market rate of interest, then it had no bearing on the value of the Ruth deal. The decision by Ruppert to loan Frazee money would have been made on the same basis that Ruppert would make any other decision regarding his personal finances: what would earn him the best return given his current financial situation?

Until such time as evidence regarding the details of the alleged loan surfaces, we cannot make a complete analysis. However, it seems reasonable to assume that the cost to the Yankees of Babe Ruth was the purchase price of $100,000 plus interest, and no more. This analysis of the return to the Yankees on the purchase of Ruth will proceed along these lines.

The purchase of Ruth returned immediate dividends for the Yankees. Yankees home attendance more than doubled from 619,000 in 1919 to almost 1.3 million in 1920. As a result, home receipts more than doubled each of the next three years. The team appeared in the World Series in 1921, 1922, and 1923, earning an additional $150,000 in revenues, and the Yankees' share of road receipts more than doubled in Ruth's first three seasons in New York. While attendance did increase around the league during the decade following World War I, the Yankees were an outstanding outlier. From 1920 through Ruth's final season with the Yankees in 1934, the Yankees failed to lead the league in attendance only twice. The first instance was 1925 when Ruth played in only 98 games due to injuries and suspensions. This was the fewest number of games he would play as a Yankee. In 1934 the Yankees also failed to lead the league in attendance during Ruth's final season in New York. Prior to Ruth's arrival the Highlanders/Yankees had finished in the top five of MLB attendance only three times, peaking at third in 1918. After the arrival of Ruth they led the league in attendance during 13 of his 15 years with the team. After his departure the Yankees led the league only three times in the next six years.

Was $100,000 an unusual amount of money to spend for one player? Certainly it was an enormous sum, but it was not as breathtaking as it may at first seem. The purchase and sale of ballplayers was more frequent in those days than it is today. Selling players was a very common way for an owner to make ends meet when finances got tough. On more than one occasion Connie Mack settled his bills by dismantling a World Series championship team by peddling his players for cash. Mack was not the only owner to follow this path to success. In fact, the Red Sox were on the buying side of this very formula when they won the World Series in 1918. So when the Red Sox sold Ruth, the sale itself was not unusual. Even selling a future Hall of Fame player was not unusual. As mentioned earlier, the Red Sox had previously sold Cy Young and Tris Speaker. What made this sale unique was the enormous impact that Ruth had on the Yankees, both on the field and at the box office.

By way of comparison, consider another young left-hander who was sold to New York by Boston in 1919 for the princely sum of $55,000. He subsequently led New York to pennants and World Series victories. That lefty was pitcher Art Nehf, and the teams were the Braves and the Giants.[15] Nehf led the National League in complete games in 1918 with 28 and won a total of 32 games in 1917 and 1918. In 1919 he won 17 games, splitting his time between the Braves and the Giants. He averaged 20 wins for the next three seasons as the Giants won two pennants and two World Series. Art Nehf was a good investment at $55,000. While Ruth cost nearly twice as much, he was an everyday player coming off a home-run record-setting season. The price may have been a stretch at the time, but it was not preposterous.[16]

ANALYZING THE FINANCIAL RETURN

In analyzing a financial return for Babe Ruth, we must consider the original investment (the purchase price of $100,000), the change in revenue resulting from the investment (more about this later), and the additional costs (interest on the promissory notes and salary and bonuses paid to Ruth). The return on that investment is calculated as the additional revenue Ruth generated less the additional costs to the Yankees due to Ruth as an annual percentage of the $100,000 purchase price. This is a standard return on investment calculation.

Interestingly, Ruth cost the Yankees less than his $20,000 salary and signing bonus during his first two years. According to the Yankees' ledgers, the Red Sox paid part of Babe Ruth's salary in 1920 and 1921. When they purchased Ruth from the Red Sox, the Yankees inherited the remaining two years of Ruth's three-year, $10,000 per year contract. Fearing that Ruth might threaten to hold out, the Yankees negotiated with the Red Sox to have the Sox pay half of any salary increase or bonus the Yankees offered to Ruth for the duration of the two years of his contract, up to $5000 per year. Indeed, the Yankees and Ruth agreed to raise his salary to $15,000 per year for the remaining two years on his Red Sox contract, plus a bonus of $5000 each year. As a result the Yankees only had to pay $15,000 per year through 1921, while the Red Sox had to pay the remaining $5000 of his contract each of those years. The Red Sox are the first documented example of a team paying the salary of a player they had sold or traded to another team. Such arrangements are commonplace today, in an era of salary-dumping trades, but in 1920 the environment was quite different, making this arrangement ground-breaking.[17]

The Yankees were not always that savvy about making deals however. They did let Ruth talk them into a contract clause for 1921 which paid him $50 per home run: the same year Babe shattered the record by blasting 59. The $2,950 the Yankees paid him that year was just a hair less than twenty percent of his salary. It was the largest performance bonus the Yankees would pay for more than a quarter of a century, and the last time Ruth ever had a performance clause in his Yankees contract.

CALCULATING REVENUES GENERATED BY RUTH

A player's value to a team is measured by his impact on team revenues. In Ruth's day, this was primarily done through his impact on attendance. Economic research shows that the most important thing a team can control that will affect its attendance is the quality of the team, measured by winning percentage. The population of the city and its income level are also important determinants of attendance, but a team can't alter those variables. Putting a better team on the field, however, is well within the control of the team. Research also shows that a better player will contribute more to his team's ability to win, thereby contributing more to the total revenue of the team.[18] This concept is known in the economics literature as marginal revenue. A baseball player's marginal revenue is the additional revenue that a team earns as a result of the player being on the team.

There is a second way that a player can impact team revenues, and that is through what we call the "superstar" effect.[19] Some players are so popular that fans will go out to see them just because they are in the game, regardless of how good their team actually is. LeBron James is a good example of this. When his team is on the road, games sell out, even when he visits poor teams that have plenty of empty seats for every other game. Babe Ruth may not have been the first baseball superstar, but he was arguably the trendsetter when it came to selling tickets. While there are models to estimate the superstar impact of players, I do not attempt to do so in this article because of a scarcity of necessary data.

I use Wins Above Replacement (WAR) to calculate Ruth's impact on the Yankees winning percentage.[20] WAR is a measure of the number of games a player is responsible for his team winning above a replacement player. For example, in 1929 Babe Ruth had a WAR of 8.0, meaning that the Yankees would have won eight fewer games if Ruth was removed from the roster and a typical replacement player was added in his place.

Calculating a player's marginal revenue using WAR is a simple two-step process. First, regress ticket revenue on a series of variables, including team winning percentage.[21] Then, using a player's WAR, determine how many games the team would win without him. In the preceding case of Ruth in 1929, his WAR was 8.0, meaning that with an average replacement player in the lineup instead of Ruth, the Yankees would have won eight fewer games, thus their winning percentage would have been .519 instead of .571, a difference of .052. Multiplying this by the coefficient on winning percentage in the regression yields the marginal revenue of Babe Ruth to the New York Yankees in 1929. This actually underestimates Ruth's contribution to the bottom line, because it assumes that his impact on the team revenues came only through his impact on the quality of the team, and not at all because of the superstar effect. Given Ruth's talents, fame, and celebrity, his superstar impact was undoubtedly quite significant.

Team revenue in Ruth's day was simpler to calculate than it is in the twenty-first century because there was no television revenue, and there was little if any radio revenue. However, there are still some tricky revenue sources to consider. After calculating the impact of a player on the winning percentage of his team, and

the ticket revenue value of that additional winning percentage, we must then calculate his impact on other important (though far smaller) sources of revenue. In addition to winning percentage, concession revenue, revenues from road games, World Series revenues (important for the Yankees, who appeared in half the World's Series played during Ruth's tenure with the club), and exhibition game receipts, which became increasingly important after Ruth joined the team, are analyzed. The impact on the concession, road and exhibition game revenues is calculated by looking at the ratio of each to home revenues and taking a straight percentage impact. The idea here is that Ruth did not necessarily change the ratio of concessions to home attendance, but the increase in home attendance increased concession revenues by the same relative amount.

A quick glance at Tables 1 and 3 reveals that the financial return earned by the Yankees on the purchase of Babe Ruth was nothing less than spectacular. And Table 2 reveals that despite his status as the highest paid player in the game, the Yankees were exploiting Ruth's ability to draw crowds and generate profits. This is demonstrated by looking at the ratio of Ruth's salary to his marginal revenue. Economic theory predicts that in a competitive market a player will be paid his marginal revenue. Baseball in the 1920s was hardly a competitive labor market. With the reserve clause in

Table 1. Ruth Impact on Yankee Revenues

Year	Ruth WAR	Change in win average due to Ruth	Increased home gate revenue ($)	Increased exhibition game earnings ($)	Increased road receipts ($)	Net World Series receipts* ($)	Increased concession earnings ($)	Total increased Yankees revenues ($)
1920	11.9	0.077	102,869	2,614	32,493	–	–	137,976
1921	12.9	0.084	117,656	4,794	31,407	70,376	–	224,234
1922	6.3	0.041	57,199	1,417	20,025	12,529	–	91,170
1923	14.1	0.093	132,157	4,300	42,559	–	17,190	196,206
1924	11.7	0.077	106,318	3,459	34,238	–	12,500	156,514
1925	3.5	0.023	31,391	1,021	10,109	–	4,573	47,095
1926	11.5	0.075	103,143	3,356	33,215	85,517	15,365	240,597
1927	12.4	0.081	111,215	3,618	35,815	–	15,765	166,413
1928	10.1	0.066	88,969	3,489	31,603	56,902	15,425	196,388
1929	8	0.052	72,049	1,883	31,267	–	9,777	114,976
1930	10.3	0.067	89,280	1,396	24,991	–	11,663	127,330
1931	10.3	0.067	91,885	2,480	32,745	–	12,337	139,447
1932	8.3	0.054	73,563	1,986	26,215	–	7,627	109,390
1933	6.4	0.043	58,236	1,572	20,753	–	6,867	87,428
1934	5.1	0.033	45,201	1,220	16,108	–	5,657	68,187
Total			**1,281,132**	**38,605**	**423,544**	**225,324**	**134,746**	**2,103,351**

* Net World Series receipts attributable to Ruth. Calculated by adjusting Yankees record by Ruth's WAR. If doing so dropped the Yankees out of first place these World Series revenues would not have been earned, thus they are considered a function of Ruth.

Sources: Wins above replacement: Baseball-Reference.com; all other data from Haupert Player Salary Database, New York Yankee Financial Ledgers, and Haupert, Michael, "Babe Ruth: Better than the Dow Jones," Outside the Lines, spring 2008, 1, 12–17.

Table 2. Babe Ruth Earnings in Perspective

Year	Contracted salary	Ruth net earnings ($) (salary + bonus – fines)	Average earnings U.S. production worker ($)	Ruth earnings/ average U.S. earnings	Ruth marginal revenue (MR) ($)	Contracted salary as % of MR	Net earnings as % of MR
1920	15,000	18,570	1,080	17.2	137,976	14.5	13.5
1921	15,000	39,638	960	41.3	224,234	8.9	17.7
1922	52,000	54,104	880	61.5	91,170	57.0	59.3
1923	52,000	52,669	960	54.9	196,206	26.5	26.8
1924	52,000	47,758	1,020	46.8	156,514	33.2	30.5
1925	52,000	42,622	1,000	42.6	47,095	110.4	90.5
1926	52,000	49,605	1,020	48.6	240,597	21.6	20.6
1927	70,000	76,191	1,040	73.3	166,413	42.1	45.8
1928	70,000	70,000	1,040	67.3	196,388	35.6	35.6
1929	70,000	70,000	1,040	67.3	114,976	60.9	60.9
1930	80,000	84,098	1,060	79.3	127,330	62.8	66.0
1931	80,000	79,192	1,020	77.6	139,447	57.4	56.8
1932	75,000	77,184	900	85.8	109,390	68.6	70.6
1933	52,000	42,029	880	47.8	87,428	59.5	48.1
1934	35,000	35,711	1,060	33.7	68,187	51.3	52.4

Sources: U.S. production worker wages: Measuring Worth.com; Haupert, Michael, "Babe Ruth: Better than the Dow Jones," Outside the Lines, spring 2008, 1, 12–17.

Table 3. Yankee Earnings on Ruth Compared to Alternative Investments

Year	Ruth MR	Cost of Ruth including interest payments ($)	Yankee net earnings on Ruth ($)	Yankees return to investment on Ruth (%)	DJIA	Annual growth rate of DJIA (%)	Moody's seasoned AAA corporate bond yield (%)	Moody's seasoned BAA corporate bond yield (%)
1920	137,976	17,820	120,156	120.2	108.85	32.02	5.75	7.78
1921	224,234	37,388	186,846	186.8	72.67	-33.24	6.14	8.50
1922	91,170	56,854	34,316	34.3	78.90	8.57	5.34	7.70
1923	196,206	52,669	143,537	143.5	98.06	24.28	5.04	6.98
1924	156,514	47,758	108,756	108.8	96.54	-1.55	5.09	7.24
1925	47,095	42,622	4,473	4.5	119.46	23.74	4.95	6.44
1926	240,597	49,605	190,992	191.0	158.75	32.89	4.82	6.09
1927	166,413	76,191	90,222	90.2	155.16	-2.26	4.66	5.61
1928	196,388	70,000	126,388	126.4	203.55	31.19	4.46	5.35
1929	114,976	70,000	44,976	45.0	297.70	46.25	4.62	5.63
1930	127,330	84,098	43,232	43.2	248.10	-16.66	4.66	5.92
1931	139,447	79,192	60,255	60.3	170.71	-31.19	4.42	6.41
1932	109,390	77,184	32,206	32.2	71.59	-58.06	5.20	9.13
1933	87,428	42,029	45,399	45.4	59.29	-17.18	4.44	8.01
1934	68,1867	35,711	32,476	32.5	96.73	63.15	4.35	7.01

Source: Dow Jones Industrial Average, Moody's Yield data: Measuring Worth.com

place Ruth never had a chance to sell his skills on the open market like modern free agents do. Because of the reserve clause, the Yankees were able to keep his services while only paying him a fraction of his marginal revenue. And while Ruth was being paid only a fraction of his marginal revenue, he was being paid a considerable amount more than the average American worker in his day. Keep in mind that this is a conservative estimate of the financial impact of Ruth on the Yankees. No attempt has been made to estimate the superstar effect of Ruth.

Perhaps no better anecdotal evidence for the importance of Babe Ruth to the Yankees can be provided than the 1925 season, the worst in Ruth's career. He played in only 98 games that season, batting .290—52 points below his career average—and hit only 25 home runs, his lowest output since before he became a full-time player in 1919, and a depth to which he would not sink again until 1934, his final year in a Yankees uniform.

The impact of his absence from the lineup was felt by the Yankees on the field and in the pocketbook. On the field, the Yankees collapsed from an 89-win season and second-place finish in 1924 to seventh place and 69 wins in 1925. It was the only year that the Yankees had a losing record in Ruth's tenure with the team. At the box office, the absence of Ruth and the poor performance of the team was just as evident. The Yankees attendance fell 33 percent to under 700,000, the first time they failed to draw over a million fans since the arrival of Ruth and the only time except his final season with the team they would not lead the league in attendance. Overall revenue in 1925 was off 25% from the year before, dropping the Yankees below the league average in profits for the only time during the decade.[22]

RUTH AS A FINANCIAL INVESTMENT

So how good a financial investment was Babe Ruth? Table 1 details Ruth's contribution to various Yankees revenue sources. Note that Ruth's actual compensation in most years differed from his contracted salary (Table 2). The presence of frequent bonus clauses was the primary reason for this difference, but a regular series of fines levied on the Babe by the Yankee brass accounted for several instances in which Ruth actually earned less than his contract stipulated. The years from 1924–26 were particularly tough for the Babe, especially 1925, when he received nearly $10,000 less than his contracted $52,000 salary. A contributing factor to Ruth's sizeable fines during that three year period was the appearance of a temperance clause in his contract. From 1922 through 1926 Ruth's contract prohibited him from drinking or staying out late during the baseball season at the risk of an unspecified financial penalty. Even a cursory look at any of the Ruth biographies suggests that he ignored this clause with regular abandon.

More often than not, however, Ruth earned more than his contracted salary due to the frequent bonuses and World Series shares he earned. Sometimes Ruth was paid a signing bonus, and several times he received a bonus in the form of a percentage of the gate for his participation in exhibition games. As noted earlier, in 1921 he had a performance bonus clause in his contract, which proved quite lucrative for the Babe.

Ruth was the major draw for Yankees exhibition games, and in order to maximize the benefit of that attraction, the Yankees gave Ruth great incentive to participate in them. By the end of his career, though he was past his prime as a player, he was still a major gate attraction and the Yankees paid him 25 percent of the net proceeds from exhibition games in which he played. During the Ruth era, the team's revenues from exhibition games exploded. Prior to 1920, the most the Yankees ever made from exhibition games was $3,800 in 1916. From 1920–34 they never earned less than $12,000, and seven times took in $20,000 or more, topping $35,000 in 1921.[23]

Ruth's highest earning year for the Yankees was 1930 when he netted more than $84,000 in salary and exhibition game receipts. Relative to his salary however, Ruth's biggest year was 1921 when he earned more than 250 percent of his $15,000 salary through a combination of a signing bonus, a home-run bonus, and receipts from exhibition games. And yet, that year he earned less than 18 percent of the revenue he generated for the Yankees. 1921 was a pretty good year for Ruth—and by extension, the Yankees. His performance that year is still the all-time high for extra base hits and total bases, and it ranks in the top five all-time for runs scored, slugging, offensive WAR, runs created, and OPS as well. He hit an amazing 12 percent of the total home runs in the league, personally out-homering five other teams. Besides home runs, he also led the league in on base percentage, slugging, OPS, runs scored, total bases, RBIs, walks and runs created. He firmly established himself as the undisputed gate attraction in the game and a goldmine for the Yankees.

PROFITING FROM THE BABE

The net profits to the Yankees from their investment in Ruth are found in Table 3. The Yankees profited from the presence of Ruth on the roster in every year, though they barely covered his salary in 1925. They more than made up for this in other years however, earning more than $100,000 in net profit on Ruth on six separate occasions. Babe was a colossal moneymaker for the Yankees. During his career, they earned more than one million dollars (not adjusted for inflation) in profit on Ruth.

Over the course of his career, the total return earned by the Yankees on their investment in Babe Ruth was 1254 percent. Because of its volatility, the stock market returned a net gain of only 17 percent during the period. Bonds did much better at 205 percent, but still fell far short of Ruth. It turns out that Babe Ruth was indeed a wise investment for the Yankees. It would have been difficult for Jacob Ruppert to find any other investment that could have done nearly as well.

Despite the riches the Yankees were earning from Ruth, Yankees general manager Ed Barrow wasn't particularly appreciative of the Babe in the waning years of his career. In a letter addressed to sportswriter F.C. Lane in March of 1933, Barrow complained that Ruth "is greatly overpaid." Adding that he hoped "the Colonel will stand pat on his offer of $50,000 and call the big fellow's bluff about retiring."[24] The Colonel did not stand pat, eventually offering Ruth $52,000 plus 25 percent of the net receipts from exhibition games, though ultimately only paying him $42,000. It was not one of the Babe's better years, though he did return a nice profit of about $45,000 for the Colonel's investment. This was certainly better than Ruppert could have done by investing in the stock market, which lost 17 percent that year. The 45 percent return also outperformed the bond market that year by a substantial amount.

The return on Ruth fell the next year, his final season in New York, to its second lowest, returning the team just over $32,000 in net profits. This was at a much reduced salary of $35,000, however. The Yankees, because they were able to reduce Ruth's salary toward the end of his career, were able to ride him for a couple of final years of profitable employment before finally shipping him off.

When he was ingloriously dispatched to the Braves in time for the 1935 season the Yankees received nothing in return. Their records indicate that he was sold to the Braves without monetary consideration. It was indeed a quiet ending to the most famous financial investment in Yankees history. ∎

Notes

1. Thanks to Ken Winter, who was my coauthor on much of the background research for this paper, and Clifford Blau for his careful fact checking. Thank you also to two anonymous referees whose careful reading and valuable comments helped to improve this article. Any remaining errors or oversights are strictly the fault of the author.
2. *The New York Times*, January 6, 1920, 16.
3. While the thought of retiring might strain credibility, Ruth was, in fact, in Hollywood at the time the sale was announced, making *Headin' Home*, which would be released later that year by Kessell & Bauman, indicating his attraction beyond the ballfield. In fact, over the length of his career, Ruth made substantial amounts of money outside of the game, appearing on vaudeville, in movies, endorsing products, and making public appearances.
4. Ibid.
5. *The New York Times*, January 7, 1920, 18.
6. *The New York Times*, January 7, 1920, 22.
7. Ibid.
8. *The New York Times*, January 8, 1920, 18.
9. *The New York Times*, January 9, 1920, 18.
10. *The New York Times*, January 12, 1920, 11.
11. According to Rodney Fort (http://www.rodneyfort.com/SportsData/BizFrame.htm) Frank Farrell purchased a 75% share of the Baltimore franchise in 1903 for $180,000. That translates into a market value of $240,000 for the team. The franchise was relocated to New York for the 1903 season and ultimately became known as the Yankees.
12. Michael Haupert and Kenneth Winter, "Pay Ball: Estimating the Profitability of the New York Yankees 1915–1937," *Essays in Economic and Business History*, vol XXI, 2003, 89102.
13. Yankee Stadium opened in 1923. Prior to that the Yankees played in their own stadium, American League Park, from 1903–12. From 1913 through 1922 they shared the Polo Grounds with the Giants.
14. *New York Yankees Financial Ledgers*. National Baseball Library, Cooperstown, New York.
15. The deal also brought four players to the Braves according to Baseball-Reference.com.
16. Kenneth Winter and Mike Haupert "Yankee Profits and Promise: The Purchase of Babe Ruth and the Building of Yankee Stadium," in Wm. Simons, ed., *The Cooperstown Symposium on Baseball and American Culture*, Jefferson, North Carolina: McFarland & Co., 2003, 197–214.
17. *New York Yankees Financial Ledgers*. National Baseball Library, Cooperstown, New York.
18. The seminal work on this topic was done by Gerald Scully, "Pay and Performance in Major League Baseball," *The American Economic Review*, 64, no. 6 (December 1974), 915–30.
19. David J. Berri, Martin B. Schmidt and Stacey L. Brook, "Stars at the Gate: The Impact of Star power on NBA Gate Revenues," *Journal of Sports Economics* 5:1 (February 2004), 33–50.
20. WAR values are from Baseball-Reference.com, accessed during the spring of 2015.
21. I regressed attendance x average ticket price on winning percentage, winning percentage in the previous year, games behind (or ahead) in previous year, World Series appearance in previous year, age of team, and gross domestic product (GDP). The regression covered the New York Yankees from 1903–42 (years for which I had sufficient financial data). Only winning percentage, previous year winning percentage, and GDP were significant.
22. Emanuel Celler, *Hearings of the Monopoly Subcommittee of the House Judiciary Committee*, 1951.
23. *New York Yankees Financial Ledgers*. National Baseball Library, Cooperstown, New York.
24. Letter from Edward Barrow to F.C. Lane, March, 1933, F.C. Lane papers, BA MSS 36, National Baseball Hall of Fame Library, National Baseball Hall of Fame and Museum, Cooperstown, New York.

Remembering the 1951 Hazard Bombers

Sam Zygner

Nestled in Perry County in southeast Kentucky—the heart of the Appalachian coal country—lays the quaint city of Hazard, population just over 4,400 souls. The county and the city are named for Commodore Oliver Hazard Perry, a naval commander during the War of 1812. At the Battle of Lake Erie, he uttered the famous words, "Don't give up the ship," and, "We have met the enemy and they are ours."[1] The same pugnacious spirit that characterized Perry was also reflected in a group of young minor league ballplayers who in 1951 captured not only the hearts of their community, but a Mountain States League pennant.

Even today, locals still talk about the magical season. They recount the exploits of an upcoming Brooklyn Dodger pitching star, a Costa Rican flamethrower who dealt with blatant racial prejudice, and a determined, hard-hitting player-manager who led the team to one of the all-time great seasons in minor league history. They were known as the Hazard Bombers.

BOMBERS TAKE FLIGHT

As World War II came to an end, life in America returned to normality. Servicemen left the horrors of war behind with a sanguine eye to the future. They also sought the need for entertainment, and a reconnection with our national pastime.

Minor league baseball, like many things, had been severely curtailed during the hostilities due to manpower shortages. As an example, in 1944 only ten leagues were operating. Following the war, circumstances changed dramatically and minor league baseball experienced a period of unprecedented growth.

By 1948, there were 58 officially recognized leagues including the spanking new Class-D Mountain States League, formally organized on February 1, 1948. The original MSL lineup consisted of towns in eastern Tennessee and southwest Virginia and Kentucky and featured a 120-game schedule beginning on April 29.[2] Although Hazard was not part of the original circuit, that soon changed.

When the first week of June 1948, rolled around, the Oak Ridge Bombers were leading the league in the standings, but struggling to draw fans through the gates. Grasping the opportunity to bring baseball to his hometown Hazard, the ambitious owner of the Mary Gail mine, Max Smith, purchased the struggling Oak Ridge club and relocated them.[3] The Bombers (65–43) were an instant success and finished their first campaign in second place. They nearly took the championship before falling to the Morristown Red Sox in the finals, three games to two.[4]

There were high expectations going into the 1949 season, but the outcome was very disappointing to Hazard supporters. The Bombers (35–89) sank to the bottom of the standings, finishing 48 games behind the first-place Harlan Smokies. Especially upsetting to Smith and the local fandom was the success of their biggest rival, the Smokies, who cruised through the postseason and captured the league crown.[5]

Smith was determined that there would not be a repeat of 1949. His first move was signing a new manager. He found his man in former major leaguer Max Macon and inked him to a two-year contract to serve as a player-manager. Macon, the one-time St. Louis Cardinal (1938) and Brooklyn Dodger pitcher (1940, 1942–43), was known for his "never-give-up" attitude. After his arm gave out, he re-invented himself as a first baseman with the 1944 Boston Braves. His last appearance in the big leagues was on April 17, 1947, after which he spent the rest of the season with the Braves American Association Triple-A affiliate in Milwaukee.[6] He was hired for his first managerial job with the Modesto Reds of the Class-C California League in 1949.[7] Despite a losing record of 54–85, he proved himself a capable leader, and could still swing a productive bat coming off a season in which the left-handed thumper hit .383 and slugged five home runs in 107 games.[8]

THE 1951 SEASON

In 1950, the Bombers' fortunes turned for the better. Under Macon's guidance, Hazard (76–49) finished in second place, five games behind the league champions, Harlan. Macon won the batting crown with a .392 average and the club drew a league-leading 55,184 in attendance. Although they were eliminated in the playoffs by Middlesboro, three games to none, the outlook for the 1951 season was promising.[9]

A key to Macon's success was his strong relationship with the Dodgers. He was able to partner Hazard with the big league club which provided him a pipeline of top-flight talent. Hazard was the only team in the MSL with a major league affiliation. Moreover, during spring training at Vero Beach, he was able to scout several young prospects. Many of these players were handpicked by him and played vital roles in the team's success. One pitcher who made a positive impression, and would make his mark during the 1951 campaign, was a tall, imposing right-hander from Port Limon, Costa Rica, Danny Hayling.

In order to steady his inexperienced stable of young arms, Macon recruited a veteran catcher, Lou Isert, who also served as his assistant coach. Isert already had six seasons under his belt in the lower minor leagues, having risen as high as the Class-B Southeastern League.[10] During the course of the year, the veteran backstop proved invaluable to his manager as one of his best hitters and capable right-hand man.

Macon was confident his team was a champion-ship club going into his second season. Many prognosticators like *Middlesboro Daily News* columnist Julian Pitzer agreed and wrote, "Hazard has the advantage of its working agreement with the Dodgers of Brooklyn. Therefore, this might be the year when the Bombers make the grade. That's our reason for giving them first."[11]

The team opened the season at aptly named Bomber Field. The ballpark had been built by team owner Smith prior to the 1950 season and featured box seats, reserved seats, and a roof which partially covered the grandstand. The evening of April 29 was especially exciting for local fans since the hometown team kicked off the season against their nemesis, Harlan. The Bombers took the field decked out in their home white uniforms with blue numbers trimmed with red piping, spanking new red, white, and blue striped stirrup socks, and blue caps featuring a prominent red "H" outlined in white. All eyes were on the field as the 1,638 fans got accustomed to a host of new faces.[12] The only three returnees from the previous season were Macon, outfielder Ken Cox, and infielder Ralph Torres.

As his opening night starter, Macon chose 19-year-old Juan Jose (Ravelo) Torres. The Cuban right-hander had struck out 12 in an exhibition game against Middlesboro a few nights earlier, impressing his skipper. Ravelo repeated with another dominating performance, silencing the Smokies' hitters by allowing only two batters to reach base on free passes and none by base hit. It was a grand start for the rookie, hurling a no-hitter in his professional debut. The final score showed Hazard 10 Harlan 0.[13]

The Bombers continued to play well during the early part of the season. Ravelo nearly repeated his previous performance by shutting out the Big Stone Gap Rebels, 10–0, this time allowing three hits.[14,15] Hazard opened the season with a six-game winning streak before Ravelo finally faltered, dropping a decision to Harlan on May 7 by the score of 6–3.

Through the month of May, Hazard jockeyed for the MSL's top spot with Morristown and Harlan. Although Ravelo drew a great deal of early attention for his pitching prowess, his mound mate Hayling, who had so impressed Macon during spring training, was quietly building what turned out to be a record-breaking season. By month's end the 6'3" Costa Rican fireballer sported a glossy 7–0 record, including his first shutout against the Norton Braves on May 24.

Macon, with an eye on improving his club, received additional help in May with the arrival of pitcher John Joseph Podres. Born and raised in Witherbee, New York, "Johnny" as his friends called him, enjoyed hunting and fishing in his beloved Adirondack Mountains, playing baseball, and following the Brooklyn Dodgers. He realized his childhood dream when he was signed out of Mineville High School by Brooklyn in 1951. Pat Salerno Jr. remembers his father competing against Podres in high school and shared one of his dad's memories of the future big leaguer in *Adirondack Life*: "So he would go to his room, turn the radio on and listen to Brooklyn Dodgers games…At 13 and 14 years old, all he wanted to be was a Brooklyn Dodger. He was a small-town boy who made it big."[16] Podres became a legend after earning the win in the deciding seventh game of the 1955 World Series, defeating the New York Yankees, 2–0, helping bringing "Dem Bums" their only world championship while in Brooklyn.

Left-handed Johny Podres would eventually be a World Series hero for the Dodgers, but in 1951 he was fresh out of high school and after struggling at Class B was shipped down to Class D Hazard.

An immensely talented left-hander with a blazing fastball, Podres began the year at Class-B Newport News. However, his struggles getting batters out consistently and need to strengthen some baseball fundamentals prompted the parent club to make a move. Podres had a record of 0–2 and 5.72 ERA in seven appearances, when the Dodgers brass felt that demoting him to Class-D ball would help him gain confidence. Bob York, who worked for the Bombers in various capacities, remembers how Podres was "a little green" when he first arrived, and how he received instant coaching from Macon.

"I remember Max Macon. Johnny Podres refused to get in front of a ball hit back through the mound. And one of the funniest things was Max Macon went and got a bat and made Podres stand on that mound and he hit those balls right back through the middle, over that mound, and Podres was just terrified."[17]

On May 21, Podres made his first start against Big Stone Gap and it wasn't pretty. Teammate Ed Bobrik recounted his roommate's inauspicious debut.

> A few weeks later a fellow by the name of Johnny Podres reached our club and Max puts him with me, and we roomed together. Podres was pitching, and the score after the first inning was ten to nothing in favor of the other team…He comes back to the bench at the end of the inning and says, "Jesus, I don't know what's going on…Gee, I don't know what's wrong with me."
>
> Well, listen. Next time you go out don't be throwing fastballs all the time. Mix them up. Throw some slow curves and stuff like that. Well, he did and he shut them out the rest of the way.[18]

Hazard came back to win the game, 12–11. Podres's second appearance of the year was in relief against Middlesboro during a May 27 doubleheader, where he earned his second victory. He then followed up with another decision against the Norton Braves two days later during a 7–6 win. From that point on, Podres was

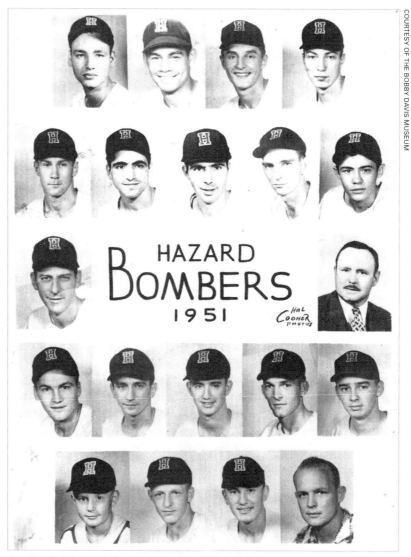

Top Row (L–R):   J. Ravelo, D. Hayling, E. Bobrik, J. Podres
Second Row (L–R):   K. Johnson, R. Coluni, L. Isert, M. Sanders, R. Torres
Third Row (L–R):   M. Macon, Max Smith (team owner)
Fourth Row (L–R):   R. Dacko, J. Tondora, J. Chapman, K. Cox, E. Catlett
Bottom Row (L–R):   C, Crook Jr. (batboy), H. Snyder, T. Kazek,
                       B. Mansfield (business manager)

nearly unhittable. "He was the first left-hander I ever saw that could throw where he was looking," said teammate George McDuff. "Most of them looked where they threw. But he had control."[19]

Following a May 26 loss to Middlesboro, Hazard stood at 17–8. The Bombers then went on a tear, winning 31 of 36 games. By July 2, Hazard stood at 48–13, five games ahead of Harlan. Fueled by the dominant performances of Podres (10–1) and Hayling (16–0), and excellent work from Bobrik (7–2) and Ravelo (10–3),[20] Hazard boasted the league's top staff. In addition, the Bombers were hitting .300 as a group including: Macon (.395), James Blaylock (.356), Donald Hilbert (.329), and John Tondora (.324).[21] It was amazing that the Smokies were as close as they were in the pennant race.

Hayling picked up his seventeenth consecutive win on July 10 in a slugfest victory over the Middlesboro Athletics, 12–10. It looked as though the A's were going to end Hayling's skein at 16 games after staking themselves to a 10–7 lead going into the eighth inning. Not a team to throw in the towel, the Bombers lived up to their name, exploding for five late runs to overcome the deficit.[22] Although not a gem by pitching standards, the big Costa Rican with the unruly fastball that did not always go where directed was thankful for the more than ample run support from the league's most potent offense.

After 18 straight wins, Hayling's remarkable win streak came to an end. On July 16, Hazard won the first game of a doubleheader, topping Pennington Gap, 3–1. The second game was a polar opposite slugfest, and Macon called on Hayling for late inning relief with his charges holding onto a one run lead. The Miners were not to be denied and came back to win the game, 13–11, sending Hayling to the showers.[23]

Except for his teammates and a few front office personnel, the darker-skinned Hayling faced discrimination throughout the season for being perceived as black. The pressure to keep his winning streak alive was nerve-racking, but it paled in comparison to the hurt he felt being the target of prejudicial slurs and verbal threats throughout the league by opposition fans and players alike that were still entrenched in bigotry and the old "Jim Crow" way of thinking. Changes relating to racial bias were slow in coming to this area of the country and it was not until the beginning of the 1951 season that the first black ballplayer, Bob Bowman of Middlesboro, crossed the color line in the MSL, four years after Jackie Robinson's debut with the Dodgers.[24] In spite of the harassment, Hayling maintained a positive attitude and displayed an extraordinary amount of intestinal fortitude in the face of adversity.

McDuff, who speaks with a smooth Texas drawl and was a fellow hurler, had only a month-long stay in Hazard, yet he struck up an instant friendship with Hayling. He witnessed a frightening example of intimidation handed out to his teammate by a narrow-minded baseball fan that occurred after a game in which Hayling had hit an opposing batter with an errant pitch.

He hit that boy in the head and put him in the hospital. So, he was in a coma for several days. He was in the hospital two or three weeks.

And boy it was bad news. I remember going in and Danny and I, we were walking pretty close

together. A guy butted in between me and Hayling and he said, "Hayling, are you going to pitch tonight?"

And he [Hayling] said, "No."

So he said, "Well, you better not get over the coaches line because I'll be there on that little nob" There was a little hill over there by center field. He says, "I'll be over there with my rifle and if you get on out of the coaches box, I'm going to pick you off."

Apparently word got out to the local fans about the trouble Hayling was facing…I know when we were getting ready to go and there were two men who walked up in suits and they were talking to Macon.

"We understand there is going to be trouble up there tonight." And they said, "If there's trouble you all just stay in the dugout because there are about two other of us that have tickets and we'll be scattered out through the stands."

And he pulled his coat back and he had a shoulder holster with a pistol. And he said, "If there's any trouble we'll settle it."[25]

On the other hand, the Hazard community warmly embraced the big right-hander with the same gusto as the rest of the Bombers. He was accepted as one of their own.

Many of the players interacted with folks in the community. During the club's off time the popular hangouts for the team were Don's Restaurant, the drugstore, and the local pool hall where fans went, hoping to socialize with the Bombers. Bobrik remembered how supportive everyone in Hazard was and with a chuckle in his voice exclaimed, "If we played a game in town, and if you were the winning pitcher, you got a free steak dinner at one of the drug stores, and you would get a free shirt from one of the clothing stores."[26]

Hayling, who was one of the best-fed players, reached the twenty-win milestone on July 26, defeating Big Stone Gap, 9–7, putting the Bombers 5½ games ahead of surging second-place Morristown. The same day, Earl Catlett and Joseph Chapman were purchased from the last place Jenkins Cavaliers,[27] and joined recently signed 18-year-old Dodger prospect, pitcher Theodore "Ted" Kazek, as insurance for the pennant race.[28] Not done dealing, Smith also acquired Battle "Bones" Sanders from rival Harlan in early August.[29] Sanders, was one of two managers piloting the Smokies during the season and was their best hitter. He had played three seasons with the San Francisco Seals of the Pacific Coast League 1945–47, batting .310 in 107 games in 1945.[30] Sanders finished the MSL season belting 25 homers and driving in 132 runs.[31] Although not documented, it is suspected that Harlan was shedding its best player over financial concerns.

On August 25, Podres won his twentieth game of the season and clinched the pennant as the Bombers edged Pennington Gap, 4–2.[32] With the last out, all of the Hazard squad swarmed the field in celebration. Macon declared that he received so many handshakes and slaps on the back that it felt like he had been in a brawl. The Bombers must have partied pretty hard that night as the next day the Norton Braves laid a thumping on Hazard starting pitcher Hallard Snyder and his teammates, to the tune of 25–4.

By the season's conclusion, Podres had garnered his twenty-first win and Hayling his twenty-fourth. Podres led the league in strikeouts with 228, in ERA at 1.67, and win percentage at .875. Hayling finished with the most wins and tied Podres for most shutouts with four. Bobrik (12-3) finished third in the league in ERA at 2.84.[33]

On the offensive side, Macon finished fourth in the race for the batting title, hitting .409. Astonishingly, he was second on his own team to Ken Cox, who in 72 games batted a glossy .415. Both Bombers were outdistanced by Orville Kitts of Morristown, who had an impressive .424 batting average. Macon had one consolation; he led the league in RBIs with 148.[34]

Final Standings

	W	L	GB
Hazard Bombers	93	33	–
Morristown Red Sox	86	39	6.5
Harlan Smokies	82	43	10.5
Middlesboro Athletics	59	66	33.5
Pennington Gap Miners	54	71	38.5
Norton Braves	53	72	39.5
Big Stone Gap Rebels	49	75	43
Jenkins Cavaliers	24	101	68.5

MSL PLAYOFFS

In the opening round of the playoffs, Hazard squared off against Harlan in a best-of-five format. As expected, the series featured a high degree of competitiveness as tempers flared during every game. However, the Bombers were not to be denied and swept the Smokies in three games. In the final contest, Hayling and Podres teamed up to win a 9–8 slugfest. Macon led the attack, driving in four runs, and the fiery Isert plated three.[35] In her book *Ball, Bat, and Bitumen*, L.M. Sutter shared an incident defining just how competitive the rivalry was:

Harlan manager John Streza was at bat and after being driven back by two inside pitches, claimed the Hazard hurler was throwing at him. Streza got on first and there made a derogatory racial statement with reference to the Hazard club. After the inning, Lou Isert, on his way to the third base coaching box, passed Streza and told him, '[Y]ou'd be afraid to make that statement in our ballpark.' Heated words ensued between the two and Streza is said to have held Isert by his hair and kicked him with his knee several times before the fray was broken up. Both players were ejected from the game.

Having dispatched the Smokies, Macon set his eyes on Morristown for the MSL title. In game one of the best of five, Podres was masterful, striking out 13 Red Sox. Robert McNeil, who had won 17 games during the regular season, was almost as good, collecting 12 whiff victims. But, in the tenth inning, the game winner came when Joe Chapman tripled and scored when Sanders drove him in.[36]

Game two pitted Kazek (4–3, 7.44) against Porter Witt (21–5, 2.84). After falling behind 4–1 in the first inning, Macon replaced his starter with Snyder, who kept Morristown in check the rest of the way. The Bombers scored once in the fourth, and three apiece in the fifth and sixth to pull ahead, 8–6. Between Macon's single, double and home run, which netted five runs batted in, shortstop Robert Coluni's three base knocks, and Sanders's four hits, it proved too much offense for their beleaguered opponents as the Bombers pummeled the Red Sox, 13–6.[37]

Game three was an almost foregone conclusion with Hayling on the hill. Morristown drew 10 walks but mustered only six hits off the big righty, who as usual went the route for the complete game win. Red Sox pitchers gave up 13 free passes and allowed 35-year-old Macon to steal two bases in the Bombers' 10–3 win. Hazard had its first league championship.[38]

Macon's proficiency as a hitter and his ability to motivate his players proved to be a major force in the success of the team. Pitcher Bobrik described his skipper fondly: "He was a quiet man. He didn't raise a ruckus with us. But, he was manly you know. We were kids and all that, but he was manly to us. He didn't give us a hard time. He didn't rant at us, or shout at us. He was low-key and I enjoyed playing for the man. He was really tops in my book. I can't say enough about him."[39]

With Macon's departure at the close of the season, as well as the absence of the star power of Hayling and Podres, some of the magic that so spellbound the community of Hazard was gone. Increasingly, television was providing a more attractive distraction and the popularity of minor league baseball was in its waning days.

In 1952, Hazard (87–32) nearly repeated its performance, repeating as pennant-winners, this time under manager Mervin Dornburg. The Bombers were knocked out in the playoffs against Morristown, three games to one. Their nemesis, Harlan (73–45), finished the regular season in second place and won the championship, upending Morristown in the finals, three games to none.[40] Sadly, it was also Hazard's last year of minor league ball. Their attendance dipped to 14,600 and, due to financial reasons, the team folded.

In 2001, as part of minor league baseball's 100th anniversary, historians Bill Weiss and Marshall Wright researched and evaluated what they considered the 100 greatest minor league teams of all time. The list includes clubs from every decade of the twentieth century and introduced baseball aficionados to some teams who were otherwise lost to history. Coming in at number 81 were the Hazard Bombers.[41]

Although professional baseball has never returned to Hazard, old-timers still share their fond memories from that wonderful 1951 season. It was baseball at its best serving as a catalyst for the community by creating a source for local civic pride. The success of Podres and Hayling, especially the latter's win streak, drew national media attention to an otherwise inconspicuous hamlet in Kentucky. The team's championship served as the icing on the cake to the greatest team in Mountain States League history.

So, if you ever find yourself driving through Hazard, and are inspired to visit the Bobby Davis Museum on Walnut Street, be sure to stop. Within its walls, in an enclosed glass case, resides an original Bombers uniform worn by batboy Claude Crooke with the number "1." You will also see two autographed team baseballs, and a black and white photograph featuring each member of the Bombers who brought a championship to a sleepy town in Kentucky, named after a naval commander with the fighting spirit, like the team, that also won the day.

EPILOGUE

Ed Bobrik pitched only one season of professional baseball. He developed a back condition and was unable to throw a fastball anymore, cutting short his dream of reaching the big leagues. He later worked for the airlines for 37 years in communications, electronics, and mechanics before retiring in Goodyear, Arizona.

Danny Hayling moved up to the Class-A Pueblo Dodgers in 1952, but suffered a broken ankle in June.[42]

He bounced around the minor leagues for several years without repeating past successes until 1960 when he won 22 games for the Class-D Hickory Rebels of the Western Carolina League.[43] He later played in Cuba, Mexico, Nicaragua, Panama, and Puerto Rico. He received the keys to the city of Hazard, is a member of the Sally League Hall of Fame (1994), and is regarded as the greatest ballplayer to ever come out of Costa Rica. He departed this world on January 14, 2009, in his home country.[44]

Max Macon moved on to Miami, Florida, for the 1952 season where he became manager of the Class-B Florida International League Miami Sun Sox. Once again, he proved a capable player-manager, leading the Sun Sox to the pennant and league championship in a tightly fought race with the Miami Beach Flamingos. He remained a skipper in the minor leagues until 1963 and finished his career for Class-A Jamestown in the New York-Pennsylvania League. His lifetime mark was 1,100–949, including stops at Triple-A Montreal of the International League, and St. Paul of the American Association. Macon died on August 5, 1989, in Jupiter, Florida.[45]

George McDuff finished the season with two wins and two losses in 44 innings. He also pitched in the mid-season Mountain States League All-Star game, but unfortunately took the loss. The 6'2" Texan pitched for four seasons in the minor leagues with stops in Lubbock in the Class-C West Texas-New Mexico League (1952, 1954, and 1955), and Class-B Big State League in Austin (1955). He currently resides in Lubbock and is still active in his landscaping business. He and his wife Beverly are avid Texas Tech sports supporters.

Johnny Podres went on to a successful career as a major league pitcher. Long-suffering Brooklyn Dodger fans will always remember him as the one who ended the cries of, "Wait 'til next year." Over the course of his 15-year career, mostly with the Dodgers, then the Detroit Tigers and San Diego Padres, he won 148 and lost 116 games with a 3.68 ERA. He later became a major league pitching coach for 13 years spending time with the Boston Red Sox, Minnesota Twins, Philadelphia Phillies, and Padres. He passed away on January 13, 2008, in Glens Falls, New York.[46] ∎

Acknowledgments
Special thanks to Ed Bobrik, George McDuff, and Bob York for sharing their personal experiences. Also, I am indebted to fellow SABR members William Dunstone, Frank Hamilton, Ed Washuta, and Robert Zwissig for providing invaluable statistical information on the MSL. Thanks to Alberto "Tito" Rondon for his research and input on Danny Hayling. Thank you to Martha Quigley of the Bobby Davis Museum and Ed Bobrik for contributing photographs. And last, but

not least, I am grateful to my wife Barbra for her journalistic skills and continuing support in all of my research and writing endeavors.

Notes

1. http://cityofhazard.com/history.html. "History of Hazard and Perry County."
2. *Middlesboro Daily News*, "Mt. States Champs Lose 10–0 Game In Opener," 4.
3. L.M. Sutter, Ball, Bat, and Bitumen: *A History of Coalfield Baseball in the Appalachian South* (Jefferson, North Carolina: McFarland & Co. Inc., 2009), 130.
4. http://baseball-reference.com/bullpen/Mountain_States_League. Accessed April 22, 2015.
5. Ibid. Harlan (83–41) won the regular season pennant and the league championship defeating Morristown three games to two.
6. Baseball-Reference.com
7. Ibid. Macon was 4–11 during his rookie season with a 4.11 ERA and was used more as a reliever than a starter. In three seasons he was with Brooklyn he was 13–8, in a similar role, with a 4.47 ERA. Nineteen-forty-four was his best season as a hitter in a Boston Braves uniform batting .273, with three home runs and 36 RBI's.
8. http://californialeague.webs.com/seasons/1949.pdf. Accessed April 22, 2015.
9. Baseball-Reference.com, "Mountain States League History."
10. Baseball-Reference.com. Isert played for Class-D Thomasville and Albany of the Georgia-Florida League (1940), Class-D Greeneville of Appalachian League and Class-D Owensboro of the Kentucky-Illinois-Tennessee League (1941), Class-D Centreville of the Eastern Shore League (1946), Class-D Natchez of the Evangeline League (1947), Class-B Gadsden and Anniston of the Southeastern League (1947), Class-B Vicksburg of the Southeastern League (1948), and Class-C Lafayette of the Evangeline League (1949) prior to landing in Hazard.
11. Julian Pitzer, "Sport Slants," *Middlesboro Daily News*, April 28, 1951, 4.
12. *Middlesboro Daily News*, "Mt. States Champs Lose 10–0 Game In Opener," 4.
13. *The Sporting News*, "Ravelo Tosses a No-Hitter In Mountain States Opener," May 9, 1951, 32.
14. *Middlesboro Daily News*, "Morristown Scores Fifth Straight Win," 6.
15. *The Sporting News*, "Coastal Plain Has 7 New Pilots," May 16, 1951, 33.
16. Paul Post, "From Mineville High to the Majors," *Adirondack Life*, October, 2013.
17. Bob York, telephone interview, April 6, 2015.
18. Ed Bobrik, telephone interview, March 19, 2015.
19. George McDuff, telephone interview, April 2, 2015.
20. *The Sporting News*, July 18, 1951, 32.
21. *Middlesboro Daily News*, "Mountain States League Leaders," July 3, 1951, 2.
22. *Middlesboro Daily News*, "Hayling Chalks Up 17th Consecutive Win For Hazard," July 11, 1951, 4.
23. *The Sporting News*, "Rookie Sets Hurling Record," July 25, 1951, 38.
24. *The Sporting News*, "First Negro to Join O.B. Club in Dixie Makes Debut," May 16, 1951, 32.
25. George McDuff, telephone interview, April 2, 2015.
26. Ed Bobrik, telephone interview, March 19, 2015.
27. Julian Pitzer, "Sport Slants," *Middlesboro Daily News*, July 27, 1951, 8.
28. *The Sporting News*, August 1, 1951, 32.
29. L.M. Sutter, Ball, Bat, and Bitumen: *A History of Coalfield Baseball in the Appalachian South* (Jefferson, North Carolina: McFarland & Co. Inc., 2009), 133–34.
30. Baseball-Reference.com
31. *1952 Sporting News Guide*, 449.
32. *The Sporting News*, "Late Change In Managers," September 5, 1951, 36.
33. *1952 Sporting News Guide*, 453.
34. *1952 Sporting News Guide*, 448.
35. *Middlesboro Daily News*, "Hazard Tops Harlan Three Straight," September 4, 1951, 4.
36. *Middlesboro Daily News*, "Hazard Wins 1st Playoff Game 2–1," September 6, 1951, 6.
37. *Middlesboro Daily News*, "Hazard Win No. 2 In Playoff Finals," September 7, 1951, 4.
38. *Middlesboro Daily News*, "Hazard Wins 3rd Straight Over Morristown To End Mountain States Season," September 8, 1951, 4.
39. Ed Bobrik, telephone interview, March 19, 2015.
40. Baseball-Reference.com
41. http://milb.com/milb/history/top100.jsp
42. *The Sporting News*, June 25, 1952, 34.
43. Baseball-Reference.com
44. http://nacion.com/obituario, "El ultimo out del Duque de Hazard," January 15, 2009. Retrieved April 23, 2015. Thanks to Barbra Zygner and Tito Rondon for providing the translation into English.
45. Baseball-Reference.com. Also added on was Macon's record at Modesto which wasn't included on his lifetime stats.
46. Baseball-Reference.com.

Connie Mack's Income

Norman L. Macht

For most of the first 100 years of major league baseball, owning a team could be profitable or perilous. Some club owners made fortunes and wore handmade silk shirts. Others lost their shirts, whatever they were made of. Some did both in their lifetimes.

Connie Mack was in the latter category. The patterns of his Athletics' fortunes both on and off the field as well as his personal income resemble the blueprint of a theme park roller coaster.

At the end of the 1932 season, in which every major league team lost money, Mack said, "I feel that I've been a failure, not in playing results but financially… Any man who can't make ends meet must be a failure. And I didn't make ends meet for the Athletics."

Was Mack a financial failure? In this excerpt from *The Grand Old Man of Baseball*, the third and final volume of my Mack biography, I tried to assess his record as a businessman through 1932, and his personal finances for his lifetime.

* * * * *

Accurate information about the early days of the business of baseball is hard to pin down. Newspaper accounts were often estimates—or just guesses. Recently discovered A's ledgers—found since the publication of the first two volumes in this trilogy—give us what seems to be an accurate, authentic source. But the profit and loss figures, for example, differ—sometimes drastically—from other sources such as the official report of the congressional Organized Baseball Hearings of 1951, the so-called Celler Committee. Maybe different bookkeeping methods account for the differences. So a researcher seeking accuracy has to make choices.

I have chosen to go with the unaudited entries made by longtime A's secretary Bob Schroeder in the ledgers that begin in 1910. Where other sources are used, I identify them.

Was Connie Mack a financial failure?

Not when you consider that every American League team operated at a loss in 1932. Only the sale of Simmons, Haas, and Dykes enabled the A's to show a profit.

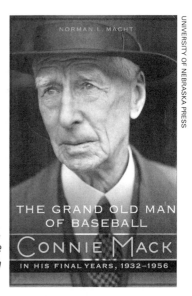

The cover photo of volume 3, which covers Mack's life from 1932 until his death in 1956.

Measured by the preceding thirty-one years, Mr. Mack was a very successful businessman.

When Connie Mack rode into Philadelphia in 1901, he was staking a claim on a gold mine richer than anything the forty-niners had found in California. Big league baseball was a very profitable business, a fact that led tycoons in other businesses to invest in the Federal League. Baseball was the only form of professional sports entertainment for the masses. Horse racing ran a distant second, and prize fighting was far behind in the competition for the dimes of the sporting crowd.

As much as he scoffed at writers' estimates of how much money he had taken out of the business, by the standards of the time—especially the pre-World War I time—Mack was a wealthy man.

He did not become wealthy on his salary, which was never more than $20,000 a year. He started in Philadelphia at $3,500. In 1902 his partners raised him to $5,000. Club ledgers show his salary at $10,000 in 1910, remaining there until 1922, when it was doubled. (He later took a cut in pay from 1934 through 1936 and again in 1943.)

The bulk of his early income probably came from dividends declared by the club's board of directors. A 1907 *Sporting News* article signed "Veteran" estimated that in the first six years of their existence, 1901–06, the Athletics earned over $100,000 in each of their pennant-winning years, 1902 and 1905, and "big profits" in the other years. At that time Mack owned 25 percent of the stock; therefore his share of the dividends "must total over $100,000." This is guesswork and assumes that all the profits were paid out in dividends, an assumption for which we have no confirmation. The A's were probably just as profitable in 1907 and 1909, when they finished second, but they may have lost money in 1908, when they finished sixth and attendance fell almost 30 percent.

In 1912 Ben Shibe loaned Mack $113,000 to buy out the newspapermen who had been given a 25 percent interest in the team in 1901. After giving five shares each to his sons, Roy and Earle, Mack now owned just under 50 percent of the stock.

The ledgers show profits totaling about $250,000 for 1910 through 1914 but do not show any dividends paid until November 1914, when $12,000 was distributed. Another dividend of $50,000 was paid on January 2, 1915.

From 1914 through January 12, 1931, Connie Mack received $255,011 in dividends, most of them in the 1920s. None were paid thereafter.

Mack also profited from outside investments. He opened a bowling alley in 1903 and sold it at a profit a few years later. He and John Shibe bought five acres in the exclusive Bala neighborhood of Philadelphia in 1906 and built twelve homes.

Owning a piece of the Athletics provided another source of income. The sale of food and drinks and scorecards, advertising in scorecards and on outfield fences, and the renting of cushions was an important part of the baseball business from the beginning. In the nineteenth century the ballgame was sometimes an incidental attraction to lure patrons to an adjacent beer garden. As early as the 1880s a club could earn a thousand dollars for scorecard rights alone. Even minor league teams received offers every spring for scorecard and refreshment privileges.

Some clubs ran their own concessions operations; some leased the scorecard and concessions privileges to pioneers in the catering business, such as Harry M. Stevens, Ed Barrow, and the Jacobs brothers (Marvin, Charles, and Louis), who went on to create Sportservice, for a percentage of the gross or a fee based on attendance.

The Athletics may have been unique: they did both. Connie Mack and the Shibes formed a separate partnership to manage the concessions and paid the club a pittance to lease the privileges. There is no record of when the Athletics' owners decided to take this direction. They may have started the business that way in 1901. It might have coincided with the opening of Shibe Park in 1909.

The 1910 club entries show $3,000 in income from the sale of privileges, two-thirds for refreshments and one-third for scorecard advertising. The same annual payments were made by John Shibe, who ran the catering business until his death in 1937, when a new Shibe Park Concessions Company was formed. While the Pirates might earn $35,000 a year from concessions privileges at seven cents a head in the 1930s and the Yankees $159,000 at eighteen cents a head in the 1940s, the new partnership of the Macks and Shibes paid the same $3,000 a year to the Athletics until 1939, when they raised it to $5,000. In 1941 it was raised to $5,500 and remained there through 1945, when it went up to $20,000.

A 1929 survey estimated that 5.5 percent of major league revenue came from concessions; for some clubs they were the most profitable part of the business. Those profits never appeared on the Athletics' profit and loss statements. They were distributed to the Athletics' stockholders on a per-share basis. Prior to 1914 Connie Mack owned 25 percent; after that, 50 percent, until his distribution of stock to his sons in 1946, when he was left with 20 percent.

What did Connie Mack's share of those concessions profits amount to from 1910 through 1950? We can only estimate based on various bits of information from occasional *Sporting News* articles on this side of the business, a 1937 *Fortune* article, and citations from the work of Steven A. Reiss in *Baseball in America and America in Baseball*.

To begin, it's necessary to understand that the Athletics never sold outfield fence signs, which were worth as much as $25,000 in some cities. They gave away scorecards for many years, and they never sold beer. A 1959 *Inquirer* story (when there was talk of the Phillies' building a new park in New Jersey because of Pennsylvania's Sunday curfew law and ban on the selling of beer in ballparks) cited "recent figures" that the average fan spent seventy-five cents during a game. "In Philadelphia it's only twenty-five cents. The difference is beer."

So the anecdotal figures—the reported 1929 Cubs' sales of sixteen cents a head and profits per head of more than twenty cents in 1946; the 1937 *Fortune* estimate that on a hot day sales might be eighteen cents a head; the fifty or fifty-five cents a head reported sales at big doubleheaders in the 1940s; the 1949 Cardinals reporting sales of sixty-three cents a head—must be discounted for the A's.

From the day the Phillies moved into Shibe Park in August 1938, the concessions company split the profits from sales at the Phillies' games with their tenants. It kept all the receipts from the Eagles and Villanova football games played at Shibe Park and catered events at other venues.

So what figures should we use? We're talking about a long-ago world of nickels and dimes. Hot dogs, sodas, and peanuts sold for ten cents until the 1940s, when Durk's hot dogs went up to fifteen cents. A 1940 Shibe Park menu lists sandwiches at fifteen and twenty cents, a hot plate of ham or steak with two vegetables for forty cents.

Let's go with an average gross of eight cents a head from 1910 to 1920, twelve cents in the 1920s, ten cents in the 1930s, and twenty cents in the 1940s, with a 50 percent profit margin.

For 1910–19 Connie Mack would have received an average of $4,700 a year. For the 1920s the average would have been $17,400 a year. For the 1930s the average would have been $10,000 a year. For 1940 through 1945 Connie Mack would receive $34,000 a year; in 1946, $49,000. After he gave shares to his sons in 1946, Mack held 302 shares. In the postwar boom years, 1947–49, he received 20 percent of $135,000 or $27,000 a year. Each of his sons got $90 a share on 163 shares or $14,670.

So over forty years Connie Mack received a total of about $655,000 as his share of the concessions profits. Had the total profits gone to the club, they would have added more than $1.5 million to the working capital.

In 1951 Penn Sportservice began paying $200,000 to the club for the concessions privileges.

By the 1920s Connie Mack was proud to be worth a million dollars. In a revocable trust dated April 23, 1928, Mack provided for his wife and three adult children, all from his first marriage. His wife, Katherine, had a ⅝ interest, and Roy, Earle, and daughter Marguerite, ⅛ each. Mack put into the trust his 747 shares of the Athletics. Dividends totaling almost $50,000, paid in 1928 and 1929, and Mack's income from the concessions went into the trust.

The farsighted trust, effective for the life of the beneficiaries, described all sorts of contingencies on the death of any of them, with the A's stock or (if sold) the proceeds passing to grandchildren and their heirs.

Then the stock market crashed and cleaned him out. He never made back the million. Mack revoked the trust in 1930. The securities were returned to him, and all accumulated income was distributed to the four beneficiaries.

From the day he arrived in Philadelphia, Mack had supported his mother and three children, along with various relatives and in-laws. In 1910 he started a second family, which produced five children. By the end of his life he was still subsidizing some of his children and was generous with relatives, grandchildren, old-time players, and countless others. When Connie Mack died in 1956, his estate, except for the proceeds from the 1954 sale of the team, would total less than $60,000. ■

Contributors

MATTHEW M. CLIFFORD is a freelance writer from the suburbs of Chicago. He joined SABR in 2011 with intentions to enhance his research abilities and literary talents to help preserve accurate facts of baseball history. Clifford has a background in law enforcement and is certified in a variety of forensic investigative techniques, all of which currently aid him with historical research and data collection. He has recorded and reported several baseball card errors and inaccuracies of player history to SABR and the research department of the National Baseball Hall of Fame. Clifford has published in the SABR Biography Project and *The National Pastime*.

ROB EDELMAN teaches film history courses at the University at Albany. He is the author of *Great Baseball Films* and *Baseball on the Web*, and is co-author (with his wife, Audrey Kupferberg) of *Meet the Mertzes*, a double biography of *I Love Lucy*'s Vivian Vance and famed baseball fan William Frawley, and *Matthau: A Life*. He is a film commentator on WAMC (Northeast) Public Radio and a contributing editor of Leonard Maltin's Movie Guide. He is a frequent contributor to *Base Ball: A Journal of the Early Game* and has written for *Baseball and American Culture: Across the Diamond*; *Total Baseball*; *Baseball in the Classroom*; *Memories and Dreams*; and *NINE: A Journal of Baseball History and Culture*. His essay on early baseball films appears on the DVD *Reel Baseball: Baseball Films from the Silent Era, 1899–1926*, and he is an interviewee on the director's cut DVD of *The Natural*.

RUSSELL FRANK's baseball career began in the New York City suburbs, where he was a Mickey Mantle worshiper and a no-field, no-hit second baseman/rightfielder for Milk Maid Ice Cream, a Peewee League team. It ended 25 years later in Sonora, California, with Live Theatre, a slow-pitch softball team. While playing third base, he failed to get his glove up fast enough to catch a line drive, which caught him below his left eye, breaking the zygomatic arch. Asked by a concerned teammate if he knew his own name, the prostrate Frank said, "Well, it isn't Brooks Robinson." He has since retreated to the safety of the Pennsylvania State University's Department of Journalism. And yes, he's still a Yankees fan.

MICHAEL HAUPERT is Professor of Economics at the University of Wisconsin–La Crosse. He is an avid baseball fan and appreciates the ability to combine his hobby with his work. He has published on the economics of baseball in several academic journals, including *NINE*, *Cliometrica*, *Black Ball*, and *Base Ball*. He is currently working on a labor history of professional baseball.

DOUGLAS JORDAN is a professor at Sonoma State University in Northern California where he teaches corporate finance and investments. He's been a SABR member since 2012. The article "That Record Will Never Be Broken!" is his second contribution to the *BRJ*. He runs marathons when he's not watching or writing about baseball. You can contact him at douglas.jordan@sonoma.edu.

DAVID KRELL is the author of *Our Bums: The Brooklyn Dodgers in History, Memory and Popular Culture* (McFarland, 2015). David has spoken at SABR's 19th Century Conference, Negro Leagues Conference, and Annual Convention. He has also spoken at the Cooperstown Symposium on Baseball and American Culture, Queens Baseball Convention, and Hofstra

WILLIAM LAMB: Prior to his retirement in 2007, Bill Lamb spent more than 30 years as a state/county prosecutor in New Jersey. He is the editor of *The Inside Game*, the newsletter of SABR's Deadball Era Committee and the author of *Black Sox in the Courtroom: The Grand Jury, Criminal Trial and Civil Litigation* (McFarland, 2013). He can be contacted via wflamb12@yahoo.com.

NORMAN L. MACHT's thirty-year project documenting the life of Connie Mack concluded with the publication of the third and final volume on October 1. Now living in Escondido, California, at 86 he is not contemplating another thirty-year project. Maybe twenty years.

BRIAN MARSHALL is an Electrical Engineering Technologist living in Barrie, Ontario, Canada, and a longtime researcher in various fields including entomology, power electronic engineering, NFL, Canadian Football, and recently MLB. Brian has written many articles, winning awards for two of them, with two baseball books on the way, one on the 1927 New York Yankees and the other on the 1897 Baltimore Orioles. Brian is a long time member of the PFRA. While growing up, Brian played many sports including football, rugby, hockey, and baseball, and participated in power lifting and arm wrestling events. He aspired to be a professional football player, but when that didn't materialize he focused on Rugby Union and played off and on for 17 seasons in the "front row."

JOHN McMURRAY is Chair of both the Deadball Era Committee and the Oral History Committee for the Society for American Baseball Research. He is a past chair of SABR's Ritter Award subcommittee, which annually presents an award to the best book on Deadball Era baseball published during the year prior. He has contributed many interview-based player profiles to *Baseball Digest* in recent years and writes a monthly column for *Sports Collectors Digest*.

DAVE OGDEN is professor in the School of Communication at the University of Nebraska at Omaha. Before coming to UNO in 2001, he was an associate professor at Wayne State College. His work can be found in *NINE: The Journal of Baseball History and Culture*, the *Journal of Leisure Research*, the *Journal of Black Studies*, *Journal of Sport Behavior* and *Great Plains Research Journal*. He is co-editor of the books, *Reconstructing Fame: Sport Race and Evolving Reputations*, *Fame to Infamy: Race, Sport, and the Fall from Grace*, and *A Locker Room of Her Own*, all published by the University Press of Mississippi. Ogden received his Ph.D. in 1999 from the University of Nebraska-Lincoln.

J.G. PRESTON lives in Benicia, California, and is press secretary for Consumer Attorneys of California. He previously served as editor of the Minnesota Twins program magazine, wrote feature articles for the Twins' program and yearbook, and wrote the script for a video biography of Kirby Puckett narrated by Bob Costas. He writes about baseball history at http://prestonjg.wordpress.com.

STUART SHAPIRO is an Associate Professor and Director of the Public Policy program at the Bloustein School for Planning and Policy at Rutgers University. He received his Ph.D. from the Kennedy School of Government in 1999. He studies and writes about the interaction between politics and regulatory policy-making. A lifelong Yankees fan, he has written two articles for the *Baseball Research Journal* in 1999 and 2001.

JOHN SHOREY is a professor of history and political science at Iowa Western Community College. Along with his survey courses in history and government, Shorey developed a course on "Baseball and American Culture" that he has taught at Iowa Western since 1998. Shorey has conducted research on various baseball topics, and has presented his research at the *NINE*'s Conference in Phoenix, the annual symposium on Baseball and American Culture at the National Baseball Hall of Fame, and at Indiana State's Conference on Baseball in Literature and Culture.

STEVE STEINBERG and **LYLE SPATZ** are the co-authors of *The Colonel and Hug: The Partnership that Transformed the New York Yankees*, the stories of Jacob Ruppert and Miller Huggins and how, a century ago, they laid the foundation for the future Yankees' greatness. Steve's and Lyle's previous collaboration, *1921: The Yankees, the Giants, and the Battle for Baseball Supremacy in New York*, was awarded the 2011 Seymour Medal. Steve has also written *Baseball in St. Louis, 1900–1925* and many articles revolving around early twentieth-century baseball,

including a dozen for SABR publications. He has been a regular presenter at SABR national conventions. Lyle has recently published *Willie Keeler: From the Playgrounds of Brooklyn to the Hall of Fame*. He has also written biographies of Bill Dahlen and Dixie Walker, among other books, and has edited books on the 1947 Brooklyn Dodgers and the 1947 New York Yankees.

CORT VITTY resides in Maryland with his wife Mary Anne and their pet golden-doodle Sparkle. A New Jersey native, Vitty graduated from Seton Hall University and continues to root for the New York Yankees. He's been a SABR member (Bob Davids Chapter) since 1999 and in addition to this essay, his original compositions have been featured in the *Baseball Research Journal* and *The National Pastime*. He has contributed to several SABR book projects and his work is also posted at Seamheads.com and Philadelphia Athletics.org.

KEVIN WARNEKE, who earned in doctoral degree in leadership studies from the University of Nebraska–Lincoln, has worked as journalist, magazine editor, public relations administrator, fundraiser and non-profit executive. He has taught journalism, public relations and development courses at the University of Nebraska at Omaha for the past 25 years.

ROBERT D. WARRINGTON is a native Philadelphian who writes about the city's baseball history.

SAM ZYGNER, a SABR member since 1996, is Chairman of the South Florida Chapter and author of *The Forgotten Marlins: A Tribute to the 1956–1960 Original Miami Marlins*. He received his MBA from Saint Leo University and his writings have appeared in the *Baseball Research Journal*, *The National Pastime*, and *NINE*. A lifelong Pittsburgh Pirates fan, he has shifted his focus to Miami baseball history.

THE SABR DIGITAL LIBRARY

The Society for American Baseball Research, the top baseball research organization in the world, disseminates some of the best in baseball history, analysis, and biography through our publishing programs. The SABR Digital Library contains a mix of books old and new, and focuses on a tandem program of paperback and ebook publication, making these materials widely available for both on digital devices and as traditional printed books.

GREATEST GAMES BOOKS

BRAVES FIELD:
MEMORABLE MOMENTS AT BOSTON'S LOST DIAMOND
From its opening on August 18, 1915, to the sudden departure of the Boston Braves to Milwaukee before the 1953 baseball season, Braves Field was home to Boston's National League baseball club and also hosted many other events: from NFL football to championship boxing. The most memorable moments to occur in Braves Field history are portrayed here.
Edited by Bill Nowlin and Bob Brady
$19.95 paperback (ISBN 978-1-933599-93-9)
$9.99 ebook (ISBN 978-1-933599-92-2)
8.5"X11", 282 pages, 182 photos

INVENTING BASEBALL: THE 100 GREATEST
GAMES OF THE NINETEENTH CENTURY
SABR's Nineteenth Century Committee brings to life the greatest games from the game's early years. From the "prisoner of war" game that took place among captive Union soldiers during the Civil War (immortalized in a famous lithograph), to the first intercollegiate game (Amherst versus Williams), to the first professional no-hitter, the games in this volume span 1833–1900 and detail the athletic exploits of such players as Cap Anson, Moses "Fleetwood" Walker, Charlie Comiskey, and Mike "King" Kelly.
Edited by Bill Felber
$19.95 paperback (ISBN 978-1-933599-42-7)
$9.99 ebook (ISBN 978-1-933599-43-4)
8"x10", 302 pages, 200 photos

BIOPROJECT BOOKS

WHO'S ON FIRST:
REPLACEMENT PLAYERS IN WORLD WAR II
During World War II, 533 players made the major league debuts. More than 60% of the players in the 1941 Opening Day lineups departed for the service and were replaced by first-times and oldsters. Hod Lisenbee was 46. POW Bert Shepard had an artificial leg, and Pete Gray had only one arm. The 1944 St. Louis Browns had 13 players classified 4-F. These are their stories.
Edited by Marc Z Aaron and Bill Nowlin
$19.95 paperback (ISBN 978-1-933599-91-5)
$9.99 ebook (ISBN 978-1-933599-90-8)
8.5"X11", 422 pages, 67 photos

VAN LINGLE MUNGO:
THE MAN, THE SONG, THE PLAYERS
Although the Red Sox spent most of the 1950s far out of contention, the team was filled with fascinating players who captured the heart of their fans. In *Red Sox Baseball*, members of SABR present 46 biographies on players such as Ted Williams and Pumpsie Green as well as season-by-season recaps.
Edited by Bill Nowlin
$19.95 paperback (ISBN 978-1-933599-76-2)
$9.99 ebook (ISBN 978-1-933599-77-9)
8.5"X11", 278 pages, 46 photos

ORIGINAL SABR RESEARCH

CALLING THE GAME:
BASEBALL BROADCASTING FROM 1920 TO THE PRESENT
An exhaustive, meticulously researched history of bringing the national pastime out of the ballparks and into living rooms via the airwaves. Every play-by-play announcer, color commentator, and ex-ballplayer, every broadcast deal, radio station, and TV network. Plus a foreword by "Voice of the Chicago Cubs" Pat Hughes, and an afterword by Jacques Doucet, the "Voice of the Montreal Expos" 1972-2004.
by Stuart Shea
$24.95 paperback (ISBN 978-1-933599-40-3)
$9.99 ebook (ISBN 978-1-933599-41-0)
7"X10", 712 pages, 40 photos

BASEBALL IN THE SPACE AGE:
HOUSTON SINCE 1961
Here we have a special issue of *The National Pastime* centered almost entirely on the Houston Astros (né Colt .45s) and their two influential and iconic homes, short-lived Colt Stadium and the Astrodome. If you weren't able to attend the SABR convention in Houston, please enjoy this virtual trip tour of baseball in "Space City" through 18 articles.
Edited by Cecilia M. Tan
$14.95 paperback (ISBN 978-1-933599-65-6)
$9.99 ebook (ISBN 978-1-933599-66-3)
8.5"x11", 96 pages, 49 photos

NORTH SIDE, SOUTH SIDE, ALL AROUND
THE TOWN: BASEBALL IN CHICAGO
The National Pastime provides in-depth articles focused on the geographic region where the national SABR convention is taking place annually. The SABR 45 convention took place in Chicago, and here are 45 articles on baseball in and around the bat-and-ball crazed Windy City: 25 that appeared in the souvenir book of the convention plus another 20 articles available in ebook only.
Edited by Stuart Shea
$14.95 paperback (ISBN 978-1-933599-87-8)
$9.99 ebook (ISBN 978-1-933599-86-1)
8.5"X11", 282 pages, 47 photos

THE EMERALD GUIDE TO BASEBALL: 2015
The Emerald Guide to Baseball fills the gap in the historical record created by the demise of *The Sporting News Baseball Guide*. First published in 1942, *The Sporting News* Guide was truly the annual book of record for our National Pastime. The 2015 edition of the *Emerald Guide* runs more than 600 pages and covers the 2014 season; it also includes a 2015 directory of every franchise, rosters, minor league affiliates, and career leaders for all teams.
Edited by Gary Gillette and Pete Palmer
$24.95 paperback (ISBN 978-0-9817929-8-9)
8.5"X11", 610 pages

SABR Members can purchase each book at a significant discount (often 50% off) and receive the ebook editions free as a member benefit. Each book is available in a trade paperback edition as well as ebooks suitable for reading on a home computer or Nook, Kindle, or iPad/tablet.
To learn more about becoming a member of SABR, visit the website: sabr.org/join